CAROLINAS
MONTH-BY-MONTH GARDENING

First published in 2014 by Cool Springs Press, a member of Quayside Publishing Group, 400 First Avenue North, Suite 400, Minneapolis, MN 55401

The information in this book is true and complete to the best of our knowledge. All recommendations are made without any guarantee on the part of the author or Publisher, who also disclaims any liability incurred in connection with the use of this data or specific details.

Cool Springs Press titles are also available at discounts in bulk quantity for industrial or sales-promotional use. For details write to Special Sales Manager at Cool Springs Press, 400 First Avenue North, Suite 400, Minneapolis, MN 55401 USA. To find out more about our books, visit us online at www.coolspringspress.com.

Library of Congress Cataloging-in-Publication Data

Polomski, Robert, 1960-
  [Month-by-month gardening in the Carolinas]
  Carolinas month-by-month gardening : what to do each month to have a beautiful garden all year / Bob Polomski.
      p. cm.
  Carolinas month by month gardening
  "First published in 2001 as Month-by-month gardening in the Carolinas by Cool Springs Press."
  Includes bibliographical references and index.
  ISBN 978-1-59186-586-5 (softcover)
  1. Gardening--North Carolina. 2. Gardening--South Carolina. I. Title. II. Title: Carolinas month by month gardening.

  SB453.2.N8P66 2014
  635.09756--dc23

                    2013039028

Acquisitions Editor: Billie Brownell
Design Manager: Brad Springer
Layout: Danielle Smith

Printed in China
10 9 8 7 6 5 4 3 2 1

CAROLINAS

MONTH-BY-MONTH GARDENING

What to Do Each Month to Have
a Beautiful Garden All Year

BOB POLOMSKI

COOL
SPRINGS
PRESS
Home and Garden Experts™

Dedication

To my spouse and soulmate, Susan Reynolds Polomski. Thank you for making me complete.

Acknowledgments

I am grateful to Billie Brownell and Cool Springs Press for the opportunity to revise this book and for their unflagging support during the entire process.

Contents

Introduction

WELCOME TO GARDENING IN THE CAROLINAS

Whether you are new to gardening or new to gardening in the Carolinas, you will quickly discover that success depends on knowing how to do certain tasks and when to do them. Creating a flower bed that draws admiring looks from passersby; complementing the look and style of your home with well-placed trees, shrubs, and groundcovers; and brightening your indoor living area with the colorful blooms and enchanting fragrances of indoor plants does not happen by chance. You can be assured that they were achieved with careful planning, know-how, and proper care.

Carolinas Month-by-Month Gardening helps you achieve these goals, guiding you throughout the year. Each month, follow the calendar format to remind you when it's time for certain garden and landscape tasks. Every season in the Carolinas presents a gardening opportunity. Start vegetables in the summer for a fall garden. Divide and replant fall-flowering perennials in the spring when their new growth emerges. Start or renovate a warm-season lawn in late spring and early summer. Just knowing how and when each task should be done makes gardening easier and more fun, and greatly improves your chances of success.

Ten categories of plants are described in this book. Each chapter takes you month-by-month through the year with reminders and step-by-step approaches that sharpen your gardening skills.

With the help of several seasoned gardeners from both North Carolina and South Carolina, I have attempted to place each activity into its appropriate month for both states. However, some fine-tuning will be necessary in your own garden and landscape. The seasons do not always arrive when they are expected, and most landscapes have microclimates within them.

INTRODUCTION

GARDENING IN THE CAROLINAS: GEOGRAPHY & CLIMATE

North and South Carolina share a 400-mile stretch of coastline. A band of sand, the Carolina Sandhills, runs through the midsection of both states, and in the west rise two mountain ranges—the Blue Ridge and the Great Smokies.

These divide the Carolinas into three distinct gardening areas, each with prevailing climates and soil types: Coastal Plain, Piedmont, and Mountains. Use the map on Page 224 to locate your area. In this book I use these terms when special advice applies to these distinct areas.

The Coastal Plain extends westward from the coast, gradually rising to the Piedmont. The soils of the Coastal Plain range from well-drained loamy sands near the coast to the coarse-textured sands of the Carolina Sandhills, which were once sand dunes comprising a prehistoric shoreline during the Ice Age. The Carolina Sandhills vary in width from 5 to 30 miles and extend from Rockingham and Pinehurst in North Carolina, southward through Aiken, South Carolina, and into Georgia. The mild winters across the Coastal Plain are offset by the suffocating heat and humidity of its long summers. However, summer's wrath is tempered along coastal areas, which enjoy lower temperatures than inland areas thanks to welcome sea breezes.

The climate along the coast north of Cape Hatteras is suitable for growing plants adapted to cool northern areas. By contrast, from Bald Head Island, North Carolina, through South Carolina, the coastal climate is subtropical.

The Piedmont lies between the Coastal Plain and the Mountains. This plateau of rolling hills is comprised largely of heavy red clay soils that color a gardener's tools, clothing, and carpeting. These poorly drained soils can dry to concrete hardness in midsummer and become wet and sloppy hog wallows in late winter. Fortunately, organic matter incorporated into these clay soils can convert them into a respectable growing medium.

Summers in the Piedmont are also hot and humid with correspondingly high nighttime temperatures. Winter is shorter than in the Mountains and seldom colder than 10 degrees Fahrenheit. Snowfall averages less than a foot per year across the Piedmont, often covering the ground for a short period of time before melting.

In the Mountains, the highest peaks, over 6,000 feet, are in North Carolina. Soils range from excellent loams in bottomland and coves, to shallow rocky soil over bedrock at the higher elevations. Although the large differences in elevation result in large variations in climate (meteorologists claim that North Carolina has the greatest variety of climate of any state east of the Rocky Mountains), cold-tolerant plants can be established here more successfully than elsewhere in the Carolinas.

The Mountains are the coolest region of the Carolinas throughout the year. Winters are colder but often interrupted by warm days, especially in the lower valleys. In the higher valleys of the North Carolina mountains and at elevations above 3,500 feet, temperatures may drop, albeit infrequently, to 0 degrees Fahrenheit.

In summer, hot, humid days give way to cool night temperatures that offer respite to plants and gardeners alike.

Autumn is the driest season in the Carolinas, with October and November being the driest months. Most rain falls during July and August; however, during most summers in the Carolinas a certain amount of drought occurs, sometimes quite severe. Tropical storms and hurricanes pose a threat to the Carolinas usually between August and October.

For climate and weather information specific to your locality, contact your County Cooperative Extension Service office.

GENERAL GARDENING PRACTICES

BUILDING HEALTHY SOIL

Gardeners often get caught up in the beauty of their plants without remembering that the foundation for any healthy garden, landscape, or lawn is soil. Good soil allows air, water, and nutrients to be absorbed by plant roots and lets those roots roam freely.

How do you build healthy soil? Begin with a soil test through your local Cooperative Extension Service center. The test will tell you the pH level of the soil and the levels of nutrients available for plant growth. Stated in numbers, pH is a measurement of the acidity or alkalinity of the soil. On a scale of 0 to 14, a pH of 7 is neutral. Numbers below 7 indicate acid conditions and readings above 7 are basic or alkaline. Soil pH affects not only plant health, but also the availability of nutrients. If the soil is too acidic or too alkaline, minerals such as nitrogen, phosphorus, potassium, calcium, and magnesium can be "tied-up" and unavailable to your plants. Adding more fertilizer will not help. The soil pH will have to be corrected by mixing in the recommended amount of limestone to raise the pH or "sweeten" the soil, or adding sulfur if you need to lower the soil pH.

Maintaining the right soil pH is very important. It affects the uptake of nutrients by plants and creates an environment that supports helpful soil-dwelling organisms, including earthworms.

■ *Organic matter, such as compost, manure, or "green" manure cover crops, improves soil fertility and structure.*

Analysis	Results		Low	Medium	Sufficient	High	Excessive
Soil pH	**7.1**						
Buffer pH	**7.80**						
Phosphorus (P)	**12**	*lbs/acre*					
Potassium (K)	**145**	*lbs/acre*					
Calcium (Ca)	**1533**	*lbs/acre*					
Magnesium (Mg)	**119**	*lbs/acre*					
Zinc (Zn)	**4.5**	*lbs/acre*					
Manganese (Mn)	**29**	*lbs/acre*					
Boron (B)	**0.5**	*lbs/acre*					
Copper (Cu)	**1.5**	*lbs/acre*					
Sodium (Na)	**12**	*lbs/acre*					
Sulfur (S)		*lbs/acre*					
Soluble Salts		*mmhos/cm*					
Nitrate Nitrogen		*ppm*					
Organic Matter		*% (LOI)*					

Calculations

Cation Exchange Capacity (CEC)	Acidity	Ca	Mg	K	Base Saturation Na	Total
6.1 *meq/100g*	**1.6** *meq/100g*	63%	8%	3%	0%	74%

Recommendations

Crop	Lime
WarmSeasonGrsMaint(sq ft)	No Lime Required

■ *The first step in knowing your soil is to having it tested by your local Cooperative Extension Service Center. Follow soil test recommendations to create a suitable environment for plants and the beneficial subterranean organisms that contribute to plant growth and development.*

The results of your soil test will indicate the amount of limestone or sulfur required to bring the soil pH into an ideal range, between 5.8 and 6.5 for most vegetable and flower gardens, shrubs, trees, and lawns. Mix pulverized or pelletized limestone into the top 6 inches of soil to raise the pH; mix in sulfur to lower it.

The soil test also measures the levels of phosphorus, potassium, calcium, and magnesium. Because calcium and phosphorous move slowly in the soil, these minerals should be incorporated into the top 6 inches of soil.

Knowing what nutrients are already present will save you money. If your test shows your soil already has high levels of phosphorus and potassium, there's no need to add a fertilizer containing these two nutrients.

Good gardeners also add organic matter, which improves soil tilth—its physical condition or structure. When added to clay soil, organic matter holds the clay particles apart, improving air and water movement in the soil. This translates to deeper and more extensive root development by our plants.

The kind of organic matter you mix into your soil is your choice. My grandfather liked to use rabbit and chicken manure for his vegetable and flower beds. My mother used fish in her rose garden. As a child I buried fish heads, tails, and other inedible parts around her roses. If you are squeamish about using these organic materials, then add compost or shredded leaves. Cover crops or "green manure" such as crimson clover or annual rye are relatively inexpensive sources of organic matter. Sow these crops in the fall and then turn them under in the spring to enrich the soil.

Organic fertilizers derived from naturally occurring sources are a good alternative to synthetic plant foods. They include composted animal manure, cottonseed meal, and bloodmeal, among many others. Although they contain relatively low concentrations of actual nutrients compared to synthetic fertilizers, they increase the organic matter content in the soil and improve soil structure.

To avoid damaging soil structure, never dig or cultivate when the soil is too wet or too dry. Follow this simple test: if the soil sticks to your shovel, the soil is too wet. Postpone digging until the soil to dries out.

Coarse-textured sandy soils have excellent drainage but hold little water. Add organic matter to them to increase fertility and water retention.

IMPORTANT NOTE: Sand has often been touted as the perfect fix for improving drainage in clay soils. Unless you add it at the rate of at least 6 inches of sand per 8 inches of soil, your soil will be better suited for making bricks than growing plants. Sand will not fix clay soils: organic matter will.

PLANTING

Plant properly. The health and long-term survival of plants that you set into their new home—indoors or out—is affected by how they're planted. Follow the "how to" instructions in the book to learn about proper planting. Your plant's survival is counting on it.

ASSESSING LIGHT LEVELS

We all know that in order to thrive, plants need light. It can get confusing, though, when you're looking at plant labels or reading a gardening book and see references to terms that seem vague or unfamiliar. In order to select appropriate plants for your landscape ("right plant—right place") you should assess the light levels in different parts of your garden and landscape. The following terms are used to describe degrees of light.

"Full sun" is an area that receives at least six or more uninterrupted hours of sun each day. This light exposure is well suited for fruiting vegetables, roses, fruits, and a wide range of flowering plants. If you're new to the South ("not from around here"), you'll quickly discover that plants growing in full sun in cooler regions of the Northeast, for example, may need some afternoon shade in our warmer region.

"Part sun" or "part shade" refers to those areas that receive direct sun for two to six hours a day, but not more than six hours of uninterrupted sun at a time in a given location. This location may receive dappled shade throughout the day. This light level will accommodate a wide variety of plants.

■ *Water newly set-out plants immediately after planting. Pay especially close attention to watering the first few weeks, while plants develop their root systems. To promote deep root growth, water thoroughly and deeply. Allow the soil surface to dry before watering again.*

"Light shade," sometimes called "high shade," is an area beneath tall deciduous trees or pines that receives little or no direct sun—only reflected light.

"Full, dense or deep shade" receives no direct sunlight and little reflected light. It can be complete shade from a building, such as the north side of your house or very dense shade cast by the canopy of a Southern magnolia whose evergreen foliage is so thick that it never allows any sunlight to reach the ground.

WATERING

Anyone can water; however, watering efficiently to meet the demands of the plant, while conserving water requires some attention to detail. Each monthly chapter in this book provides information on when and how often to water. The aim is to avoid the common mistakes of overwatering or underwatering—two practices that can injure or kill plants.

Water needs depend on the plant and the situation. Moisture-loving plants require more frequent watering than plants adapted to dry conditions. Newly set-out plants need to be watered after planting and during their establishment period. Once they become established, however, they may not require supplemental watering even during the hot, dry summer months. Some shrubs and trees are quite drought tolerant and can withstand long periods without rain or irrigation.

Soil also affects watering. Plants growing in clay soils need to be watered less often than plants growing in sandy soils because sandy soils drain so rapidly.

Whether you water with a garden hose or an automatic below-ground irrigation system, water wisely. Refer to the "Water" sections in each month for information on watering efficiently.

FERTILIZING

Fertilizing could be the gardening practice that causes the greatest confusion. Besides knowing when, how often, and how much to fertilize, the choices seem endless. Should you choose a fast- or slow-release nitrogen fertilizer? Would your plants prefer a diet of organic or inorganic nutrients? What do those numbers on the bag mean? Should

---

Ready to Use [1]

FERTIFEED
All Purpose Plant Food

12-4-8 [2]

FertiFeed Ready To Use All-Purpose Plant Food
Net Weight 4lb. 12oz. (2.15kg)

GUARANTEED ANALYSIS [3]

Total Nitrogen (N)..12%

    10.2% Urea Nitrogen*

    1.8% Ammoniacal Nitrogen

Available Phosphate (P_2O_5)..4%

Soluble Potash (K_2O)..8%

[5] Sulfur (S)...2%

    2% free Sulfur (S)

Manganese (Mn)..0.05%

    0.05% Chelated Manganese (Mn)

Zinc (Zn) 0.05%

    0.05% Chelated Zinc (Zn)

[6] Inert Ingredients..76%

[4] Derived from urea, isobutylidene diurea, ammonium phosphate, and potassium sulfate. Potential acidity 0 lbs. calcium carbonate equivalent per ton.

*Contains 6.8% water-insoluble isobutylidene diurea.

Information regarding the contents and levels of metals in this product is available on the Internet at http://www.regulatory-info-sc.com

KEEP OUT OF REACH OF CHILDREN

---

[1] **The fertilizer brand name**
There are different brands of fertilizer, just like there are different brands of clothes.

[2] **Fertilizer analysis or grade**
All fertilizers are labeled with three numbers that indicate the guaranteed analysis, or fertilizer grade. These three numbers give the percentage by weight of nitrogen (N), phosphate (P_2O_5) and potash (K_2O) as listed in the "Guaranteed Analysis." Often, to simplify matters, these numbers are said to represent the primary plant minerals (or "nutrients") nitrogen, phosphorus, and potassium, or N-P-K. This 4-pound 12-ounce (76-ounce) bag of 12-4-8 fertilizer contains 9 ounces of nitrogen, 3 ounces of phosphate, and 6 ounces of potash.

[3] **Guaranteed Analysis**
The guaranteed analysis, or grade, lists the percentages of nutrients in the fertilizer and their sources.

[4] **Derived from**
The label tells you the inorganic or organic sources that were used to manufacture this fertilizer.

[5] **Nutrients other than N-P-K**
These are micronutrients, other nutrients that plants need in smaller amounts than nitrogen, phosphorus, and potassium. Besides the primary elements, the fertilizer may contain secondary minerals—such as calcium, magnesium, and sulfur—and trace elements—such as manganese, zinc, copper, iron and molybdenum.

[6] **Other ingredients**
Other ingredients make the fertilizer easier to spread. Inert ingredients, also called filler or carrier, make the fertilizer easier to spread.

you choose the 10-10-10 or the 16-4-8? Dry or liquid fertilizer? Before making an application, realize that fertilizing should be guided by soil test results, the appearance of the plants, and the purpose of fertilizing them before making an application.

Fertilizers are minerals added when the soil does not supply enough of these nutrients. The three most important nutrients—nitrogen, phosphorus, and potassium—are represented by three numbers on a fertilizer bag. For example, 16-4-8 gives the percent by weight of nitrogen (N), phosphate (P_2O_5), and potash (K_2O). In this case, nitrogen makes up 16 percent of the total weight, phosphate–which supplies phosphorus–accounts for 4 percent, and potash, a source of potassium, makes up 8 percent. The remaining weight (the total must add up to 100 percent) is comprised of a nutrient carrier.

A fertilizer containing all three nutrients, such as a 16-4-8, is referred to as a "complete" fertilizer. If soil tests indicate high levels of phosphorus and potassium, then apply only an "incomplete" fertilizer, one that supplies only nitrogen, such as 21-0-0.

In addition to the primary elements (N-P-K), the fertilizer may contain secondary plant nutrients including calcium, magnesium, and sulfur, or minor nutrients such as manganese, zinc, copper, iron, and molybdenum. Apply these nutrients if dictated by soil test results.

You can choose dry or liquid fertilizers. Dry fertilizers are applied to the ground around your plants. They are available in fast- or slow-release nitrogen forms.

Fast- or quick-release nitrogen fertilizers dissolve readily in water and are almost immediately available to plants. They can also be quickly leached out of the root zone in fast-draining, sandy soils.

Liquid fertilizers can be absorbed through the leaves as well as roots of plants. These have to be applied more frequently than granular types, usually every two to four weeks.

Slow-release fertilizer makes nutrients available to the plant for an extended period of up to several months. While more expensive than conventional fertilizers, they reduce the need for supplemental applications and the likelihood of fertilizer burn. Select a slow-release fertilizer that has at least one-half of the total amount of nitrogen listed as "water insoluble nitrogen."

Alternatives to synthetic slow-release fertilizers are organic fertilizers derived from naturally occurring sources such as composted animal manure, cottonseed meal, and bloodmeal, among many others. As the organic materials slowly decompose, the minerals are released over a long period of time. Although they contain relatively low concentrations of actual nutrients compared to synthetic fertilizers, they increase the organic matter content in the soil and improve soil structure.

A slow-release fertilizer is a good choice, especially for sandy soils, which tend to leach, or for heavy clay soils where runoff can be a problem. If the soil is properly prepared at the start, supplemental fertilization may not be necessary for several years after planting. When fertilizing your perennials, let their growth rate and leaf color guide you. Rely on soil test results to help you make the right decision. If the bed is already highly fertile, the soil test will save you from the other, equally undesirable results of overfertilizing, such as encouraging a lot of leafy growth at the expense of flowers.

PRUNING

Pruning improves the health and appearance of plants. It can be as simple as snipping the dead heads of spent flowers from your zinnias (deadheading) or removing a large limb from your maple tree. In the following chapters, read the step-by-step instructions for pruning roses, shrubs, and trees.

You'll find that pruning will require you to have a purpose in mind. It can be to encourage more flowers on perennials, to reduce the height of plants, or to create a strong structure of trunk and limbs to support future growth in young trees.

Sometimes fertilizer products and pest control products (herbicide, insecticide, fungicide) are in the same aisle, and sometimes they're in different aisles. Sometimes organic or natural remedies are shelved together with conventional remedies; sometimes they're separated. When shopping for fertilizer or pest control, always carefully read the labels on products so that you know that what you're buying is what you need.

CONTROLLING PESTS

You are bound to confront the three most common pests in your Carolina garden: insects, diseases, and weeds. (Deer, voles, and rabbits can also be considered pests and are addressed in appropriate months.)

Deal with them sensibly. Follow the principles of Integrated Pest Management or "IPM." IPM is a common sense approach to managing pests that brings Mother Nature into the battle on the gardeners' side. It combines smart plant selection with good planting and maintenance practices, and an understanding of pests and their habits. It starts with planning and proper planting to produce strong, healthy plants that, by themselves, can prosper with minimum help from you. As in

nature, an acceptable level of pests is accommodated. Control is the goal, rather than elimination.

Several techniques can be used in a home garden/landscape IPM approach.

IPM CULTURAL PRACTICES

- **Proper soil management**—Maintain the appropriate soil pH for your plants by testing your soil at least every three years. Add generous amounts of organic matter to buildup soil fertility.

- **Plant selection**—Match plants suited to the soil and climate of your area, and select species and cultivars resistant to pests. These plants are resistant—not immune—to damage.

Expect them to exhibit less insect or disease injury than susceptible varieties growing in the same environment.

- **Watering**—*Water late at night or early in the morning when dew has formed.* Avoid watering in early evening when leaves may remain wet for an extended period of time, which favors fungal infections.

- **Mulching**—Apply a shallow layer of organic mulch such as compost, shredded leaves, or wood to conserve moisture, suppress weeds, and supply nutrients as they decompose.

- **Sanitation**—Remove dead, damaged, diseased, or insect-infested leaves, shoots, or branches.

IPM MECHANICAL CONTROLS

- **Handpicking**—Remove any insects by hand or knock them off with a strong spray of water from the hose.

- **Exclusion**—Physically block insects from attacking your plants. Aluminum foil collars can be placed around seedlings to prevent cutworms from attacking plant stems. Plants can be covered with muslin or spun-bonded polyester to keep insects out.

IPM BIOLOGICAL CONTROLS

- **Predators and parasites**—Some bugs are on our side. Known as beneficial insects, they are the natural enemies of damaging insects. They fall into two main categories: predators and parasites. Predators hunt and feed on other

■ *Lightweight floating row covers admit air, water, and light but exclude pests. Rest the cover loosely on the tops of plants or support it with wire hoops.*

insects. They include spiders, praying mantids, lady beetles, and green lacewings. Parasites, such as braconid wasps and *Trichogramma* wasps, hatch from eggs inside or on another insect, and they eat their host insect as they grow.

Releasing beneficial insects into your landscape or garden may offer some benefit, but it is better to conserve the beneficial insects already there. Learn to distinguish between pests and beneficial insects in your garden and landscape. Avoid applying broad-spectrum insecticides that will harm beneficial insects if it looks as if the harmful insects are already being kept to tolerable levels.

- **Botanical pesticides and insecticidal soaps**— Botanical pesticides or "botanicals" are naturally occurring pesticides derived from plants. Two common botanicals include pyrethrins, insecticidal chemicals extracted from the pyrethrum flower (*Tanacetum cinerariifolium*), and Neem, a botanical insecticide and fungicide extracted from the tropical Neem tree (*Azadirachta indica*), which contains the active ingredient azadirachtin.

Insecticidal soaps have been formulated specifically to control insects. They are most effective in controlling soft-bodied pests such as aphids, scale and mealybug crawlers, thrips, whiteflies, and spider mites. Generally, they have little effect on beetles and other hardbodied insects (an exception being cockroaches). The soaps must come into direct contact with the pest to be effective. The soap penetrates the outer cuticle of the insect's body and dissolves or disrupts the cellular membranes causing dehydration and death. Soaps can also block the spiracles or breathing pores in the insect's body, interfering with respiration. In some cases, soaps may also act as an insect growth regulator, affecting the metabolism of cells and metamorphosis.

Certain common dishwashing liquids and laundry detergents, when mixed with water, have also shown insecticidal and miticidal properties. When applied to an assortment of vegetable crops,

Palmolive®, Dawn®, Joy®, Ivory®, and Dove®, for example, have effectively reduced populations of whiteflies, aphids, and spider mites. However, dishwashing and laundry detergents are not labeled as insecticides. Although they may be insecticidal, they are chemically different from the registered insecticidal soaps. Furthermore they may prove phytotoxic, causing injury by dissolving the waxy cuticle of the plant's leaf surface. It is better to save these soaps for the washing of clothes and cleaning of dishes for which they were originally designed.

■ *Insecticidal soap is a specially formulated insecticide that kills soft-bodied insects, such as aphids. Use an insecticidal soap in your garden rather than dish soap from your kitchen to avoid causing injury to your plants.*

"Natural" pesticides break down rapidly when exposed to sunlight, air, and moisture and are less likely to kill beneficial insects than insecticides that have a longer residual activity.

- **Microbial insecticides**—These insecticides combat damaging insects with microscopic living organisms such as viruses, bacteria, fungi, protozoa, or nematodes. Although they may look like out-of-the-ordinary insecticides, they can be applied in ordinary ways—as sprays, dusts, or granules. The bacterium *Bacillus thuringiensis* (*B.t.*) is the most popular pathogen. Formulations from *Bacillus thuringiensis* var. *kurstaki* (*B.t.k.*) are the most widely used to control caterpillars—the larvae of butterflies and moths.

- **Horticultural oils**—When applied to plants, these highly refined oils smother insects, mites, and their eggs. Typically, horticultural oils such as Sunspray®, Scalecide®, and Volck®, are derived from highly refined petroleum products that are specifically manufactured to control pests on plants. Studies have shown that horticultural oils derived from vegetable oils, such as cottonseed and soybean oil, also exhibit insecticidal properties.

Dormant applications generally control aphid eggs and the egg stages of mites, scale insects, and caterpillars like leafrollers and tent caterpillars. Summer applications control adelgids, aphids, mealybugs, scale insects, spider mites, and whiteflies.

Oils have limited effects on beneficial insects, especially when applied during the dormant season. Additionally, insects and mites have not been reported to develop resistance to petroleum or vegetable oils.

- **Traditional, synthetic pesticides**—Synthetic pesticides, developed by people, should be your last resort when confronted by damaging pest levels. Use them sparingly to control the targeted pest. Specific names of synthetic pesticides are avoided in this book because products and their labels change rapidly along with the pesticide registration and use process. When buying any pesticide, read the label and follow all directions and precautions before mixing and applying it, and before storing or disposing of it.

FURTHER HELP

Clemson University and North Carolina State University have Extension offices or centers in every county of the Carolinas. Many are staffed by Master Gardeners trained in horticulture. These volunteers are also available to answer your questions at many arboreta, botanical, and other public gardens.

Help is available from the Garden Clubs of North Carolina and South Carolina and an array of web-based societies devoted to specific plants, and from seminars and informative newsletters.

Now, let's get started!

HOW TO USE THIS BOOK

This book is a month-by-month guide to the activities you, the gardener, need to do in order to have a productive and successful gardening experience. The plants featured in this book are divided into ten groups, arranged alphabetically in each month to help you find the information you need both seasonally and by plant type.

Annuals are relied upon to deliver brilliant color and a long-lasting display of flowers all season long. Find when to start them from seed indoors, when to transplant them outside, and how to care for them during the year so they look their best.

Bulbs, **corms**, **rhizomes, and tubers** are unique belowground storage organs that encompass an exciting array of beautiful and durable plants. For simplicity's sake, I refer to them collectively as "bulbs." Use this book to learn when to plant them and how and when to divide them.

Edibles—herbs and vegetables—can be grown and harvested year-round in most of the Carolinas. Knowing when to start seeds indoors and when to set transplants in the garden will keep your garden productive throughout the year.

Cool- and warm-season **lawn grasses** can be grown in the Carolinas. The timing of certain cultural practices differs for each type. Follow the cultural requirement for your particular lawn to keep it healthy, dense, and attractive.

Perennials are technically termed "herbaceous" perennials to separate them from woody shrubs and trees. These flowering plants, ferns, and ornamental grasses deliver unique colors and textures with flowers, leaves, and seedheads. Perennials have specific needs regarding pruning, deadheading, dividing, and transplanting.

The **rose**—our national emblem—has been around since ancient times and continues to infatuate gardeners with its grace and beauty. Its popularity has skyrocketed with the introduction of easy-care shrub roses. Provide these flowers with the attention they deserve, and you will be rewarded with exquisite flowers.

Shrubs come in a dizzying array of shapes, sizes, forms, and colors. Some have soft, naturally billowy forms; others sport showy, fragrant flowers or brightly colored berries; and still others deliver stunning fall color. Planting, pruning, fertilizing, and keeping an eye out for pests should be done at specific times of the year.

Trees are permanent landscape investments that grow in value with each passing year. Select them carefully, place them wisely, and plant them properly. Insects and diseases are a constant threat, but pest-resistant trees help.

Vines and groundcovers are the workhorses of the landscape: they combine functionality with beauty. Vines have traditionally been used to hide chain-link fences and unsightly views and to provide some shade and privacy on the front porch. Groundcovers are called upon to control soil erosion on steep slopes, to hide red clay in places where nothing else will grow, and to replace lawn grass in shady or wet areas.

Water gardening offers a different set of challenges and experiences than does "terrestrial" gardening. Water and bog plants encompass a wide range of unique plants that like "wet feet." Select the right kinds of plants for your water garden and give them the proper care each month.

Now, let's look at these plants and their monthly needs in more detail.

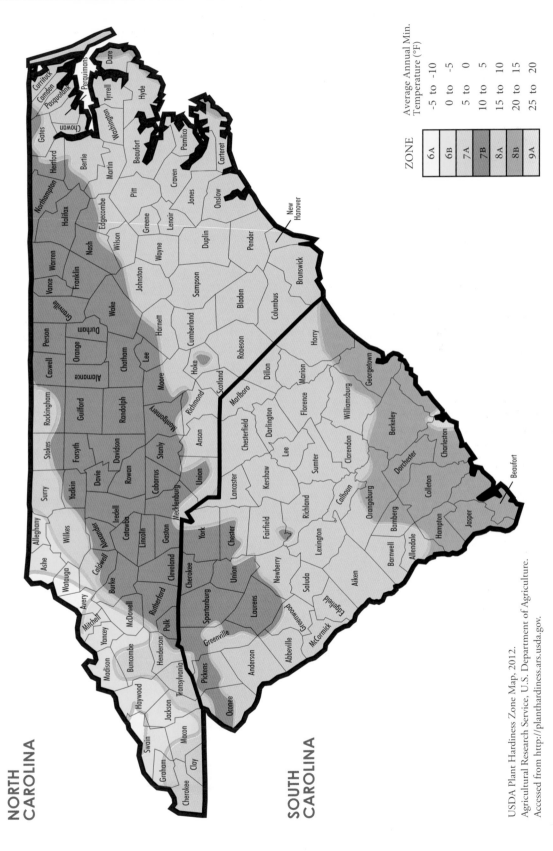

NORTH
CAROLINA

SOUTH
CAROLINA

ZONE   Average Annual Min.
            Temperature (°F)

6A	-5 to -10
6B	0 to -5
7A	5 to 0
7B	10 to 5
8A	15 to 10
8B	20 to 15
9A	25 to 20

USDA Plant Hardiness Zone Map, 2012.
Agricultural Research Service, U.S. Department of Agriculture.
Accessed from http://planthardiness.ars.usda.gov.

January

Winter is my least favorite season. I don't think I have seasonal affective disorder, but my mood brightens when I'm in the presence of flowering plants. Although many shrubs and trees showcase colorful stems or bark, berries, or evergreen leaves in winter, they don't compare to the emotional rush that's triggered by winter blooms. A serious consequence to blooming in winter is the ever-present danger of losing the flowers to freezing temperatures. Nevertheless, their appearance and fragrance during the winter months is a chance worth taking.

A tree that blooms sporadically from fall through winter on mild days with a larger show in early spring is the winter flowering cherry (*Prunus subhirtella* 'Autumnalis') with semi-double pink flowers.

In late January and February, I look forward to the spicy sweet-smelling blooms of Japanese flowering apricot (*Prunus mume*). This tree was one of the late J. C. Raultson's favorite trees. Over 300 named cultivars offer single or double flowers in white through shades of pink to red.

Other winter flowers that raise my spirits are the many cultivars of Japanese camellias that bloom from late fall to early spring. Rightfully, they've earned the nickname of "winter rose."

Witchhazels offer an interesting floral display in winter: their spiderlike flowers are comprised of four straplike petals that look like strands of confetti that have exploded from the bud. Among the best choices for the garden are the hybrids between the Asian species (*Hamamaelis × intermedia*; photo on left). These plants produce the showiest flowers and become multi-stemmed shrubs ranging from 6 to 15 feet high. My favorites among the two dozen cultivars include 'Arnold Promise', 'Jelena', 'Primavera', and 'Ruby Glow'.

Paperbush (*Edgeworthia chrysantha*) is an uncommon deciduous shrub that bears extremely fragrant creamy yellow flowers in midwinter.

Finally, in very early spring I look forward to smelling the fragrant flowers of Cornelian cherry dogwood (*Cornus mas*), a multi-stemmed small tree. The glowing yellow flowers eventually give rise to fruits that turn dark red in late summer.

These are just a few of my favorite winter-flowering plants that take me to my happy place when the days are cold and dreary. Perhaps they'll do the same for you.

PLAN

ANNUALS

Organize your seed packets to create a sowing schedule. Look up the date of the last expected freeze in your area (see the map on p. 223). Check the instructions on the seed packets to find the number of weeks of growth required before each seedling can be transplanted outdoors. Count the weeks back from the last expected freeze to know when to sow your seeds.

■ *A square-foot garden can increase your yield and reduce your workload in the garden.*

BULBS

As you scour the garden catalogs and websites with spectacular pictures and mouth-watering descriptions of summer- and fall-flowering bulbs, pay attention to bloom time, color, height, and hardiness.

EDIBLES

Intensive gardening can be accomplished in a number of ways to increase production from a limited space. Shift the garden layout from rows to raised beds, which utilize most of the ground formerly used for pathways. Make these permanent rectangular beds as long as you like and 3 to 4 feet wide so they can be worked from either side. Plant intensively in these beds. Consider "square-foot gardening," where the bed is divided into square blocks. Each plant or seed is planted in the center of each square. See Mel Bartholomew's *All New Square Foot Gardening, Second Edition* (Cool Springs Press, 2013).

Another intensive gardening approach is vertical gardening, which exploits the air space above the bed. Vining and sprawling plants like cucumbers, melons, pole beans, and indeterminate tomatoes can be supported with trellises, nets, strings, or poles. Because they occupy little garden space, the remaining space can be planted with low-growing vegetables.

LAWNS

If you're planning on hiring a lawn-care service company, be realistic about what you expect from your lawn and from the company. Here are a few pointers:

1. Know what services you want. Get several estimates. Ask neighbors and friends for recommendations.

2. Obtain a written service agreement. Find out if the service is automatically renewed each year and request an annual written confirmation. Ask if there are penalties if you cancel your service agreement.

3. Ask if the company is licensed and insured. Don't be afraid to ask for proof.

■ *Besides being easy to maintain, well-designed and well-constructed raised beds can be attractive accent features in your garden.*

4. Ask if the company is a member of a state or national trade association, such as the Professional Lawn Care Association of America. Trade associations help keep their members informed of the latest technical information and the safe use of pesticides.

5. Pesticides and other lawn-care chemicals should be used only as needed. Ask the company what chemicals it plans to use.

6. A company should always provide advance notice of chemical applications so lawn furniture and toys can be removed from the lawn.

7. Check with the Better Business Bureau to see if there have been any complaints lodged against the company. Ask the company for references from local customers.

PERENNIALS & ORNAMENTAL GRASSES

As you design your garden, take the traditional route and use perennials in island beds or borders. An island bed can be viewed from all sides. A perennial border is often called a mixed border because it can include annuals, shrubs, and trees to create a variety of colors and textures. A border is usually backed up to a wall, fence, or hedge. It should be wide enough to accommodate a generous helping of plants; this means it should be at least 8 feet in width, including a 2-foot space in the back to allow for air movement and room for you to maintain the planting.

Perennials can also be used as:

1. Pockets of color. Light up your landscape with long-blooming perennials. Tuck them in around your shrubs to add color and texture, and use them alone or in concert with annuals and bulbs to add some pizzazz to the front of your home, along walkways, or at the corners of your patio.

2. Groundcovers. Evergreen daylilies, hellebores, and wild gingers can be used to cover large areas of ground.

3. Containers. Perennials can be grown with annuals and bulbs in containers to bring color where you want it—on the front porch, deck, patio, or near the swimming pool. Select compact, long-blooming perennials such as 'Stella de Oro' daylily, goldmoss sedum (*Sedum acre*), and the Galaxy series of yarrow.

ROSES

Whether you plan to sprinkle a few roses amongst your perennials and shrubs or have thoughts of producing an ever-blooming rose border, sit down and take the time to select the right roses for your purpose. Aside from saving you money and sleep, along with alleviating frustration, choosing roses that match your site and your management style will pay big dividends in beauty. Unless you're willing to commit to a regular pesticide program, select durable, easy-care roses.

Compare your wish list with varieties recommended by the Carolina District Rose Society (www.carolinadistrict.org), covering North and South Carolina, and one of the eighteen geographical districts of the American Rose Society. Also, take a look at the *Handbook for Selecting Roses*, published yearly by the American Rose Society (www.ars.org). It covers both old garden and modern roses that are evaluated by rosarians across the country. The scores will give a clue as to how your choices measure up against others in their class. If it turns out some varieties you have picked have not been tested by the rosarians in the Carolina District Rose Society, you may enjoy taking it upon yourself to give it a trial in your own garden.

Consider All-America roses as well. All-America Rose Selections, Inc. (AARS) is a nonprofit research organization founded in 1938 for the purpose of evaluating and identifying roses that

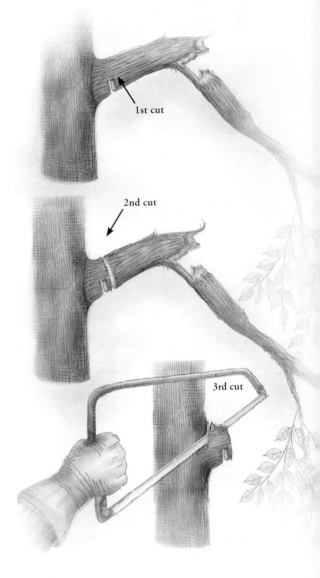

■ *When pruning a large tree limb, start with a small cut from underneath, then move to the top of the limb and cut all the way through, just to the outside of the first cut. This keeps the bark from tearing when the limb breaks loose. Finish the job by trimming the stub so it's flush with the branch collar.*

HERE'S HOW

TO PRUNE TREES

1. Thin-out dying, dead, or pest-ridden twigs and branches. "Thinning" is a term that describes the removal of a branch where it joins the limb or trunk. Thinning opens up the center of the tree to sunlight and reduces the number of new shoots that sprout along the branches. A lot of growth can be removed by thinning without dramatically changing the tree's natural appearance or growth habit and giving it the "just-pruned" look.

   Heading cuts are usually reserved for shrubs and are generally undesirable on mature trees. Young trees can be headed-back to encourage branching on long leggy branches. Never head-back or "top" the limbs of mature trees—their structure is weakened or lost with the production of numerous snakelike sprouts, and the stubs that result are exposed to attack from insects and diseases.

2. Next, remove one of any two branches that are rubbing or crossing over each other. Wounds develop on rubbing branches, creating entryways for invading insects and diseases.

3. Look for codominant limbs. Remove branches that form a narrow, V-shaped angle with the trunk. Branches that have included bark are weakly attached.

4. Remove upright-growing side limbs that are growing taller than the main trunk.

5. Do not coat the wounds with pruning-wound paints. There is no scientific evidence that dressing wounds prevents decay.

stand head-and-shoulders above others. Six types of roses can vie for the All-America title each year: hybrid teas, floribundas, grandifloras, miniatures, climbers, and landscape roses. AARS roses are evaluated in test gardens throughout the United States by commercial rose producers. They are scored on such characteristics as vigor, growth habit, hardiness, disease resistance, and flower production.

Before you order, make sure you've got enough room in your garden. Order the plants early and they will arrive at the right time for your area.

SHRUBS

When scouring the catalogs with gorgeous images of attractive shrubs, check to see if they come with the added bonus of pest resistance. Avoid adding another plant to your landscape that will result in a battle with pests during the hot, humid summer months! Have you forgotten about your fights with euonymus scales, Entomosporium leaf spot on your Indian hawthorns, and lace bugs

on your azaleas and cotoneasters? You can always practice "tough love" gardening by getting rid of the infested plants, but this can quickly become an expensive practice. Use the catalogs as a starting point, and continue your search for pest-resistant plants in print and electronic media, and during visits to local nurseries and garden centers.

TREES

If you're planning on pruning your trees this winter, have a purpose in mind as described in the steps above.

VINES & GROUNDCOVERS

Think about some troublesome areas that would benefit from a colorful vine or groundcover. Look for multi-season ornamental characteristics in the plants. The leaves of evergreens offer year-round interest. Deciduous plants can offer attractive leaves, and fall color that can enhance the architectural features of a trellis or latticework. Don't forget about fragrant flowers, colorful fruit, and unique seedpods.

As you compile your list of favorites, remember the importance of matching the vine or groundcover to the site. Avoid the disappointment you will have if you try to force a vine or groundcover to grow where it just doesn't belong.

WATER GARDENS

Whether you have a small container or a large pond, sit down and select the right plants for your water garden. As you compile your list, study the ornamental features of each plant and their optimum water depth, but most important, know the plant's mature spread. Avoid focusing on the intense 6- to 7-inch-wide flower of the hardy water lily 'Escarboucle' without knowing that the plant will spread up to 7 feet. 'Pink Shadow', with 3½-inch-wide off-white flowers, spreads half as much and would be a better choice for smaller pools and containers. If size is a limitation, consider dwarf cultivars, purchase fewer plants, or build a larger water garden.

PLANT

ANNUALS

Growing your own transplants from seed offers you a wider choice of varieties. It can also be a challenge. Be sure to pay attention to timing. Avoid sowing seeds too early because they may be ready for transplanting before outdoor conditions permit. See January, Plan.

There are two ways of growing transplants from seed. In the one-step method, sow seeds directly into individual containers. Transplant them directly outdoors when they can be easily handled. In the two-step method, sow seeds in trays or flats until the "true leaves" emerge, then transplant them to pots for further growth before moving them to their permanent homes outdoors. Use aluminum foil pans if nursery flats are not available. Punch holes in the bottom of the pans for drainage.

When the soil can be worked, direct-sow sweet alyssum, larkspur, and California, Iceland, and Shirley poppies later this month in the Coastal Plain. Although in the Piedmont and Coastal Plain they're better suited to fall sowing, sow them now if you didn't sow in fall. Sprinkle them on a roughly raked surface and water.

HERE'S HOW

TO SOW SEEDS FOR ONE-STEP OR TWO-STEP METHOD

1. Moisten a soil-less seed-starting mixture and fill the pots or trays to within ¼ inch of the top.

2. Mix very fine seeds with vermiculite or sand and pour into the center of a folded sheet of paper. Tap it gently over the medium to sow the seeds. If planting in individual pots, make a hole in the mix with a pencil point, chopstick, or other "dibble." Plant the seeds no deeper than recommended on the label. A general rule is to cover seeds to a depth equal to twice their diameter. Drop one or two seeds in each hole.

   When sowing medium to large seeds in the two-step method, use the end of a pencil to create furrows about 1 to 2 inches apart and about ⅛- to ¼-inch deep across the surface of the growing medium with the end of a pencil. Sow the seeds in rows for easier labeling and transplanting.

3. Press extremely fine seeds such as petunia, begonia, and snapdragon lightly into the medium, or water them in with a fine mist spray. Cover the seed if light is not required for germination. A thin layer of vermiculite will do. Otherwise, leave the seed uncovered, exposed to light.

the seed packet; if there are no instructions, provide bottom heat of 75 to 85 degrees Fahrenheit. Use a bottom-heat mat or a waterproof insulated heating cable, or set the tray on top of the refrigerator.

When the seeds have sprouted, expose them to bright light to keep them short and stocky. Remove the plastic covering and put them under fluorescent lights. Two 40-watt cool white fluorescent lights are a cost-effective choice and provide the right quality of light. Set the trays on your light stand and lower the lights so they're almost touching the topmost leaves. Keep the lights on for sixteen hours each day. An automatic timer will help. As the seed-lings grow, raise the lights. Temperature can be 60 to 70 degrees Fahrenheit, 10 degrees lower at night. Tape aluminum foil to the back and sides of the light stand to concentrate light on plants.

4. Label the pot or flat with the name of the crop and the date it was planted. Read the packet and make note of the date the seed is expected to germinate so you will know when to expect sprouts to appear.

5. Spray-mist the seeds to water them in. If watering from the top may dislodge the seeds, place the entire container into a tub, sink, or bucket containing a few inches of water. After the potting mix is saturated, set it aside to drain.

6. Cover the pots or trays with plastic wrap, or put them in a plastic bag secured at the top to retain moisture. They won't have to be watered until the plastic wrap is removed.

7. Unless the seeds require cool temperatures, move them to a location between 65 and 75 degrees Fahrenheit in bright but indirect sunlight. Germination can be hastened by providing warmth. Follow instructions on

BULBS

Coastal gardeners in Zone 8b to Zone 9a can plant tulips and daffodils that have been precooled or refrigerated for at least six to eight weeks. Refer to October, Plant for details. If you're going to be preparing a new border for bulbs, now it is appropriate to mix compost, lime, or other amendments into the bed. If the soil is wet and sticks to your shovel, wait a few days or you could do more harm than good. When the soil crumbles easily in your hand, it's a good time to dig.

EDIBLES

Some gardeners grow their seedlings indoors in the bright direct light of a south-facing window, greenhouse, or sun porch. Others prefer the outdoors, using a cold frame (see November, Plan). In the milder areas of the Piedmont and Coastal Plain, gardeners can move their seedlings outdoors during the day to expose them to full sunlight. Be aware that you will have to contend with some cloudy, overcast days. Instead of relying on sunlight, buy or build an artificial light stand and grow your seedlings under lights.

See January, Plan to find out how to organize your seed packets to create a sowing schedule for your seeds, and for step-by-step information on producing transplants from seed indoors to get a jump on the growing season.

Coastal Plain gardeners can sow basil, chives, parsley, sage, summer savory, and sweet marjoram indoors. To encourage parsley seeds to sprout more rapidly, soften the seeds by soaking them overnight in warm water. Coastal Plain and Piedmont gardeners can sow seeds of broccoli, cabbage, and cauliflower indoors for transplanting within six to eight weeks. Head and leaf lettuce can be set out four to six weeks after sowing. Piedmont gardeners can wait until next month before starting these vegetables.

Outdoors, gardeners in the warmer coastal areas can sow beets, carrots, garden peas (English peas and edible pea pods), lettuce, mustard, radishes, spinach, and turnips. Wait until later this month and early next month in the more inland areas of the Coastal Plain. Coastal Plain gardeners can plant asparagus crowns (see February, Plant for the step-by-step procedure); wait until the next month or two to plant in the Piedmont and Mountain regions.

LAWNS

Sod of cool-season grasses can be installed anytime the soil isn't frozen. Delay planting warm-season grasses until the air temperature stays consistently above 60 degrees Fahrenheit.

PERENNIALS & ORNAMENTAL GRASSES

For the cost of a commercial packet of seed, you can produce hundreds of seedlings—less than the cost of a single potted transplant. Many cultivars will not come true from seed, which means that the offspring will not be identical to the parents and, in most cases, will be inferior to the parents. These cultivars must be propagated vegetatively—by stem or root cuttings or by division. There are some varieties, however, that will come true from seed.

In the warmer parts of the Coastal Plain, start perennials from seed late this month. Perennial seeds often require a specific chilling period before germination can occur. To learn about any special treatment required to overcome dormancy and induce germination, follow the packet instructions prior to sowing the seeds. Starting perennial seeds indoors is similar to the seed-starting technique described on pages 26–27.

Some perennials will germinate readily—in one to two weeks or less than a month. Others, however, will germinate randomly over an extended period of time that can range from days to several weeks and sometimes several months. This most commonly occurs with perennial seeds that have special pregermination requirements. Refer to the seed packet for instructions. Some seeds have thick seed coats (such as wild blue indigo, lupine, and perennial sweet pea) and need to be soaked in water or scratched with a file so water can be absorbed or imbibed by the seed. Other seeds, particularly perennials from temperate regions, need to be stratified, or exposed to moist, chilling conditions for a specified time period (check the seed packet for the length of cold exposure); otherwise, they will not germinate.

Seeds such as bleeding heart (*Dicentra*), columbine (*Aquilegia*), and garden phlox can be overwintered outdoors in a cold frame (see October, Plant). Seeds can be stratified in the refrigerator in milder areas of the Carolinas. Here's how:

1. Fill a plastic bag with dampened milled sphagnum peat moss or vermiculite and place the seeds in the bag. Label the bag with the date and the name of the seeds.

2. Place the bag in the refrigerator at 40 degrees Fahrenheit for the required period of time, usually between six to eight weeks. After the required cold treatment, sow the seeds in trays or pots and move them to a cool location (less than 70 degrees Fahrenheit) in bright, indirect light so that germination will occur.

ROSES

It's time now to get the site ready for rose planting.

Remember that a grade No. 1 rose will be a better investment than lower grades (which are indicated by higher numbers).

Plant bare-root roses as discussed in the February, Plant, Shrubs and Trees. Space plants according to their growth habit and mature spread. Follow these general spacing guidelines: hybrid teas and grandifloras, 3 to 4 feet apart; floribundas, 2 to 3 feet apart. Climbers need 8 to 12 feet between plants, and miniatures between 18 and 24 inches. Species, shrub, and old garden roses can be spaced 5 to 6 feet apart.

Coastal gardeners can move their roses to other spots in the garden now. Unless the conditions are dry enough so you can work the soil without damaging its structure, Piedmont gardeners can wait until next month.

HERE'S HOW

TO PREPARE A SITE FOR ROSES

1. For individuals or groups of roses, dig and work the soil thoroughly over as large of an area as possible. Before digging, make sure the soil is dry enough to work. If the soil sticks to the shovel or your shoes, wait a few days to allow the soil to dry. Digging wet clay soil can ruin soil structure, making it more suitable for constructing bricks than growing roses.

2. Spread a 2- to 4-inch layer of organic matter such as compost on the soil surface. Add limestone to increase the soil pH of acidic soils or sulfur to decrease the pH of alkaline soils, as recommended by the soil test results. Roses can tolerate a soil pH between 5.5 and 7.0; a pH of 6.2 to 6.8, however, would be ideal. Mix the amendments into the bed 8 to 12 inches deep. Allow the bed to settle for a few days before planting.

3. Coastal gardeners can select and plant bare-root roses at the middle of the month or later. When selecting a bare-root rose, look for these features:

   • Three or more sturdy canes that show no signs of shriveling or discoloration.

   • Healthy-looking roots that are well distributed around the plants.

   • Dormant, leafless canes. A bare-root rose that has leafed out is in jeopardy, because the leaves are demanding sustenance from the roots. If you choose to purchase plants in this state, plant them immediately if the conditions are good, or pot them up and transplant them later when more favorable conditions exist.

HERE'S HOW

TO GET YOUR LAWN MOWER READY FOR SPRING

Plan to service your lawn mower yourself or take it to a lawn repair shop this month or next. A few of the items to include:

- Air filter—clean or replace it if it's damaged.

- Spark plug—clean it or replace it if it's cracked.

- Oil—check to see that it's filled to the right level. Change the oil as recommended by the manufacturer.

- Mower blade—replace it if it's chipped, cracked, or bent. Maintain a sharp mower blade to cut the grass cleanly, which improves its look and ensures rapid healing and regrowth. A dull mower blade tears the grass.

If the blades on your reel-type mower require special equipment to sharpen them (refer to your mower's instruction manual), consider leaving this task to a professional.

- Tires—examine the tires for wear and replace them if necessary.

- Screws and bolts—check for loose screws and bolts on the handle controls and the motor now and throughout the season.

If you do it yourself, be safe. Disconnect the wire from the spark plug for safety and keep the manual within reach.

The evergreen Kaleidoscope abelia (Abelia × grandiflora 'Kaleidoscope') offers multiseason interest with gold-margined leaves that turn rose-colored in winter and white flowers in summer.

SHRUBS

Set out container-grown and balled-and-burlapped shrubs when the soil is not frozen. If you were unable to move established shrubs last fall, transplant them now while they are dormant.

TREES

If you purchased a live Christmas tree, plant it outdoors as soon as possible, especially if it has already been in the house for more than three days.

VINES & GROUNDCOVERS

In the warmer parts of the Carolinas, plant vines and groundcovers now when the soil can be worked. Before you dig, test the soil for moisture by squeezing a handful. Soil that can be dug is lightly moist and will loosely hold its shape after you squeeze it. If the soil forms a sticky ball in your hand, it's too wet to work. If you dig in a wet soil, you can ruin its structure, creating large clods that will dry out and become rock-hard with few pore spaces for air and water.

At the other extreme is very dry soil, which also should not be worked. If a handful of soil when squeezed turns to dust, wait for a rain shower a day or two before digging to prevent the topsoil from eroding away.

WATER GARDENS

Planting of water gardens will occur later in spring when you'll also have to divide and repot plants. If you don't have containers, aquatic plant fertilizer tablets, and pea gravel, order them now.

CARE

BULBS

If a few mild days of winter have encouraged shoots to emerge, don't fret about the health of your bulbs. The leaves are quite cold hardy and will not require any special protection. If they are damaged, expect new leaves to emerge.

Maintain a blanket of mulch at the feet of your bulbs, especially in the Mountains where freezing and thawing can lift the bulbs out of the ground, leaving them to dry out or be harmed by cold. An insulative layer of mulch will break the cycle of freezing and thawing.

EDIBLES

Continue harvesting carrots, radishes, and turnips. Lettuce and spinach growing in a cold frame or under the protection of a fabric row cover (spun-bonded polypropylene) or plastic tunnel can also be picked.

LAWNS

If mowing is necessary, remove no more than one-third of the grass height with a sharp mower blade. Maintain bermudagrass lawns that have been overseeded with ryegrass at a height of 1 inch. Dormant lawns do not have to be mowed.

PERENNIALS & ORNAMENTAL GRASSES

Mountain gardeners should inspect their perennials to see if any have been heaved out by the freezing and thawing of the soil. Firmly press them back down into the soil to prevent them from freezing or drying out. To reduce frost heaving, maintain a layer of mulch around your perennials to insulate the soil.

Ornamental grasses don't have to be trimmed just yet. As long as they haven't been damaged by winter winds, ice, or snow, enjoy their glorious winter foliage.

ROSES

Mountain gardeners should check the winter protection on their roses. If the mulch has been scattered or blown away to expose the crown of the plant, particularly at the bud union, put it back in place.

SHRUBS, TREES, AND VINES & GROUNDCOVERS

Remove any broken storm-damaged limbs. Use pruning shears, loppers, or a saw to make clean cuts. Any major pruning should be reserved for next month or after the coldest part of winter has passed. However, gardeners in the Coastal Plain can start pruning trees later this month, although it may be safer to wait until early next month. Piedmont and Mountain gardeners can wait until next month or March.

Delay pruning or removing cold-damaged plants. Sometimes they'll sprout from the stems or the roots, depending on the plant and the extent of injury. Be patient. It may take until May or June before new leaves sprout from the seemingly lifeless branches.

Summer-flowering shrubs can be pruned later this month in the Coastal Plain, after the coldest part of winter has passed, include butterflybush, glossy abelia (*Abelia* × *grandiflora*), smooth hydrangea (*Hydrangea arborescens*), and others. They produce flowers on the current-season's growth.

SHRUBS

Protect newly planted evergreens from winter burn by shading them on the south and southwest sides with temporary burlap screens or snow fences. Established evergreens may also require similar sun and wind protection to prevent the leaves from turning brown and scorching. This is especially important in the Mountains where the soil can

■ *Moderate to heavy pruning to improve tree structure is best done when trees are dormant in late winter, right before bud-swell.*

freeze and remain frozen on sunny days. When this happens, the leaves continue to transpire or lose water, but the roots cannot replace the lost moisture from the frozen soil. Winter burn can also occur when the sun thaws the leaves, which then refreeze rapidly when the sun is blocked or at sunset when the leaf temperature drops quickly.

TREES

If you staked your newly planted tree last fall, check the rubber straps and stakes. They should be secured at the lowest point on the trunk to give it a little room to move back and forth, which encourages the development of a strong, thick trunk. In the Mountains, the stakes may have to be hammered back into the ground if they've been heaved out of the soil by cold. Make a note to remove the straps in the spring after growth has started.

VINES & GROUNDCOVERS

Check the condition of the vines growing on trellises or supports and see that they're still attached.

WATER GARDENS

Examine the tropical water lilies you overwintered indoors. Any tubers showing signs of rot should be discarded. Check to see that the sand is damp and hasn't dried out.

WATER

ANNUALS, EDIBLES, AND PERENNIALS & ORNAMENTAL GRASSES

Determine the need for watering seed-propagated plants by squeezing the top ½-inch of planting medium between your thumb and forefinger. If water squeezes out easily, there's enough moisture. If the medium feels slightly moist but water is difficult to squeeze out, add water.

BULBS

Check the potting mix in pots that will be forced indoors. The mixture should be evenly moist but not soggy. The easiest way to determine moisture is to lift the pots. A dry pot will be lighter than a wet one.

LAWNS

Dormant and overseeded lawns may need watering this month if it's been dry, warm, and windy.

SHRUBS, TREES, AND VINES & GROUNDCOVERS

During winter thaws, water fall-planted and established evergreens, especially those on the south and west sides of the house. Mulch newly planted shrubs with a 2- to 3-inch layer of compost, and keep them well watered. During mild winter spells, water fall-planted and established evergreens, especially if the winter is dry. Pay particular attention to trees planted on the southern and western sides of your home.

■ *The widely popular Nellie R. Stevens holly reliably produces bright red berries in the fall. Tolerant of heat and drought, this hybrid grows 20 to 30 feet tall and 10 to 15 feet wide.*

FERTILIZE

ANNUALS AND EDIBLES

Seedlings growing in soil-less mixes need to be fertilized when the first true leaves appear. Feed at every other watering with a water-soluble fertilizer to promote faster growth until the plants are ready to plant outdoors.

PERENNIALS & ORNAMENTAL GRASSES, SHRUBS, TREES, AND VINES & GROUNDCOVERS

Do not fertilize at this time. Wait until at least budbreak—when new growth emerges in the spring.

PROBLEM-SOLVE

ANNUALS, EDIBLES, AND PERENNIALS & ORNAMENTAL GRASSES

Damping off is a serious disease that attacks and kills seeds and seedlings. This common fungal disease attacks the seedlings at ground level, rotting the stems and causing plants to topple over. Their stems look as if they have been pinched. See February, Problem-Solve, for a description and controls.

BULBS

Check the condition of your stored bulbs such as caladiums, dahlias, and tuberous begonias. Discard

HERE'S HOW

TO START SEEDS WITH THE SEALED-LID METHOD

1. Cut a paper towel into postage-stamp-sized squares and place them on the inside of a lid.

2. Wet each square towel with a few drops of water. Then place one seed in the center of each square.

3. For small seeds, picking them up may be a challenge. Break a toothpick, wet the jagged end, and touch the seed with it. The seed readily sticks to the end and can be easily deposited on the paper.

4. Once you have placed the seeds on the lid, close the container, using the lid as the floor and the container as a makeshift greenhouse. Put the container in a warm, out-of-the-way place.

5. Depending on the type of seed, germination may take place in a few days or it may take a week or more. Inspect the seeds every now and then by looking through the underside of the lid for signs of the "seedling root" or radicle peeking through.

6. Once you see the radicle or seedling root, a welcome sign that germination has occurred, remove the container from the lid. Gently pluck the germinated seeds off the lid with tweezers and plant them in small pots filled with potting mix. Use the eraser end of a pencil to dibble a shallow planting hole. After placing the seed in the pot, run the pointed end of the pencil alongside the hole to cover the seed.

I have found the sealed-lid method to be highly efficient and economical. For example, instead of sowing a whole packet of tomato seeds, germinate only the number you want to eventually transplant in the garden.

any that show signs of rot, which attacks improperly stored tubers in warm, humid conditions. Discard all diseased tubers. Avoid damaging tubers when digging them up, and store them in a cool, dry, dark place.

LAWNS

Handpull winter annuals such as common chickweed, henbit, and hairy bittercress. Pull wild garlic when the soil is moist to remove the entire plant. If you leave the bulb behind, it will resprout.

ROSES, SHRUBS, TREES, AND VINES & GROUNDCOVERS

Apply a dormant horticultural oil in late winter or early spring before bud-break to smother overwintering insect eggs, aphids, mites, and scale insects. Read the label for any precautions regarding the recommended high- and low-temperature limits at the time of application. Special equipment (or a professional) will be needed to treat large trees.

As groundcovers are settling in, fill the open areas with mulch. An alternative to mulching is interplanting with annuals. Use transplants for small areas and direct-sow large areas. A couple of points to consider when interplanting with annuals:

1. When using a pre-emergent herbicide, you cannot seed with annuals—they will be prevented from germinating by the herbicide.

2. Select well-behaved varieties of annuals and don't plant them so densely that they'll shade or crowd out groundcovers or compete for light or nutrients. As the groundcover plants spread, fewer annuals can safely be planted without encroaching on the permanent plantings.

EDIBLES

Sowing seeds into pots and then waiting for the seedlings to emerge can be an act of faith. To avoid those feelings of helplessness and anxiety when sowing vegetable seeds, try the sealed-lid seed-starting technique. I have used it for germinating large-seeded vegetables like tomatoes, peppers,

cucumbers, squash, and melons. The materials for the sealed-lid method include a small plastic container that has a clear or translucent plastic lid such as a leftover margarine or whipped-cream container, and a piece of paper towel about 6 inches square.

WATER GARDENS

How many is too many when it comes to plants and fish for a pool? There's a way to calculate that.

HERE'S HOW

TO DETERMINE THE MAXIMUM NUMBER OF PLANTS AND FISH

*   To determine the amount of water in your pool, use this simple formula: length × width × depth × 7.5 gallons/cubic foot = total gallons in the pond

*   To determine the surface area for a square or rectangular pool, use this formula: length × width = surface area

*   To calculate the volume of a rectangular pond, multiply the surface area by the depth: (length × width) × depth = volume

*   To calculate the volume of a circular pool, use the formula: πr^2 or 3.14 × (½ the diameter × ½ the diameter) × depth = volume

*   If you plan to dig a pond rather than construct an aboveground pool, "call before you dig" to find out where your underground utilities and pipes are located. Dial 811 or visit www.nc811.org and www.sc811.org. Member companies will mark underground lines within three business days (not including the day of the call).

Also, be aware of any local building codes that may affect the placement of your water garden, its size, and depth. Anything that's deeper than a couple of feet could be classified as a pool, and pools often require fencing.

This month I take an inventory of my seed collection. First, I gather up all of the seeds that I've squirreled away in various places like the refrigerator crisper, the pockets of jackets and sport coats, and dresser drawers. Then, over several evenings and weekends, I decide what to save, trade, or toss out.

To help me decide what stays and what goes into the compost heap, I ask myself several questions: **How old is the seed?** Seeds remain viable or are capable of germinating over a certain period of time. When stored under cool, dry conditions, expect these seeds to produce a good stand of healthy seedlings: **1 year or less:** onions, parsley, parsnips, and salsify; **2 years:** corn, okra, and peppers; **3 years:** beans, cowpeas (Southern peas), and peas; **4 years:** beets, fennel, mustard, pumpkins, rutabagas, squash, Swiss chard, tomatoes, turnips, and watermelons; **5 years:** Brussels sprouts, cabbage, cauliflower, collards, eggplant, muskmelons, radishes, and spinach.

Is the seed viable? Perform a simple germination test using moistened paper towels or the sealed method technique described on p. 34. If few seeds germinate, you may want to discard the seed and buy fresh seed for the upcoming gardening season.

Is the seed the actual variety you wanted to save? Expect true-to-type varieties with self-pollinated beans, peas, lettuce, and non-hybrid tomatoes. However, surprises abound with insect-pollinated varieties of cucumber, melon, squash, or pumpkin, or wind-pollinated sweet corn, spinach, and Swiss chard.

Was the seed collected from a hybrid? Hybrid or F1 hybrid seed is the offspring of a cross made between two parent varieties. If you prefer the original hybrid, discard them.

Do you have any seeds or varieties you can swap for? In the eyes of some gardeners, a "Joe DiMaggio" or "Willie Mays" could be a 'Sweet Baby Blue' corn or a 'Super Italian Paste' tomato. Save these seeds and trade them for something else.

When I answer these questions, I find that very few seeds ever get composted. Probably because I always ask myself one final question, "Am I really sure I can't find any room for this little packet of seeds?" The answer is always, "But of course, my wife has eight dresser drawers with plenty of room!"

PLAN

ANNUALS

When planning your garden, think in splashes—not drops—of color. High-impact, car-stopping beds are achieved when annuals are planted *en masse*. Before you buy any plants or seeds, draw your garden plan on a sheet of graph paper. Draw it to scale and decide on the kinds of colors you want. As you look through catalogs, examine plant descriptions carefully. Take note of these features:

- Are they cool- or warm-season annuals?

- What is their expected height and spread at maturity? Will they require staking?

- Are they "self-cleaning?" The spent flowers of some modern varieties are shed by the plant and quickly disappear. Others need spent flowers removed (called deadheading) to eliminate the old, faded blooms. This task is necessary for cosmos, marigold, pansy, and pinks. Deadheading prevents the formation of seeds and stimulates continued flowering.

BULBS

Plan to order summer-flowering bulbs for new beds or as complements to existing plantings. Try new varieties of tried-and-true standbys, such as lilies, which offer newer colors and long-lasting color in midsummer. Experiment with some of the "little" bulbs with long flowering periods between summer and fall, such as the summer scillas (*Scilla autumnalis* and *S. scilloides*), alliums (*Allium globosum* and *A. senescens*), hardy cyclamens (*Cyclamen graecum* and *C. hederifolium*), and zephyr lilies (*Zephyranthes candida*). Though small in stature, they're ideal for adding sparkle to containers and small cozy spots in the garden.

EDIBLES

To keep your garden in continuous production, use any of three intensive approaches.

Rotate your vegetables by not planting the same vegetable or related vegetable in the same location

HERE'S HOW

TO PLANT AN INTENSIVE VEGETABLE GARDEN

1. Interplanting or intercropping involves growing different kinds of vegetables together at the same time. Combine a slow-growing or early-maturing crop with a fast-growing or late-maturing crop. The quick-growing vegetable will mature and be harvested before the slow-growing crop needs the space; thus two crops can grow in the same area without crowding each other.

2. In succession planting, a crop is grown, harvested, removed, and another planted in its place. Just avoid planting vegetables in the same family in the same place right after one another. For example, try following peas with okra, or plant cucumbers after spinach. Planting a spring, summer, and fall garden is another form of succession planting. Cool-season crops (broccoli, lettuce, peas) are followed by warm-season crops (beans, peppers, tomatoes), and these may be followed by more cool-season plants or even a winter cover crop.

3. Relaying consists of staggering the planting times of one type of crop to extend the harvest season over a long period of time instead of having one big harvest all at once. One approach is to plant one variety several times, at about two-week intervals (allow more time between early plantings in colder soil, but only ten days between the last plantings). For instance, sweet corn may be planted at two-week intervals for a continuous harvest. Another relaying approach is to make one planting of two or more varieties that differ in maturity time; for example, try fifty-day with sixty-day beans or early, mid-, and late-season varieties of sweet corn.

HERE'S HOW

TO PLANT CONTAINER-GROWN SHRUBS AND TREES

1. *Dig a planting hole twice as wide as the rootball, but no deeper. The plant should sit at the same place it was growing in the container or maybe an inch or so above the surrounding soil to allow for settling.*

2. *Place the container on its side and roll it on the ground while tapping it to loosen the roots. Upend the container and gently pull it off of the plant roots. Do not pull plant by stem.*

3. *Use your fingers to loosen any roots that may be matted, gently untangling them. Roots that are tightly coiled should be cut apart and loosened. Gently spread the roots wide so they are pointing outward as much as possible.*

4. *Set the shrub into the hole.*

5. *Backfill the hole with the original soil. Mound the soil to create a ridge around the plant to hold water. Water well and cover the soil with organic mulch, keeping it a few inches from the shrub.*

If you didn't plant sweet peas last October or November, plant them outdoors this month. You can even start the seed indoors in peat pots four to five weeks before setting them out, giving them a head start before the temperatures get too hot.

Dig up, divide, and replant overgrown clumps of liriope. Mountain gardeners can postpone this chore until late March or April. Replant the liriope divisions about a foot apart.

There are some vines that are just plain frightening. When kudzu made its American debut at the United States Centennial Exposition's Japanese Pavilion in Philadelphia in 1876, little did the organizers and visitors know that this lovely "porch vine" would eventually be billed as the world's fastest vine, growing a foot a day and up to 100 feet in a single season. The rest is history.

Vines like Japanese wisteria can become botanical pythons, strangling trees and pergolas with their sheer weight. Some vines raise concern because of their rampant freewheeling nature, not only in the garden but also in nature where they have escaped. These include English ivy (*Hedera helix*), Hall's Japanese honeysuckle (*Lonicera japonica* 'Halliana'), wintercreeper euonymus (*Euonymus fortunei*), Oriental bittersweet (*Celastrus orbiculatus*), and porcelainberry (*Ampelopsis brevipedunculata*).

Do some research. Read local gardening columns in newspapers and gardening magazine articles, and visit private and public gardens to see these vines in action in the landscape. These background checks will alert you to any landscape surprises.

WATER GARDENS

A number of plants are the "kudzus" of the aquatic world. When they escape into streams, lakes, and estuaries they form dense colonies, which interfere with boating, fishing, and other recreational activities. They degrade water quality by reducing oxygen levels in the water and displace desirable plants. Millions of dollars are spent annually to control these thugs.

The State of North Carolina Department of Environment and Natural Resources Division of Water Resources and the South Carolina Department of Natural Resources Aquatic Nuisance Species Program educate the public and the plant nursery industry about these noxious exotic aquatic weeds.

A good time to install a small water garden is in the spring when the ground can be worked.

To calculate the size of the pond liner, outline the area and decide on a depth.

■ *Use spray paint to outline the shape of your water garden.*

1. Measure the length and width of the pool. If it's a circle or irregularly shaped, draw a square or rectangle around it and use the length and width of the square or rectangle.

2. Use this equation to calculate the length and width of your pond liner:

   length = maximum length of pond
   + (2 × maximum depth)
   + (2 × edging allowance)

   width = maximum width of pond +
   (2 × maximum depth) + (2 × edging allowance)

3. Center the liner over the hole and weigh down its edges with smooth stones or bricks. Slowly fill the pond with water. As the pond fills, gradually take the weights off the edges so the water will fill into the crevices. When the water comes within 1 inch of the top, shut it off and cut away any excess material, leaving about a foot beyond the rim. Line the edge of the pond with stones, pavers, bricks, or other suitable materials.

4. For preformed pools, spread an inch or two of damp sand on the bottom. Set the form in the hole so the rim is just above ground level. Take it out and make any adjustments. When it's level, firmly pack soil around its edges. Fill the pool with water. Hide the rim with rocks or use a spreading groundcover.

CARE

ANNUALS

Indoors: Seedlings receiving inadequate light become spindly and floppy. Keep them in a south-facing window or place them under artificial lights for sixteen hours a day.

Outdoors: Pinch off pansy flowers when transplanting to encourage branching and focus the plant's efforts on rooting and getting established.

BULBS

It's not unusual for some spring-flowering bulbs to send up a few leaves in late fall or early winter. The bulbs will remain safe and still produce flowers

HERE'S HOW

TO INSTALL A WATER GARDEN

1. Outline the shape of a flexible liner with a rope or garden hose. Mark the border with spray paint, builder's chalk, lime, or sand. If you have a preformed pond, set it on the ground and mark its outline with the same marking materials.

2. Start digging from the edges to create an outline and excavate toward the center. Make the sides steeply sloped (about a 20-degree angle from the vertical) to achieve good volume relative to surface area to limit algae problems.

3. Check the edge of the pond frequently as you dig to make sure it's level by placing a carpenter's level on top of a long straight piece of lumber laid across the hole. The edge should be even all around to prevent water from overflowing before it's completely full.

4. Create an underwater shelf along the inside wall to hold potted marginal or bog plants and rocks. The shelves are typically 10 inches long and about 18 inches wide (if raccoons are in your area, these shelves will be used as fishing platforms!). You can grow marginals in shallow water by placing them on clean bricks or upside-down flowerpots.

5. Dig the hole at least 2 feet deep, allowing for a 1- to 2-inch layer of sand. With a preformed liner, dig the hole about 2 inches deeper and 3 to 5 inches wider on the sides than the liner.

6. For flexible liners, apply a 1- to 2-inch layer of damp river sand, old indoor-outdoor carpeting, or any other soft materials to protect the liner from sharp rocks.

next spring. It's not too late to send soil samples to your local Extension Center for testing. Because some additives, like limestone, take time before increasing the soil pH (ideally between 6 and 7), the sooner you submit a sample, the better.

■ *Ornamental grasses should be cut back to 4 to 6 inches in height.*

LAWNS

Maintain Kentucky bluegrass between 1½ and 2½ inches in height. Mow tall fescue between 2 and 3 inches high. Overseeded ryegrass lawns maintained at 1 inch should be mowed when the grass is 1½ inches tall.

PERENNIALS & ORNAMENTAL GRASSES

Mountain gardeners should inspect their perennials to see if any have been heaved out by alternating freezing and thawing of the soil. Firmly press them back down into the soil to prevent them from freezing or drying out. To reduce heaving, maintain a layer of mulch around your perennials to insulate the soil.

Cut shorter ornamental grasses to 4 to 6 inches in height and pampas grass from 6 to 12 inches in height. When pruning back the pampas grass, wear gloves and cinch the top-growth with rope to make removal easier.

Trim away any dead leaves or stems from asters, coreopsis, and rudbeckia. Avoid damaging the crown of new leaves at the base. Wait until new growth emerges before cutting back 'Miss Huff' and 'Chapel Hill Yellow' lantana and salvia.

ROSES

Cut and divide outdoor-growing miniature roses when they're dormant in the Piedmont and Coastal Plain. Wait until March or April in the Mountains. See April, Care.

Prune roses that produce flowers on the current-season's growth before new growth begins. Valentine's Day is often the recommended pruning time for Coastal Plain gardeners; Piedmont gardeners can wait until the end of the month or early March. Others prune when the forsythia is in full bloom. I wait for the rosebuds to start swelling before pruning.

Prune everblooming roses now, including bush roses such as hybrid teas, grandifloras, and floribundas. Miniatures and repeat-flowering climbers that produce flowers on current-season's growth may also be pruned (see March, Care for instructions). In the Mountains, wait until next month or April, after the coldest part of winter has passed.

Hybrid teas produce single flowers on long stems. Grandifloras send up clusters of large flowers on strong, straight stems. Prune both classes to outward-facing buds to develop an open, bowl-shaped habit.

■ *Prune roses while they are still dormant this month or next month.*

TO PRUNE HYBRID TEA AND GRANDIFLORA ROSES

1. Select three to six of the most vigorous, well-spaced canes (pencil size in diameter or thicker) from hybrid teas, and up to eight from grandifloras.

2. Remove the older canes that are brown or gray at the base.

3. Reduce the length of the canes by one-third or one-half. Generally, do not cut them back lower than 18 inches unless they've been damaged by pests or cold. Alternate the height of these final cuts to outward-growing buds to give your rose an informal look rather than an unnatural-looking "flat top."

Floribundas and polyanthas produce grand displays of flower clusters. They need a lighter-handed approach that will encourage the production of gobs of flowers all season long.

1. Lightly head back the canes either just below where they flowered or down to one-third their length. Cut back twiggy clusters to a strong bud. When grown as a hedge, they can be sheared with hedge clippers to remove one-third to one-half of their height.

2. Thin out the twiggy growth on the inside of the plant.

3. Remove a few of the spindly canes at the base to make room for the remaining canes. To produce the maximum number of flowers, leave more canes than you would for hybrid teas and grandifloras.

Repeat-blooming old garden roses, species, and shrub roses that flower on the current-season's wood should be pruned right before growth begins in late winter or early spring. They can be tip-pruned throughout the growing season to encourage the production of flower-bearing side shoots.

VINES & GROUNDCOVERS

In cold Mountain areas, some shallow-rooted groundcovers may have been heaved out of the ground by freezing and thawing soil. Once the soil is not frozen and is fairly dry, gently press the plants back into the ground to prevent them from drying out.

Watch for signs of heaving among your small shrubs; the freezing and thawing of the ground can force shallow-rooted plants out of the soil. Replant any that have been heaved and mulch with 2 to 3 inches of organic material to reduce fluctuations in soil temperature.

SHRUBS

Shrubs can get a new look or be renewed when they have outgrown their location (perhaps they were mistakenly planted along the foundation of a house and have begun to engulf the windows), have been seriously damaged or neglected, or have become "leggy" with most of their leaves clustered at the top, revealing bare or leafless stems below.

TO PRUNE A CRAPEMYRTLE

1. Remove all broken and diseased limbs.

2. Next, thin out all of the side branches one-third to one-half of the way up the height of the plant.

3. Remove rubbing and crossing branches and shoots growing into the center of the canopy or upper part of the crapemyrtle. Make your cuts to a side branch or close to the trunk.

4. Head-back wayward and unbranched limbs. Make each cut above an outward-facing bud. This will encourage the development of branches behind the cut and make them fuller.

5. Remove dried-up seed clusters within reach. This will give the tree a more uniform appearance and look neater.

■ **Shearing or heading back.** *Shearing concentrates the growth near the ends of the branches to create a shell of leaves with an interior.*

■ **Rejuvenation pruning.** *Rejuvenation pruning involves cutting back all of the stems to within 6 to 12 inches of the ground. This severe pruning should be done in later winter or early spring before new growth begins. Make each cut just above a bud; I like to vary the height of each pruned shoot to develop a more natural, informal shape. Shrubs that respond well to this treatment include forsythia, weigela, spirea, and hydrangea. Most broadleaf shrubs, such as azaleas, glossy abelias, nandina, and cleyera, also respond well to rejuvenation pruning.*

■ **Renewal pruning.** *Renewal pruning is an alternative to the drastic removal of top growth all at once. It involves removing the oldest stems over a period of three years. In the first year, remove one-third of the oldest, largest-diameter stems. The second year, remove one-half of the remaining old stems and head back long shoots that are growing from the previous year's pruning cuts. The third season, remove the remaining old wood at the base and head back the long new shoots. Do not use hedge shears but cut each branch separately at different lengths with hand pruners. By changing the depth of each cut, your shrub will develop a textured, natural look.*

HERE'S HOW

TO REJUVENATE OR RENEW A SHRUB

1. The drastic approach is to rejuvenate the shrub by cutting it back to within 6 to 12 inches of the ground before spring growth begins. Most broadleaf shrubs, including Japanese cleyera, azaleas, glossy abelia, and nandina, respond well to this treatment. When the new shoots emerge, pinch out the tips and thin out some of the shoots to make some room and begin developing a strong framework.

2. A milder tactic is to renew the shrub over a period of three years. Renewal pruning works well for multi-stemmed plants such as forsythia and spirea. In the first year, remove one-third of the oldest stems. In the following year, take out one-half of the remaining old stems and head back long shoots that grew from the previous pruning cuts. In the third year, remove the remaining old wood and head back the long new shoots.

Summer-flowering shrubs such as butterfly bush and beautyberry can be cut back to within 6 inches or a foot in the spring since they bloom on the current-season's growth. Wait to prune spring-flowering shrubs until after they bloom.

TREES

Ice and snow accumulation can damage your evergreens with their weight or if they are removed carelessly.

Begin pruning when the coldest part of winter has passed and before new growth begins. When pruning large, heavy limbs, follow the three-cut approach to prevent the branch from stripping bark away as it falls.

Avoid making "hat racks" out of your crapemyrtles. Follow the steps on page 47 to produce a natural-looking tree form that accentuates the flowers, beautiful bark, and elegant structure.

HERE'S HOW

TO PERFORM THE THREE-CUT METHOD FOR REMOVING LARGE LIMBS

1. Make the first upward cut about a foot from the trunk and one-third of the way through the bottom of the limb.

2. Make the second downward cut from the top of the branch a couple of inches away from the first cut, farther away from the trunk. As the branch falls, the undercut causes the limb to break away cleanly.

3. Finally, remove the stub by making the last cut outside of the branch collar (a swollen area at the base of the branch). The collar region is the boundary between the trunk and the branch that acts as a natural barrier to decay-causing organisms. Never leave a stub. Stubs usually die and are entry points for decay-causing fungi.

VINES & GROUNDCOVERS

Vines that have outgrown their spaces can be cut back now. Prune other vines that bloom on current-season's growth now. Avoid pruning vines that will be blooming in the spring on last year's growth. After the coldest part of winter has passed, prune summer-flowering vines such as Confederate jasmine (*Trachelospermum jasminoides*), trumpet-creeper (*Campsis* × *tagliabuana* 'Madame Galen'), and Japanese hydrangea vine (*Schizophragma hydrangeoides*).

Prune your clematis based on whether it flowers on last year's wood, this year's wood, or both. Experts divide the genus into three groups: Group I are all the early spring-flowering evergreen clematis and early- and mid-flowering species. This group includes *Clematis alpina, C. armandii, C. macropetala,* and *C. montana.* These clematis flower on last year's wood and should be pruned after the flowers fade but no later than July. The only pruning really needed is to remove weak or dead stems and whatever is needed to confine the plant to its allotted space.

Group II consists of clematis that also flower on last year's growth but will produce a second flush of bloom on new growth. These include mid-season large-flowered cultivars such as 'Bees Jubilee', 'Henryi', 'Nelly Moser', and 'Vyvyan Pennell'. Remove all dead and weak stems in late winter or early spring, and cut the remaining stems back to a pair of strong buds, which will produce the first blooms. Occasional pinching after flowering will stimulate branching.

Group III consists of late-flowering cultivars and species that flower on this season's growth such as *C. flammula, C. integrifolia, C.* × *jackmanii, C. viticella, C. tangutica, C. texensis,* and the herbaceous species. These can also be pruned in late winter or early spring. For the first two or three years they may be cut back to a foot from the ground. Later cut them back to 2 feet. If not cut regularly, this group can become very leggy and overgrown.

The boundaries between these three groups are not absolute. Certain Group III clematis, for example, can be treated as Group II to produce early blooms on the previous year's wood, but they serve as a rough guide to safely keeping your clematis vines within bounds.

Cut liriope back to within 3 to 4 inches of the ground using clippers, a string trimmer, or a mower set at its highest setting. If you wait, you'll have to do it carefully by hand to avoid nipping the new growth, which will be left with brown edges on the leaves throughout the season.

Dwarf mondo grass (*Ophiopogon japonicus* 'Nana') grows more slowly than liriope and usually requires cutting back every two or three years. If the leaves look unsightly, trim it lightly to encourage the production of new leaves.

WATER GARDENS

Check the tender aquatic plants you overwintered indoors. Make sure they're covered with water and don't allow them to dry out. Clean the pond of any debris.

WATER

ANNUALS
See January, Water.

EDIBLES AND PERENNIALS & ORNAMENTAL GRASSES

Do not overwater seedlings or transplants. Water them when the surface of the medium feels dry. Do not allow the pot or flats to dry out. If they're uncovered, check them daily and water as needed.

LAWNS

Moisten newly sodded areas of cool-season lawns so the sod will "knit" into the soil. Water immediately after sodding to wet the soil to a depth of 3 or 4 inches. Don't let the soil dry out until the sod has knitted or rooted into the soil. Observe established lawns for signs of drought stress and apply an inch of water per week (in the absence of precipitation).

For warm-season grasses, dormant and overseeded lawns may have to be watered if it's been dry, warm, and windy.

ROSES, SHRUBS, TREES, AND VINES & GROUNDCOVERS

Water newly set plants at planting. Keep the soil moist but avoid excessive watering, which can inhibit root growth.

Depending on the weather and rainfall, you may need to water newly planted trees daily for the first few weeks. Water the top of the rootball with 2 gallons of water per inch of trunk caliper. After that, begin cutting back—watering deeply but infrequently—eventually reaching an "as needed" basis by testing the soil and rootball for moisture.

If severe cold is forecast for your area, water evergreens before the soil freezes. The roots are not able to take up moisture when the soil is frozen.

FERTILIZE

ANNUALS

Feed indoor-grown transplants with a water-soluble fertilizer such as 20-20-20 at half strength every other week.

Coastal Plain gardeners can fertilize pansies when new growth resumes. A liquid fertilizer may have to be applied every two weeks.

BULBS

The best fertilizer for bulbs is a soil that's rich in organic matter. Adding nutrients periodically to replace nutrients absorbed by the growing plants, however, will help them bloom in top form. Spring bulbs, whose shoots have emerged, should be fertilized with a complete fertilizer such as 10-10-10. Apply 1 rounded teaspoon per square foot. Brush off any fertilizer from the leaves. If you fertilized

with a slow-release fertilizer last fall, it is not necessary to fertilize now.

EDIBLES

Fertilize indoor-grown transplants with a water-soluble fertilizer such as 20-20-20 at half-strength every other week. Outdoors, fertilize the newly emerging growth of established asparagus beds with a nitrogen-containing fertilizer. Gardeners on the coast can sidedress beets, carrots, and English peas. See March, Fertilize.

LAWNS

Do not fertilize cool-season or dormant lawns at this time. Overseeded bermudagrass and zoysiagrass lawns can be fertilized this month. Use a fertilizer recommended by soil test results. Do not apply a fertilizer containing phosphorus and potassium if adequate levels are already present in the soil.

PERENNIALS & ORNAMENTAL GRASSES

Seedlings growing in soil-less mixes need to be fertilized when the first true leaves appear. Feed at every other watering with a water-soluble fertilizer in order to promote faster growth until the plants are ready to plant outdoors. Water between feedings with plain water.

SHRUBS, TREES, AND VINES & GROUNDCOVERS

Don't be too hasty to fertilize your shrubs and trees. Wait until at least bud break—when new growth emerges in the spring.

Fertilize groundcovers and vines based on need. It's best to rely on soil test results when you are going to replace any nutrients that are deficient in the soil. Don't be too hasty to fertilize your vines and groundcovers. Fertilize when new growth begins.

PROBLEM-SOLVE

ANNUALS, EDIBLES, AND PERENNIALS & ORNAMENTAL GRASSES

Control any winter annual weeds such as bittercress, common chickweed, and henbit by handpulling. Suppress them with a shallow layer of mulch.

■ *Damping off is a serious soilborne fungal disease that attacks and kills young seedlings.*

Damping-off is a serious disease that attacks and kills seedlings. Overwatering, lack of drainage, poor ventilation, and crowding can foster an attack. With seedlings, the stem rots at or close to the soil surface. This is mainly caused by the fungi present in the seed-starting medium. Damping-off is easier to prevent than cure. Use clean containers. If necessary, disinfect them with a 10 percent bleach solution (1 part bleach to 9 parts water). Use a sterile, well-drained medium. Provide good conditions for rapid seed germination and development. Avoid waterlogging the medium when watering. Damping-off can be reduced by cutting back the frequency of watering and increasing the amount of light.

BULBS

Watch out for aphids on forced bulbs. These soft-bodied insects suck plant sap with their piercing-sucking mouthparts, causing the leaves to curl and become malformed. Aphids can be controlled with insecticidal soap and other insecticides.

A number of fungal diseases attack both growing plants and stored bulbs. Fungi invade planted bulbs through wounds, causing them to rot in the ground. The plants may look stunted, their leaves become yellow, and the plant dies. Bulbs attacked by these rots include daffodil, dahlia, gladiolus, and tulip. Stored bulbs may become infected through wounds or nicks in the tissue. Bulbs feel spongy and are discolored.

Fungicides can be used to treat healthy bulbs dug from infected beds prior to replanting in another part of the garden. The infected area can be treated with an appropriate fungicide at least six months before replanting. Depending on the disease and the course of action, the diseased bed may have to be avoided for several years. In the future, purchase and plant healthy bulbs. Because cultivars vary in their resistance to diseases, cultivate the more resistant types. Use care when digging up bulbs to avoid damaging them.

LAWNS

Handpull winter annuals. Treat wild garlic with a broadleaf herbicide when the air temperature is above 50 degrees Fahrenheit.

ROSES

Apply dormant oil spray as described in January, Problem-Solve. Cane-boring insects such as square-headed wasps and small carpenter bees bore into the pith of cut rose stems, leaving a telltale hole in the tip. The attacked cane wilts and dies back. Control them only when high numbers are present. After pruning your roses, paint the cuts on stems larger than ¼ inch in diameter with wood glue or shellac to block borers from entering.

Remove any of last year's leaves that remain after pruning. Overwintering leaves could harbor disease spores. Apply a fresh layer of compost over the old mulch.

To control blackspot on susceptible roses, apply fungicide after pruning. Powdery mildew-susceptible varieties can be treated with a fungicide (Neem oil, lime-sulfur, or others) at the first sign of the disease.

Cankers are dark areas on canes caused by fungi. These dead areas often encircle the cane completely and kill all growth above the canker. Sometimes they elongate and extend down to the crown, killing the entire plant. These fungi enter healthy canes through wounds caused by winter injury or improper pruning cuts.

Use sharp tools for clean cuts that will heal rapidly. Prune infected canes, cutting back to healthy tissue. Look at the pith or center of the cane and continue pruning back until the pith looks white. If you cut into diseased canes, disinfect your pruning shears with Lysol®, which is less corrosive than the traditional mixture of water and household bleach (4 parts water to 1 part sodium hypochlorite). This will prevent diseases from spreading to other canes.

SHRUBS
Use dormant oil sprays on landscape plants to smother overwintering insects and mites before the plants leaf out. See January, Problem-Solve.

Camellia flower blight is a fungal disease that attacks only the flowers of Japanese camellia (*Camellia japonica*). Pull off all affected flowers and discard them. At the end of the flowering season, rake up and destroy all fallen blossoms and other plant debris. This disease requires community-wide attention. Educate your neighbors and

encourage them to pick up and discard or destroy diseased flowers.

TREES
See January, Problem-Solve for insect advice.

Examine your Leyland cypress, arborvitae, and junipers for the pine-cone-shaped nests of overwintering bagworms. Pick off the egg-containing "bags" and discard them.

VINES & GROUNDCOVERS
To manage insects and mites, see January, Problem-Solve.

Some weed control will be required early in the establishment of groundcovers. It should be able to outcompete marauding weeds and stay relatively weed-free after it becomes established and spreads.

EDIBLES
Plant dormant asparagus crowns without any green shoots showing into a bed enriched with organic matter such as compost, manure, or shredded leaves.

Remove and discard the nests of bagworms hanging from the branches of your arborvitae, cedars, junipers, and Leyland cypress. These nests contain from 500 to 1,000 eggs that will hatch next month and into June.

HERE'S HOW

TO PLANT ASPARAGUS

1. Place the crown into the bottom of an 8-inch-deep furrow and cover with about 2 inches of soil (in heavier clay soils set them 6 inches deep). Set the crowns 12 inches apart in the trench.

2. As the new shoots emerge and grow, add another 2-inch layer of soil—do this every two to three weeks until the trench is filled.

3. Mulch with a 2-inch layer of compost to conserve water and control weeds.

4. Begin harvesting asparagus spears in the third year. (If you must, harvest lightly in the second year, for no more than two weeks. Harvesting too much and too early results in weak plants).

March

As we herald the arrival of spring and the many opportunities to spend cash on the latest, greatest gadgets and thingamabobs, become a frugal gardener. Here are just a few economical "green" techniques that will save you some "green" this gardening season.

- Grow your own plants from seeds, divisions, or cuttings. Share or trade open-pollinated heirloom plants with friends and acquaintances. Layering is a simple, foolproof way of propagating these pass-along plants.

- Reuse foam coffee cups, paper cups, cottage cheese tubs, yogurt containers, margarine containers, and cut-off milk cartons as seed-starting pots. Poke holes in the bottom for drainage. You can also make pots out of newspapers. The clamshells with clear lids at salad bars make ready-to-use mini-greenhouses for seed-starting or rooting cuttings.

- Use plastic milk jugs to seep-irrigate your plantings. Punch holes in the sides of a jug with a large nail spaced about 2 inches apart. Bury the jug, but leave the neck above the soil. Fill the jug with water (solutions of liquid fertilizer may be used to water and fertilize at the same time) and screw the cap on firmly. The water will gradually seep out, providing a slow, deep irrigation for nearby plants.

- When shopping for perennials, look for potted plants that contain several divisions or offsets that can be easily teased apart at planting. For the price of one pot, you can acquire several plants.

- Mulch your plantings. Fallen leaves make an attractive fine-textured mulch when they're shredded with a lawn mower.

- Harvest rainwater to irrigate your landscape and garden this spring and summer. Attractive rain barrels, clay urns with spigots at the bottom, or makeshift pickle barrels make excellent vessels for capturing and using rainwater.

- Recycle organic yard trimmings and kitchen wastes and return them back into the landscape or vegetable garden as a soil conditioner or mulch.

- Create an edible landscape that tastes as good as it looks. Plant fruiting shrubs and trees that offer the dual benefits of aesthetics and nutrition. These include pawpaw, persimmon, pineapple guava, pomegranate, jujube, blueberry, olives ('Ascolana', 'Mission', and 'Pendolino' [pollinator]), and banana (look for 'Veinte Cohol', a "short cycle" compact banana with black-mottled stems and tasty clusters of 3-inch-long bananas).

MARCH

PLAN

ANNUALS

Before visiting the garden center, make a list of the kinds and quantities of annuals you need. Planning beforehand will help you avoid over-indulging so you purchase only what you need. Here's how:

1. Measure the length and width of the flower-bed and calculate the area in square feet (area = length × width). If the bed is irregularly shaped—oval, round, or long and winding—make a rough estimate.

2. Jot down the kind of sun- or shade-loving annuals you would like to plant in the bed. Include their spacing requirements. Refer to the seed packet or catalog for the correct spacing.

3. Determine the number of plants you need.

BULBS

As your spring-flowering garden begins to go into glory this spring, take photographs so you can refer to them later in the year. The photos will come in handy when you're making plans to spruce up your garden or extend your beds with spring-flowering plants this fall. Also, sketch a planting map in your gardening journal to show where the bulbs are located. With an accurate plot plan, you will know where to plant spring-flowering bulbs this fall. You'll also be able to plan for continuous flowering by sowing or transplanting annual or perennial flowers among the bulbs after their display has ended.

EDIBLES

If you are serious about growing herbs and vegetables, document your observations, thoughts, and plans for the future. List the herbs and vegetables you planted in the garden. Include the names of seed companies, plant name, variety, planting date, and harvest date.

LAWNS

Plan to recycle your grass clippings as you mow. Returning your grass clippings to the lawn saves time, energy, and money—and look at recycling grass clippings as a way of fertilizing your lawn. Grass clippings contain about 4 percent nitrogen, ½ to 1 percent phosphorus, 2 to 3 percent potassium, and smaller amounts of other essential plant nutrients. This is basically a 4-1-3 fertilizer.

PERENNIALS & ORNAMENTAL GRASSES

Start perennials from seed, trade plants with neighbors, or purchase less expensive or smaller plants at the beginning. Know how many plants you'll need; check out this chart.

Leave your grass clippings on the lawn to break down and "feed" your lawn. Alternatively, rake up the clippings and use them as mulch or compost them.

HERE'S HOW

TO CALCULATE THE NUMBER OF PERENNIALS NEEDED

The following chart shows the number of plants per square foot for a given spacing.

SPACING MULTIPLIER	
SPACING (INCHES)	(# OF PLANTS PER SQ. FT.)
12	1.00
15	0.64
18	0.44
24	0.25
36	0.11

HERE'S HOW

TO CALCULATE THE NUMBER OF GROUNDCOVER PLANTS NEEDED

AREA (SQ. FEET)	SQUARE SPACING*							
	4 IN.	6 IN.	8 IN.	10 IN.	12 IN.	15 IN.	18 IN.	24 IN.
25	225	100	56	36	25	16	11	6
50	450	200	113	72	50	32	22	12
100	900	400	225	144	100	64	44	25
200	1,800	800	450	288	200	128	89	50
300	2,700	1,200	675	432	300	192	133	75
1,000	9,000	4,000	2,250	1,440	1,000	641	444	250
Spacing Multiplier	9	4	2.25	1.44	1	0.64	0.44	0.25

* "on center" spacing (plants are spaced from the center of one plant to the center of the next one)

For an area not found in the chart, use the following formula:
area in square feet × spacing multiplier = number of plants needed

OR use this simple formula: $N = A/D^2$

Where N = the number of plants in a given bed;
    A = the area of the bed in square inches, and
    D = the distance in inches between plants in the row and between rows.

Assume the bed measures 48 square feet (8 feet long and 6 feet wide) and you want to plant the perennials 15 inches apart. To determine the number of plants needed for the bed, use this equation:

Area of Bed × Spacing Multiplier =
Total number of plants

In our example, the perennials will be spaced 15 inches apart, so 48 square feet × 0.64 = 31

Space 31 perennials 15 inches apart to occupy a 48-square-foot bed.

ROSES

Plan to go vertical with climbing roses. Use existing structures in your landscape such as lampposts, clothesline posts, or porch columns. You can even sink an 8-foot pressure-treated 4 × 4 about 18 inches into the ground and train a climber onto it. Or link two or three posts together with chain or heavy rope to create a festoon.

■ *Introduced in 1824, the climbing yellow Lady Banks rose (Rosa banksiae 'Lutea') produces a blizzard of springtime flowers on thornless stems.*

■ *Strawberries grow well in pots or in the landscape as groundcovers.*

SHRUBS

Dense shrubs should not be planted close to the foundation or siding, or in front of foundation vents because they can obstruct airflow around and beneath your home, which can lead to moisture problems. Plan to prune these shrubs or move them to another area in the landscape. If you move them to south- or west-facing walls to insulate your house from summer's heat, keep them away from foundation vents and at least 4 feet from the foundation.

Keep shrubs away from the compressor on your split-system air conditioner. While the shade cast by the shrubs can reduce energy consumption, they should be planted far enough away so they won't obstruct airflow or service.

TREES

The first Friday following March 15 is Arbor Day in North Carolina. Plan to plant a tree or support an organization that does.

VINES & GROUNDCOVERS

Strawberries can make an uncommon groundcover for edging walkways or flowerbeds in full sun or part shade. Alpine strawberries (*Fragaria vesca*) are attractive ground-hugging choices, particularly 'Improved Rugen' and 'Semper-florens'. But when you want big, luscious strawberries on your cereal in the morning, you need to grow the cultivated strawberry (*F. × ananassa*). Although not as compact or as contained as alpines, each plant can be expected to bear a quart of homegrown berries.

Select strawberry varieties that are June-bearers or "single-croppers." These short-day plants develop flower buds in the short days of the fall and produce one heavy crop in April in the Coastal Plain and May in the Piedmont and Mountains ("June-bearer" is a bit of a misnomer). During the long days of summer they produce aboveground runners called "stolons."

Coastal Plain gardeners can plant June-bearers from November to March and Piedmont and Mountain gardeners can plant during March or April. Plan to purchase June-bearing varieties for early, mid-, and late-season harvests. Contact your county Cooperative Extension Service office for the recommended varieties for your area. Strawberries are not permanent groundcovers because they have to be replaced every two or three years, but they do add a whole new edible dimension to groundcover plantings.

WATER GARDENS

If you're planning on introducing fish to your water garden, spend some time this month learning more about them. Visit your public library, visit water specialty centers, read mail-order catalogs, and talk to other water gardeners. Not only do fish add ornamental interest and movement, but they'll improve water quality as they feast on mosquitoes and their larvae, algae, and plant debris. The plants will be fertilized by the waste created by the fish, and the submerged plants will use the carbon dioxide they exhale to produce oxygen.

Many different kinds of fish are available, such as the typical goldfish-in-a-bowl variety (which can grow up to a foot in length in ponds), long-lived colorful koi, speedy golden orfes, and mosquito fish. If you lack experience and confidence with fish, start small with a few inexpensive goldfish. As you sharpen your water-gardening skills, you can add more fish later.

PLANT

ANNUALS

Cool-season annuals to plant outside now in the Piedmont and Mountains include alyssum, calendula, pansy, snapdragon, and viola. Delay planting seeds of other annuals outside, except for the hardy ones that like to sprout in cool weather. These include alyssum, calliopsis or annual coreopsis, larkspur, poppies, and sweet William.

Plant this month in the Coastal Plains, next month in the Piedmont, and the month after that in the Mountains.

BULBS

If you received an amaryllis (*Hippeastrum* hybrids) over the holidays, move it to a permanent location outdoors in the garden if you live in Zone 7 or warmer, and if you keep it mulched during the winter months. After the last spring frost, plant your amaryllis in a well-drained fertile site in full sun to partial shade. The neck of the bulb where the leaves emerge should be 2 to 4 inches below the soil surface. Mulch with a 2- to 3-inch layer of

■ *Besides aquatic plants, long-lived koi, which have been bred in Japan since the sixth century, add color and movement to your water garden.*

compost to conserve moisture and suppress weed growth. Make a single application of a slow-release complete fertilizer after planting and then in subsequent springs when the shoots appear. Expect your amaryllis to bloom every year in early summer.

EDIBLES

Indoors in the Mountains, sow basil, chives, parsley, summer savory, and sweet marjoram. To encourage parsley seeds to sprout more rapidly, soften the seeds by soaking them overnight in warm water. Indoors, Mountain gardeners can also sow seeds of broccoli, cabbage, and cauliflower for transplanting within six to eight weeks.

Piedmont gardeners can sow warm-season vegetables in flats or trays—try eggplant, New Zealand spinach (a heat-tolerant substitute for spinach), pepper, and tomato. Vegetables that resent any root disturbance, such as cucumber, muskmelon, summer squash, and watermelon, should be sown in individual pots or peat pellets. Avoid sowing seeds too early or they may be ready for transplanting before outdoor conditions permit.

Sweet potatoes are started from "slips"—shoots that sprouted from last year's crop. Purchase them as transplants or start your own by placing a sweet potato in a glass half-filled with water. Place it in bright light. Detach the plants from the mother root when they are 6 to 8 inches long, pot them up, and then plant them in the garden about three weeks after the last freeze.

In the Coastal Plain, plant perennial herbs such as chives, oregano, and thyme when they become available in garden centers. Coastal Plain and Piedmont gardeners can sow parsley and dill. Sow beets and Swiss chard in the Coastal Plain and Piedmont. Because each "seed" is actually a dried fruit containing up to six seeds, expect a cluster of seedlings to emerge. When their first true leaves appear, thin the bunches by pinching off the extra seedlings near ground level.

In coastal areas after the last freeze, set out eggplant, onion, pepper, and tomato but be prepared to cover them in case of a late freeze. Be careful when purchasing tomato or pepper transplants that are already in bloom. Once the plant starts flowering, it

HERE'S HOW

TO PLANT ANNUALS

1. Moisten the potting medium before taking the plant out of the container. This will keep the soil intact when you slide it out.

2. Dig a hole a little wider than the rootball and the same depth. Plants growing in peat pots can be planted pot and all. Moisten the plants in the peat pot before planting.

3. Hold your hand over the top of the pot with the plant stems between your fingers. Tip over the pot and gently tap the plant into your hand. Annuals growing in cell-packs can be pushed out from the bottom with your thumb. If they are reluctant, slit the walls of the container and peel it away. If there is a mat of tangled roots on the base, tease the bottom third of the rootball to loosen it up.

4. Plant the rootball level with the soil surface. Remove any exposed portion of peat pots (the exposed peat can act like a wick, drawing moisture away from the roots and soil, causing the plant to dry out quickly).

5. Pinch off any open flowers to direct the plant's energy into building roots for speedy establishment.

6. Firm the soil around each plant with your fingers and water. Allow the plants the correct spacing. Refer to the seed packet for suggested spacing.

7. Once you have finished planting, cover the bed with a 2- to 3-inch layer of mulch, tapering to a ½-inch layer near the crown but not covering it. During the next few weeks, keep the plants well watered to help them become established.

is forced into the dual responsibility of maintaining flowers and trying to produce roots; it will concentrate on fruiting rather than growing. The end result will be a small plant that bears little fruit. You're always better off planting one that's not in bloom.

Sow seeds of butter beans (lima beans), pole beans, snap beans, sweet corn, summer squash, and watermelon.

Piedmont gardeners can buy seed potatoes and cut them into egg-sized pieces containing one or two eyes. Allow the cuts to dry and callous for a day or two before planting. Plant them when the soil temperature remains above 50 degrees Fahrenheit.

In the Piedmont and Mountains, plant asparagus crowns before new growth emerges from the buds. Set out transplants of broccoli, cabbage, and cauliflower

as well, up to four weeks before the last spring freeze. Sow seeds of carrots, lettuce (leaf and head), garden peas, mustard, radishes, rutabaga, and spinach.

Mountain gardeners can sow mustard, garden peas, radishes, spinach, and turnips.

LAWNS

Wait until next month to plant warm-season grasses.

If you didn't seed thin or bare patches of cool-season grasses last fall, which is the best time to seed Kentucky bluegrass and tall fescue, you can attempt to seed now; however, be prepared to accept some losses. Cool-season grasses prefer cool temperatures, especially for seed germination, and the longer you delay seeding, the less time the seedlings will have to become established before the arrival of summer's heat. And be mindful that

HERE'S HOW

TO SOD A LAWN

1. Measure the area to be sodded and calculate the amount of sod you'll need.

2. Schedule delivery only after you prepare the bed and are ready to install. Insist on prompt delivery after the sod is harvested.

3. Keep the sod in a shady place to prevent it from drying out. Lay it as soon as possible.

4. Start sodding from the longest straight edge such as a driveway, curb, or sidewalk. Stagger the blocks or strips as if laying bricks. Butt the sod firmly and stretch each piece so it lies flat against the soil. In dry, hot weather, lightly wet the surface before laying and water each small area well immediately (within one hour) after laying. Use a knife, spade, or sharpened concrete trowel to trim the pieces.

5. On steep slopes, lay the sod across the angle of the slope; it may be necessary to peg the sod to the soil with homemade wooden stakes to keep it from sliding.

6. Immediately after laying the sod, tamp down the sod or roll the lawn perpendicular to the direction the sod was laid with a lawn roller (water-ballast roller). This eliminates any air spaces between the soil and the sod and ensures good sod-to-soil contact.

7. Water immediately afterward to wet the soil below to a depth of 3 or 4 inches. Don't let the soil dry out until the sod has "knitted" or rooted into the soil. More thorough watering can then be done as the roots begin to penetrate the soil.

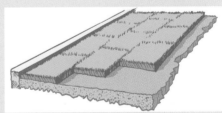

8. Start mowing when the sod is firmly rooted and securely in place.

■ *Place the sod pieces tightly together in a staggered, checkerboard pattern, similar to bricks in a wall.*

what you do for your lawn grass seedlings will also benefit emerging weeds. Even if you get a fairly good stand, you'll have a long road ahead to keep the young lawn alive during the summer months.

If you can justify the expense, install tall fescue or Kentucky bluegrass sod; you'll need plenty of water to help it through the summer.

PERENNIALS & ORNAMENTAL GRASSES

Plant perennials when they become available from local nurseries or when they arrive in the mail from catalog orders. Plant dormant bare-root plants soon after receiving them.

Dig up, divide, and replant established perennials if they've become too crowded and flowering has been sparse. Some fast-growing perennials need to be divided between one to three years after planting—these include aster, astilbe, beebalm, boltonia, garden mum, garden phlox, rudbeckia, Shasta daisy, and many others. To avoid interrupting flowering, dig up summer- and fall-blooming perennials when the new growth is a few inches high.

Divide ornamental grasses before new growth emerges. Cut back the old culms to within 4 to 6 inches of the ground and use a sharp shovel or large knife to slice one or more wedges out of the crown. Immediately plant them elsewhere.

■ *Cut back clumps of ornamental grasses in the spring, being careful to cut only the brown foliage.*

TO PLANT BARE-ROOT PLANTS

1. Remove the plastic wrapping and shake the packing material loose from the roots. Soak the roots in a bucket of water at least an hour before planting.

2. Dig the planting hole wide enough to accommodate the roots when they're spread out.

3. Create a cone of soil in the bottom of the hole and tamp down the top firmly. This will prevent the plant from settling too deeply.

4. Set the plant over the cone and drape the roots evenly over the top.

5. Backfill the hole. Work the soil in among the roots with your fingers. If the perennial has settled too deeply, lift it gently to raise the crown to the proper level.

Uncover the trays or pots overwintered outdoors and move them to a cold frame for protection from freezing temperatures. The perennial seedlings will emerge over a range of weeks (sometimes longer). Transplant tray-grown seedlings to individual pots after they've developed one or two sets of true leaves.

ROSES

Plant potted roses when they become available in the Piedmont and Coastal Plain. Plant them as early as possible to get them settled in before summer's heat and humidity arrive. In the Mountains, plant dormant bare-root roses about four weeks before the last expected freeze. At the higher elevations in the North Carolina Mountains, where the temperature may drop to 0 degrees Fahrenheit, wait until after the last freeze before planting.

SHRUBS, TREES, AND VINES & GROUNDCOVERS

Plant balled-and-burlapped or container-grown plants. Birch, black gum, dogwood, fir, hickory, magnolia, pecan, red oak, and walnut are best moved and planted in early spring while they're still dormant. Plant them as early in the season as possible to help them get established before the heat of summer begins.

Avoid two common mistakes: over- and under-watering. A few weeks after planting, start cutting back on watering to every few days or longer, especially with cloudy, rainy, or cool weather. Also, remove any berms you create to prevent excess water. See page 65. Eventually water on a weekly or "as needed" basis by testing the soil and rootball for moisture.

SHRUBS

Propagate shrubs with long pliable stems (such as forsythia and winter jasmine) or difficult-to-root plants (such as rhododendron) by ground-layering.

WATER GARDENS

Plant aquatics in nursery pots, laundry baskets, shallow pans, and large tubs. Use a heavy clay-based garden soil. Avoid amending it with peat moss, vermiculite, or perlite, which tend to float away. Submerged plants can be planted in containers filled with sand or tied to a stone so they're kept just below the water surface.

■ *Check the water percolation rate by filling an 18-inch-deep hole twice with water. If the second filling takes more than twenty four hours to drain, consider improving the drainage by creating raised beds or using drain tile.*

HERE'S HOW

TO PROPAGATE MORE SHRUBS BY GROUND-LAYERING

1. Before growth begins, bend one or two young, healthy stems to the ground.

2. Wind the underside of the stem and cover it with soil. Hold it in place with a piece of wire bent to a hairpin shape and pushed into the ground. Do not bury the shoot tip.

3. If you layer now, the shoots will usually be rooted by the end of the growing season. Then sever the new plant from the parent and transplant it. Shoots layered later in the summer should be left through the winter and separated in spring.

After you pot up your plant, add a 1-inch layer of pea or aquarium gravel on the surface to prevent the soil from muddying up the water. Before submersing the container, water it thoroughly and then place it in the pool.

In the warmer parts of the Carolinas, hardy water lilies may need to be divided every year or two. They can be divided at any time during the growing season, starting six weeks before the last expected freeze. Here's how:

1. Lift the pot out of the pool and take the clump out of the pot.

2. Look along the length of the rhizome for buds or growing points called "eyes." Tiny lime-green or bronze leaves may be emerging from the growing point.

3. With a sharp knife or pruning shears, cut sections of the rhizome into 3- to 4-inch-long pieces or divisions that have eyes and accompanying roots.

4. Repot the division, making sure that the growing point is above the soil level.

HERE'S HOW

TO PROPERLY PLANT A CONTAINER-GROWN OR BALLED-AND-BURLAPPED SHRUB OR TREE

Select the right location by matching the shrub or tree to the site. Sun-loving trees require at least six hours of direct sun a day. Shade-loving shrubs will tolerate less than two hours of direct afternoon sun, and thrive in a location that provides filtered sun. Also, pay attention to drainage. In general, plants prefer well-drained soils. If you have some areas of your garden that tend to be on the wet side, otherwise known as "hog wallows," then choose shrubs and trees that are adapted to those boggy conditions, such as anisetree (*Illicium* spp.), Virginia sweetspire, and river birch.

1. Check the water percolation rate by filling an 18-inch-deep hole twice with water. If the second filling takes more than twenty four hours to drain, consider improving the drainage by creating raised beds or using drain tile. If the soil in the proposed planting site is a dense clay subsoil, it is unrealistic to expect any tree to develop to its full potential without extensive work to help improve the soil.

2. Estimate the depth of the planting hole. Find the topmost root on your shrub or tree by removing soil or media from the surface of the rootball. Measure the distance from where the topmost root emerges from the trunk to the bottom of the rootball. Dig a hole that's slightly shallower than this distance. On wet soils or in areas with high water tables, dig a slightly more shallow hole so the plant rests slightly higher than the surrounding soil.

3. Dig a wide, shallow hole at least two to three times the diameter of the rootball. For shrubs, dig similar sized holes or rototill an entire bed and then dig the hole slightly wider than the rootball but not deeper than the height of the rootball (see step 2, the distance from the topmost root to the bottom of the rootball).

4. Examine the rootball and treat any defects. Shrubs and trees growing in plastic or other hard-sided containers may have roots circling around the outside of the rootball. To prevent these circling roots from eventually

choking your shrub or tree, redirect their growth laterally into the surrounding soil. Spread out or cut any circling or kinked roots. Do not cut roots larger than about one-third of the trunk's diameter or you may harm the tree. On pot-bound shrubs or trees with roots growing around the periphery of the rootball, use a spade to slice the outer edge of the rootball from top to bottom. If a mat of roots has formed on the bottom of the rootball, prune off the mat.

5. Place the shrub or tree in the hole and check its depth. It's always best to plant too high rather than too deep. Lay your shovel across the hole

straw. Extend the mulch layer to the outermost reaches of the branches. Also, maintain a hand's width of space between the mulch and trunk to keep the bark dry and to discourage rodent feeding. If the tree needs to be supported, stake it at the lowest point on the trunk that will keep the tree erect. Inspect the staking hardware six to twelve months after planting and remove it if the unsupported tree stands erect.

9. Limit pruning to only broken, dead, or diseased branches. Any corrective pruning can be conducted after a full season of growth in the new location.

10. Water frequently. Water—not fertilizer—is the most important ingredient for helping shrubs and trees get established in the landscape. During establishment, trees should be irrigated two to three times weekly with 2 gallons per inch trunk caliper. All this water should be applied only to the top of the rootball.

to see that the rootball is slightly above the handle. The topmost root should be slightly above (up to 1 inch for small trees and up to 3 inches for tall ones). On poorly drained soils or soils with high water tables, plant with up to one-third of the rootball above the ground. If the hole is too deep, put some soil in the bottom of the hole, tamp it down with your feet to give the plant some solid footing, and put the plant back in the hole. For balled-and-burlapped shrubs and trees, remove any string, rope, synthetic burlap, strapping, plastic, and other materials that will not decompose in the soil.

6. Once it's in place, start backfilling—returning the soil into the planting hole. Lightly firm the soil around the rootball to stabilize it. Do not cover the top of the rootball with soil and do not place mulch on top of the rootball.

7. Water the rootball and backfill. Fill in any holes or depressions with additional backfill soil. Do not firmly pack backfill soil because this could cause too much soil compaction, especially in clay soil. The water infiltrating the backfill soil will eliminate many of the large air pockets. The presence of small air pockets could even be of benefit because they could allow more air to reach the roots. If water drains away, create a temporary berm or basin with backfill to retain water.

8. Apply a 2- to 3-inch layer of mulch such as compost, leaf litter, shredded wood, or pine

MARCH

HERE'S HOW

TO POT UP WATER GARDEN PLANTS

1. Fill a 5-inch pot with soil and plant the tuber about ¼ inch deep. Add a layer of pebbles or gravel to the top and label it.

2. Move the pots to an aquarium or a large bucket. Add enough water so the tops of the pots are covered by 3 inches of water. The water should be 70 to 80 degrees Fahrenheit, so an aquarium heater may be necessary.

3. In two to six weeks, when new leaves have formed, move the plants into bright light.

4. Transplant the tubers into permanent containers (see May, Plant). Wait until the water warms up to 70 degrees Fahrenheit before placing them in your water garden. Very cold water can shock the plants, slowing down the growth of leaves and flowers for many weeks.

Divide both Asian (*Nelumbo nucifera*) and American lotus (*N. lutea*) at the same time you divide hardy water lilies.

About a month before the last expected freeze, check to see if the tropical water lilies you stored indoors over the winter have sprouted. If they haven't, put the tubers in water near a sunny windowsill to coerce them into growth. Once they've sprouted, pot them up in temporary pots.

CARE

ANNUALS

Pinch out the growing tips of plants that have become rangy. They will branch from below the pinch and regain their bushy form.

Cut off dead blooms to encourage continued flowering of pansies.

Also see February.

BULBS

After flowering, the leaves of your spring-flowering bulbs will turn an unsightly yellow. Temper your urge to remove the leaves, or braid them into attractive ponytails. The bulbs need the leaves to harvest energy that's channeled to the bulb for next year's flowers. Bulbs that were forced indoors can be fertilized while in bloom, and then planted in your garden to allow the leaves to mature and replenish the bulb. Expect the bulbs to flower again next year.

Snip off the spent blooms of spring-flowering bulbs to prevent seedpods from forming. If you expect them to repeat their show next spring, allow leaves to mature and die down naturally before removing. Unless the leaves have an opportunity to store a good supply of carbohydrates and nutrients in the underground bulb, the plants won't flower next year.

LAWNS

There are two kinds of mowers: rotary mowers and reel mowers. Rotary mowers have a whirling blade that cuts the grass at high speeds. It can be used to mow lawns down to an inch. Reel mowers have a series of blades that cut the grass like scissors. The blades press against a bar at the bottom to slice the grass, giving the lawn a highly finished look.

Mow cool-season lawns at the proper height; check out this chart.

COOL-SEASON LAWNS SUGGESTED MOWING HEIGHTS	
LAWN GRASS	MOWING HEIGHT (INCHES)
Kentucky bluegrass	Winter: 1.5 to 2.5 Summer: 2.5 to 3
Fine fescue	Winter: 1.5 to 2.5 Summer: 2.5 to 3
Tall fescue	Winter: 2 to 3 Summer: 2.5 to 3.5
Ryegrass (overseeded)	Winter: 1 to 2.5

PERENNIALS & ORNAMENTAL GRASSES

Press back any perennials that may have frost-heaved over the winter. Maintain a 2-inch layer of

LAWNS

Wait until next month to fertilize hybrid bermudagrass and zoysiagrass. Kentucky bluegrass or tall fescue can be fertilized this month according to the results of a soil test. If the lawn has good color and vigor, however, postpone any fertilizer applications until the fall.

PERENNIALS & ORNAMENTAL GRASSES

Most perennials benefit from a boost with fertilizer as new growth begins in the spring. Select a slow-release fertilizer according to soil-test results. Follow the label directions regarding the amount and frequency of application. Water the fertilizer in to make it available to the plants.

ROSES

Fertilize roses after pruning and before they leaf out. Follow soil-test results to supply the necessary nutrients. Use a slow-release fertilizer that contains at least one-third of its total nitrogen in a slowly available form.

SHRUBS, TREES, AND VINES & GROUNDCOVERS

Evaluate their growth and appearance to decide if fertilizing is necessary. Look for these signs of "hunger" or mineral deficiency: stunted growth, smaller than normal leaves, poor leaf color, early leaf drop. Be aware that these same symptoms of poor growth can be the result of the following causes: heavily compacted soil; stresses induced by insects, diseases, and weeds; or adverse weather conditions. Before you fertilize, determine the cause of the problem and correct it. Having your soil tested is one way of getting to the "root" of the problem. Rely on soil-test results to supply the minerals that are deficient in the soil.

If needed, fertilize them after they leaf out. Use a slow-release fertilizer that contains one-half of the nitrogen in a slowly available, water-insoluble form.

Sweep any fertilizer from the leaves of groundcovers to avoid "burning" them.

ANNUALS

Spider mites can be a problem on indoor seedlings.

Damping off can be triggered by waterlogged conditions in the growing medium. See February, Problem-Solve for more information.

Pre-emergent herbicides are available for use around many common bedding plants. These herbicides kill germinating weed seedlings before they appear. When selecting a pre-emergent herbicide, keep these pointers in mind:

- Identify the weed that you want to control.

- Select a herbicide that will control this weed but can be applied to the flowering annuals you're growing.

- Read the label carefully and apply only as recommended. For example, some pre-emergent herbicides are safe to use only on established bedding plants. If applied shortly after transplanting, injury may result.

BULBS

Gray mold, or botrytis blight, is a springtime disease that is most active during cool and wet weather. It attacks dead or dying leaves and flowers and can quickly spread to healthy tissues. Bulbs and corms may also be infected, leading to rot. A wide range of plants is infected, including amaryllis, bulbous iris, dahlia, hyacinth, and tulip. Warm, humid, rainy conditions foster this fungal disease, which produces yellow, orange, brown, or reddish brown spots on the leaves and flowers. The spots on the leaves and flowers grow together, causing them to collapse and become slimy. Eventually they're covered with a telltale gray fuzzy mold.

To control botrytis, collect and discard faded flowers. Fungicides can be applied at the first sign of disease. Provide good air movement by not overcrowding the plants. Use wide spacings to allow leaves and flowers to dry off quickly. Avoid overhead watering; this fungus spreads through splashing water and wind. Most important, keep the plants healthy. Examine your stored bulbs and discard any that show signs of rot.

If weeds occur in bulb beds, do not remove them by cultivation. Pull them by hand so the bulbs and roots will not be disturbed.

EDIBLES

Look for imported cabbage worm caterpillars on cabbage, cauliflower, and, to a lesser extent, other members of the Brassica family, including broccoli, kale, and mustard. Prevent the butterflies from laying eggs in the spring by covering the young plants with a layer of spun-bonded row cover. Handpicking the larvae is another way to control them, but their camouflage makes them difficult to locate. Use a biological control, *Bacillus thuringiensis* var. *kurstaki* (*B.t.k.*), sold as Dipel®, Thuricide®, and others. Spray *B.t.k.* as soon as you see the first tiny larvae, and repeat applications as additional eggs are laid. Other less specific (and highly toxic) insecticides are available. They may kill a broad spectrum of insects and require a waiting time between application and harvest.

Also see January for disease information and February for weed information.

LAWNS

Mole crickets are serious lawn pests in the sandy soils of the Coastal Plain. Identify areas where mole cricket adults are active. Their offspring will be active there in late June and July, when you can control the young nymphs with insecticides.

Brown patch attacks warm-season grasses in the spring as the lawn emerges from dormancy, or in the fall as they're going dormant. Collect infected clippings and compost them. Avoid overfertilizing, especially with nitrogen during the fall or spring. Water during dry spells to keep the grass healthy, but avoid overwatering. Fungicides will protect healthy grass from becoming infected.

Later this month in the Piedmont, and early next month in the Mountains, apply a crabgrass preventer or pre-emergent herbicide to control summer annuals such as crabgrass and goosegrass. A pre-emergent herbicide forms a barrier at or just below the soil surface and kills the emerging seedlings when they come into contact with it. Crabgrass seed germinates when the day temperatures reach 65 to 70 degrees Fahrenheit for four or five days, coinciding with the time forsythia and crabapples bloom. Goosegrass germinates about three or four weeks after crabgrass.

Prevent winter annuals such as common chickweed and henbit from going to seed by handpulling, mowing off the flowers, or spot-treating with a broadleaf herbicide. Identify weeds after they emerge to select an appropriate post-emergent herbicide. Post-emergent herbicides are most effective when the weeds are young and actively growing, with air temperatures between 65 to 85 degrees Fahrenheit. Be sure the herbicide is labeled for use on your lawn and your lawn has fully greened up and is actively growing.

PERENNIALS & ORNAMENTAL GRASSES

Flower thrips damage bellflower, daylily, and peony flowers with their feeding. Remove and discard thrips-infested flowers.

Damping off can be triggered by sustained waterlogged conditions in the growing medium. Avoid overwatering. Water your seedlings only when the surface of the medium feels dry.

Inspect the newly emerging leaves of your daylilies for reddish brown streaks and browned-out spots. They could be afflicted with a disease called leaf-streak. This fungus overwinters in dead, infected leaves, so collect and discard diseased or dead leaves to reduce the chances of future outbreaks.

Handpull winter annuals such as henbit and common chickweed to prevent them from going to seed. Maintaining a 2-inch layer of mulch will suppress weeds.

In some cases a pre-emergent herbicide will reduce the amount of handweeding required. See May Vines & Groundcovers, for more information.

ROSES

Handpull winter annuals such as henbit and common chickweed to prevent them from going to seed. Maintain a 2- to 3-inch layer of mulch to suppress weeds.

Watch out for aphids and spider mites. Look for aphids clustered near the tips of new shoots and flower buds. Dislodge them with a strong spray of water early in the morning, giving the leaves plenty of time to dry before evening.

If your roses are plagued by blackspot and powdery mildew, either follow a weekly fungicide spray program or plant disease-resistant roses. Although these roses may still get diseases, they may be vigorous enough to outgrow infections.

Flower buds and flowers covered with a grayish brown fuzz might be infected with gray mold, a springtime fungal disease that's active in cool, wet weather. It also attacks new shoots. Collect and discard the infected flowers and prune out discolored canes back to healthy tissue. After pruning, treat plants with a recommended fungicide to protect the wounds.

Examine the new growth of your roses. Look for distorted and smaller than normal leaves and extremely thorny, thickened stems. If you see these symptoms, your rose may be infected with rose rosette disease (RRD). This fatal disease often kills roses within one to two years. If you find RRD, take action because this contagious disease can be transmitted to healthy roses by the primary vector—a tiny eriophyid mite—and potentially by you.

SHRUBS, TREES, AND VINES & GROUNDCOVERS

Mountain gardeners can apply a dormant horticultural oil spray on dormant landscape plants before new growth emerges.

Look for the grayish white webs or "tents" of eastern tent caterpillars in the crotches of trees. They feed on the leaves of crabapples, wild cherry, and apple, but they aren't fussy. When these trees are scarce, you'll find them in ash, birch, willow, maple, and oak trees. Trees are rarely killed, but the damage is unsightly. To control them, wait until evening and wipe out the nests with a gloved hand, or wrap the nest around a stick and drop the whole

nest into a container of soapy water. The bacterial insecticide B.t. (*Bacillus thuringiensis*) can be used to control the caterpillars when they are small.

See January, Problem-Solve.

Watch out for the "cool-weather" mites: southern red mites, which attack Japanese and American hollies, azaleas, camellias, and rhododendrons and spruce spider mites, which feed on arborvitae, false cypress, juniper, spruce, and other conifers. They attack in the spring and fall—at higher mountain elevations they may be active all summer long.

Look for small cone-shaped objects hanging from the branches of your arborvitae, cedars, junipers, and Leyland cypress. These are the nests of bagworms, which contain from 500 to 1,000 eggs that will hatch next month and into June. Remove the bags and discard them.

Sanitation is a cost-effective way to reduce disease problems. Rake out dead leaves from groundcovers and prune out any dead, diseased, or broken limbs from vines. Before treating with a fungicide, identify the disease and determine if chemical control is warranted.

Groundcover beds should be kept relatively free of weeds until they are dense enough to crowd them out. Instead of handpulling or mulching, control weeds with a pre-emergent herbicide, which kills germinating weeds before they appear. Early this month, Coastal Plain gardeners can apply a pre-emergent herbicide to control summer annuals such as crabgrass and goosegrass (the application is made when they germinate but before they emerge). Wait until later this month to do this in the Piedmont, and do it early next month in the Mountains.

Handpull winter annuals such as bittercress, common chickweed, and henbit to prevent them from going to seed. Maintain a 2- to 4-inch layer of mulch to suppress weeds.

A preemergent herbicide can reduce the amount of handweeding required. Pre-emergent herbicides kill germinating weed seedlings before they appear.

Grasping a lemon yellow squash flower between my fingers, I smiled and visualized the gorgeous green zucchini the blossom would become one day.

This miraculous transformation from flower to fruit occurs through pollination—the transfer of pollen or male cells from the anther to the female cells on the stigma. Squash, like most vegetables, depends on insects for pollination.

One of the best insect pollinators known since ancient times is the honeybee (*Apis mellifera*), which was introduced to North America by European settlers in the 1600s. (Native Americans called these honeybees the "white man's fly.") Honeybee pollination is not intentional, but a result of the insect's search for its favorite foods—pollen and nectar.

Although the honeybee's way of life and work ethic make it an ideal pollinator, it is the insect's physical makeup that results in efficient pollination.

Its large compound eyes offer a wide range of vision and sensitive antennae, and its tongue acts either as a spoon for licking up small drops or a pump to rapidly draw in large quantities of nectar or water. The honeybee's hairy body collects pollen as it dashes from blossom to blossom. Combs and brushes on the legs are used to remove the pollen from the flowers or from the body and stuffed into "pollen baskets" in the legs.

For honeybees, pollination is just a matter of survival—and for us too. Millions of acres of crops—even those in our own gardens—depend on, or benefit from, honeybees, which means that we need to protect them. Avoid broad control insecticides. If you use them, apply insecticides when bees aren't actively foraging in the garden. You may have to make your applications very early in the morning or late in the evening. Thinking about honeybees and seeing the blooms on my squash, cucumbers, peppers, and watermelons, I wonder about the future of this year's crop. What if there aren't enough honeybees? Would I be reduced to scurrying from blossom to blossom with a cotton-tipped swab, daubing tiny pollen grains on the impatient stigmas? It might work, but when it comes to pollination, I'd rather have it done by an expert.

PLAN

ANNUALS

In addition to using annuals to show off their flowers and leaves outdoors, make plans to cultivate a cutting garden to enjoy the flowers indoors. With careful planning you can have flowers blooming from spring until fall. A cutting garden requires regular watering, the prompt removal of dead or dying leaves, and the continuous removal of spent flowers to encourage the production of more flowers. Try these flowers in the cutting garden: celosia, China aster, gaillardia, globe amaranth, heliotrope, lisianthus, marigold, phlox, snapdragon, strawflower, poppy, and zinnia.

HERE'S HOW

TO CALCULATE SPACING

Square

Triangular

IN-ROW SPACING (INCHES)	SPACING MULTIPLIER (# OF PLANTS NEEDED PER 1 SQ. FT.)
4	10.4
6	4.6
8	2.6
10	1.7
12	1.2
14	0.8
16	0.7
18	0.5
24	0.3

For more uniform beds, plan to use a triangular spacing instead of a straight row or a rectangular grid. Triangular spacing requires more plants per square foot, but the resulting effect will be more attractive than plants placed in rows. To determine the number of plants needed for a given area, use the following formula: Area of Bed in Square Feet × Spacing Multiplier = Number of Plants Needed.

BULBS

Evaluate your spring-flowering bulbs. Note in your gardening journal which bulbs and cultivars met or exceeded your expectations. If any looked disappointing, make plans to replace them or give them another year or two to settle in.

Also include remarks about the growing environment and culture. Were winter and spring unseasonably warm or mild? Were there unexpected freezing temperatures? Did you fertilize the bulbs last fall with a slow- or fast-release fertilizer? When was the last time you tested the soil for pH and fertility levels? It is ideal to have soil tested by your Cooperative Extension Service every three years.

EDIBLES

Summer is around the corner—plan to water your herbs and vegetables efficiently when hot weather arrives. Take a look at the irrigation methods described in May, Plan, Shrubs and select an appropriate one for your garden.

LAWNS

Write in your journal when you fertilized the lawn and the amount you applied. Document insect, disease, or weed problems, and pesticide applications. Include your soil-test report. Your journal can become a teaching tool, especially when you need the assistance of a lawn-service company or county Extension agent to help you diagnose a problem.

PERENNIALS

Some perennials become top-heavy and require support to prevent them from bending or toppling over. They include delphinium, boltonia (*Boltonia asteroides* 'Snowbank'), gaura, peony, sneezeweed, balloon flower, and culver's root (*Veronicastrum virginicum*). Plan to support these plants early in

■ *Peonies are beautiful flowers that will require support to keep them from flopping over in the garden.*

their growth before they get too tall and floppy. There are a wide variety of materials to use such as specially designed peony rings, tomato cages, and plastic or bamboo stakes. Position the stakes so the plants will eventually hide the supports. When securing their stems, tie the soft twine into a figure eight to avoid binding a stem.

To avoid staking some perennials altogether, select compact, lower-growing cultivars or prune them (by pinching or cutting back) at least eight weeks before flowering to keep their height in check. See the Care section to learn more about this approach.

ROSES

If you're serious about growing roses, document your observations, thoughts, and plans for the future. Some of the following items can be noted:

- Bloom dates for each variety

- Condition of the flowers, leaves, and overall health

- Pest problems such as insects, diseases, and weeds

- Pesticides used and when they were applied

- Plants that need to be moved or replaced because they turned out to be "a lotta-care"

■ *Plants can be rooted from cuttings taken in late spring and summer from the current season's growth.*

HERE'S HOW

TO ROOT ROSES FROM CUTTINGS

1. Fill a 6-inch pot with equal parts of moist peat moss and perlite.

2. Remove a stem that has just flowered and is about the diameter of a drinking straw.

3. Count upward two or three pairs of leaves from the bottom of this cutting, and make a cut ¼ inch above the topmost bud.

4. Wound the bottom end of the stem with a razor blade or sharp knife by making a ½- to 1-inch vertical slit through the bark on the side opposite the top bud. Roots will emerge from along the edges of the wound.

5. Dip the lower end in a rooting hormone (contains indole-butyric acid or IBA) to encourage uniform rooting. Tap off the excess.

6. Using a pencil, make a hole in the rooting medium and insert the cutting. Remove leaves that may be buried in the medium. Firm the medium around it and settle them in with a fine spray of water.

7. Put the pot in a plastic bag and move it to a shaded location outside against the north wall of your house or under a tree. Alternatively, you can sink the pot in the ground in a shaded location and cover the cuttings with a clear plastic 2-liter soda bottle whose bottom has been removed. Water to prevent the cuttings from drying out.

8. Open up your mini-hothouse occasionally if there's too much condensation inside. You can unscrew the cap of the soda bottle.

9. The cuttings should root in a month and will send out new leaves if you've been successful. To see if they've rooted, give the stem a gentle tug. If it resists, it has rooted. Remove the bag. Pot up the cuttings in individual pots and keep them moist and shaded. Gradually expose the rooted cuttings to stronger light to harden them off. After a couple of weeks, transplant them.

roses. The notes you take about weather conditions, fertilizing, watering, and pest control applications are important clues.

SHRUBS

Look for shrubs that bear edible fruits like figs, pomegranate (*Punica granatum* 'Wonderful') and pineapple guava (*Feijoa sellowiana*). My favorite shrub for year-round beauty is the blueberry with creamy white or pink flowers in spring; deep blue fruit in summer; red, orange, and yellow fall color; and rosy pink stems in winter.

Rabbiteye and southern highbush blueberries can be grown in the Piedmont and dry, sandy soils of the Coastal Plain. Only the highbush blueberry can be cultivated in the Mountains because it can survive cold winter temperatures of 10 degrees Fahrenheit

■ *Cultivated since ancient times for its glossy leaves, flowers, and fruit, pomegranate (*Punica granatum*) is a deciduous to semievergreen, twiggy, multistemmed shrubby tree or large shrub that can reach a height and width of 12 to 15 feet or more.*

and lower. Blueberries are acid-loving shrubs that can be grown like azaleas and rhododendrons. Use them in borders and hedges. For highest yields, plant at least two varieties of rabbiteyes that bloom at the same time and cross-pollination will occur.

TREES

Variety is the spice of life—which also applies to the landscape. Find time to increase your tree vocabulary by learning about a few trees this month. Research native American trees that were growing in North America when the Europeans first arrived and are still in our states. This is proof of their longevity and ability to adapt to our Carolina climate, soils, and pests.

Visit parks and preserves to see native plants in their natural habitats. Undisturbed areas near your home may also give you some ideas. See what grows well in your region. Take photographs of the plants and show them to knowledgeable people to help you identify them, or use a good field guide with color photos. Visit your local library and bookstores to find reference books on native trees. Become a member of a local native plant society. The members often swap plants and seeds and are knowledgeable about what grows best in your area.

When you have found some favorites, avoid the urge to dig up native plants from the wild. There are ethical, legal, and scientific consequences to this practice. It's better to purchase nursery-propagated natives from nurseries or garden centers.

VINES & GROUNDCOVERS

Take pictures of various views to see where vines and groundcovers can be used to bring color to otherwise nondescript areas. Use variegated plants to add the illusion of light to a dark area. Shade-loving groundcovers such as hosta, ivy, variegated liriope, and wintercreeper euonymous can be suitable choices. Take a look at the color of your home, fences, and paving to see if any groundcovers can be used to unite and harmonize these features with the landscape.

WATER GARDENS

Know someone who's apprehensive about an in-ground pond? Consider water gardening in a

■ *Imperial taro (*Colocasia esculenta *var.* antiquorum *'Illustris') is one of many bold-leaved elephant's ears that make striking architectural specimen plants.*

container. Anything that holds water and does not have a toxic lining can be used. Containers can vary from plastic to concrete to ceramic to wooden barrels with plastic liners. Any of the plants used in water gardening in pools or ponds can be grown in a container. Keep in mind, however, the mature size of the plant. The plants can be grown in individual pots and the pots staged atop bricks or other supports so that their rims are at the appropriate

■ *The exquisite flowers of lotus (*Nelumbo nucifera*) last for about three days; flowers of some of the dwarf varieties last a bit longer. They give rise to interesting showerhead-shaped seed capsules.*

level. You have a wide variety of plants to choose from. Here are some of my favorites:

1. The first group of plants are those that are happy with wet feet but whose crowns can stick above the surface of the water, like striped giant reed (*Arundo donax* 'Variegata'), elephant ear (*Colocasia esculenta* 'Black Magic'), and giant taro (*Alocasia macrorrhiza*).

2. The next group of plants are those that like their crowns to be level with the water surface. These include yellow-flowered water canna (*Canna* 'Ra'), dwarf papyrus (*Cyperus papyrus* 'Nanus'), and *Hibiscus moscheutos* 'Blue River II'.

3. Third, there are plants whose crowns should always be covered by several inches of water like cultivars of lotus (*Nelumbo* 'Angel Wings' and *N.* 'Baby Doll' are both suited for pot

culture) and parrot's feather (*Myriophyllum aquaticum*). Pot the plant in a clay-based soil topped with a layer of gravel to prevent the soil from washing into the water. Put the container on rollers before planting so you can move it around easily.

PLANT

ANNUALS
Start hanging baskets early in April. Impatiens and begonias do well in shade. For sunny locations, try dwarf marigolds, petunias, scaevolas, verbenas, and annual vincas.

Portulaca is wonderful in baskets, as it tolerates hot sun and drought. For a bushier basket planting, keep the plant tips pinched. Start pots for your patio or porch.

Two weeks before the last frost, plant cleome seeds and gloriosa daisy.

Two to three weeks after the last freeze when the soil temperatures have warmed, cosmos, gomphrena, marigold, portulaca, sunflower, zinnia, and other warm-season annuals can be sown directly in the beds where they are to grow. Keep the seeded area moist until the seeds emerge. Thin out as soon as they are large enough to transplant. Any extras can be transplanted to other areas.

BULBS
Summer-flowering bulbs such as crocosmia, dahlia, and lily can be planted after the threat of freezing temperatures has passed. Mountain gardeners can wait until next month to plant.

In the warmer parts of the Carolinas, dig, divide, and replant cannas and dahlias. The best time to do this is after the eyes have sprouted but before they have grown more than an inch. Each tuber should have a short piece of old stem attached. Discard those that show signs of growth. Dust the newly cut surfaces with a fungicide before putting them in the ground.

Stake dahlia tubers at planting so you can insert the stake without skewering the tuber.

Plant gladiolus corms every two weeks until July to create a continuous succession of flowers. Plant the corms at least 4 inches deep to stabilize them as they produce their long flower stalks. You can also mound soil around the base to avoid having to stake them.

Avoid planting caladium tubers too early in the spring because they can rot. The soil temperature must be above 70 degrees Fahrenheit. Plant the tuber shallowly, only an inch or two deep. Because roots and shoots emerge from the top, place it knobby side up.

Bulbs forced indoors that have finished flowering can be moved outdoors. Cut off the faded flowers and transplant bulbs into the garden.

Wait until the last freeze before transplanting Easter lilies (*Lilium longiflorum* var. *eximium*) outdoors (they are hardy to Zone 6) in a well-drained location. Space the plants 12 to 18 inches apart. Because lilies like their "feet in the shade and their heads in the sun," mulch with a 2-inch layer of compost, pine straw, or shredded leaves. As the leaves and stems of the original shoots die back, prune them off. New growth will soon emerge, sometimes producing a second round of flowers. Easter lilies, which were forced to flower under controlled greenhouse conditions in March or April, will flower naturally in May or June. In addition, you will get a taller plant, one that grows to a height of 3 feet or more.

When the bulbs go dormant as signaled by the yellowing, dying leaves, dig up and transplant red spider lilies (*Lycoris radiata*) and magic lilies or naked lilies (*Lycoris squamigera*) immediately. Plant them shallow, with their "necks"—the point where the leaves emerge and the tunic ends—just sticking out of the ground. Planting too shallow is better than planting too deep because the bulbs possess contractile roots that will pull the bulb down into the soil until it is the right depth. When planted too deep, *Lycoris* will spend a few non-flowering years producing a completely new bulb.

EDIBLES

After the last expected freeze, set out the transplants of herbs you started indoors. Mountain gardeners can divide chives, thyme, mint, and tarragon when new growth emerges. A simple way of propagating rosemary and thyme is by layering. See March, Shrubs for planting details.

In the Coastal Plain and Piedmont after the last freeze, sow beans, corn, cucumbers, and southern peas. Avoid planting okra seeds too early. The soil temperature should be above 75 degrees Fahrenheit; soak okra seed overnight before planting in the garden.

Set out transplants of eggplant, muskmelon, watermelon, peppers, summer squash, New Zealand spinach, and zucchini after the last expected freeze when the nights are continuously above 60 degrees Fahrenheit.

Plant determinate bush-type tomatoes for canning or preserving so the fruit will ripen all at once, all within a week or two of each other. For vine-ripened tomatoes, plant indeterminate tomatoes that have an extended fruiting period; they vine, flower, and fruit all the way up to the first frost.

Without protection you can plant tomatoes one to two weeks after the last expected freeze. Plant transplants either on their side in a shallow trench with only the topmost leaves showing, or dig a deep hole with a shovel or posthole digger to set the transplants straight down.

In the Piedmont and Mountains, make another planting of beets, broccoli, cabbage, carrots, potatoes, and radishes.

LAWNS

For warm-season lawns, repair bare patches or replant large areas using seed or sprigs when the average daytime temperatures stay above 60 degrees Fahrenheit.

If the lawn is overrun with weeds or is beyond simple patching, renovate this month or in May.

Renovation is the step you should take before having to completely overhaul the lawn. Figure out how your lawn spiraled into decline, then follow these steps.

HERE'S HOW

TO OVERHAUL A LAWN

1. If your soil hasn't been tested in the past two or three years, submit a sample to your county Cooperative Extension Service office.

2. Eliminate undesirable weeds or lawn grasses. Handpull or use a herbicide. Some herbicides require a waiting period of four to six weeks before seeding, so plan accordingly. Do not apply a pre-emergence herbicide.

3. Mow the area at the lowest setting and collect the clippings. If a thick thatch layer is present (greater than ½ inch), rake it out by hand. For large areas, rent a vertical mower. This machine has revolving blades that lift the thatch layer to the surface. Set the machine so the blades cut into the upper ¼ to ½ inch of soil. Rake up the debris and compost it. Seeds falling into the furrows are more likely to germinate.

4. If the soil is compacted, use a power-driven aerifier or core aerator to improve air and water movement (see September, Plan). Core in several directions. Use the vertical mower to break up the cores.

5. Seed the bare areas with a rotary or drop-type spreader, applying half the total amount in one direction and the other half at right angles to the first. Rake the seed into the soil to ensure good seed-to-soil contact. (See if your equipment rental dealer has a slit seeder—a machine that cuts furrows and deposits the seed in the soil.)

6. Cover the area with clean straw to conserve moisture and enhance germination.

7. Fertilize the lawn one month after renovating.

For cool-season lawns, if you can justify the expense, install tall fescue or Kentucky bluegrass sod; you'll need plenty of water to help it through the summer. If you want a green lawn without sodding, sow seed as early in the month as possible, mulch with weed-free straw, and keep the seedbed moist for a few weeks to speed-up establishment. Getting your lawn through the summer will be a challenge. If you can delay seeding until fall, then wait.

WARM-SEASON LAWNS SUGGESTED MOWING HEIGHTS*	
LAWN GRASS	MOWING HEIGHT (INCHES)
Bermudagrass	
Common	1 to 2
Hybrid	¾ to 1½
Centipedegrass	1 to 2
St. Augustinegrass	2½ to 4
Dwarf	1½ to 2½
Zoysiagrass	¾ to 1½

*Measure the height of the mower on a level surface and adjust it to the proper height.

PERENNIALS & ORNAMENTAL GRASSES

Condition or harden-off the seedlings started indoors. Gradually expose them to outdoor conditions by moving them to a cold frame or a porch for at least a week before planting in the garden.

When planting ornamental grasses, follow this general rule of spacing: Place plants as far apart as their eventual height. This means that grasses that top out at 3 feet should be planted 3 feet apart from center to center.

Plant container-grown perennials now.

ROSES

When planting climbing roses next to a wall, place them at least 2 feet away from it. Plant potted roses when the soil is dry enough to be worked.

SHRUBS AND TREES

Continue planting container-grown shrubs, following the how-to instructions in March. Pay strict attention to watering to help them get established. It's not too late to plant container-grown and balled-and-burlapped trees. Pay careful attention to watering during their establishment phase and don't let them dry out.

VINES & GROUNDCOVERS

In the Mountains sow seeds of tender summer-flowering annual vines in pots this month so they'll be large enough to move outdoors after the last freeze. Gardeners in the milder parts of the Carolinas can direct-sow the seeds to the garden after the last expected freeze, and they will have flowering in midsummer to fall.

Some seeds require special treatment prior to sowing to encourage germination. The seeds of morning glory and moonflower (*Ipomoea alba*)

HERE'S HOW

TO PLANT CONTAINER-GROWN PERENNIALS

1. Hold your hand over the top of the plant stems between your fingers. Tip the pot over and gently tap the plant into your hand. If the roots are circling around the rootball, loosen them to encourage growth into the surrounding soil. The tangled roots of large-rooted hostas and daylilies can be teased apart with your fingers. Use a knife, pruning shears, or sharp spade to loosen the sides of the rootballs of fine-rooted perennials.

2. Dig a hole the same depth as the rootball and slightly wider.

3. Set the plant in the hole so the crown is at or slightly above ground level.

4. Cover and firm the soil lightly around the plant.

5. Water thoroughly to settle the soil around the roots. Depending on the weather and rainfall, you may need to water daily for the first few weeks. Mulch with a 2- to 3-inch layer of compost with a ½-inch layer near the crown but not covering it.

6. During the next few weeks keep the plants well watered to help them become quickly established. After that, begin cutting back on water, eventually watering on an "as-needed" basis. Always test the soil and rootball to see if they're moist.

should be nicked with a knife or file and then soaked overnight to allow water to be absorbed by the seed for germination to occur.

WATER GARDENS

Hardy water lilies and lotuses that have spent the winter in the deeper parts of your pool, to protect their roots from freezing, need to be returned to shallower depths when the ice has melted completely.

Hardy water lilies are sold dormant and bare-root or non-dormant with a few leaves, roots, and perhaps buds. It's important that you prevent the rhizome from drying out. Put the lily in a bowl of water before planting.

Divide your bog plants just before or as new growth is emerging. Rhizomes such as those of striped rush can be divided into sections with shoots and roots. Fibrous-rooted plants such as pickerel rush can be teased apart into separate plants. Keep these marginal plants confined to containers like a nursery pot, which makes fertilizing and future dividing easier. Use the same heavy clay soil used for planting water lilies and other floating-leaved plants.

Place them on the shelf inside the pond or set them on bricks, weathered cinder blocks, or upside down pots so they're at the appropriate depth.

Any submerged plants that have become overgrown need to be thinned out. Compost the trimmings or incorporate them into the vegetable garden. You can propagate the trimmings by anchoring them in pots filled with sand.

HERE'S HOW

TO PLANT A HARDY WATER LILY

1. Select a roomy container with a drainage hole. Hardy water lilies grow horizontally, so select a container that is wider than tall. A pot that is 7 to 9 inches deep and 15 to 17 inches wide is fine for most; more vigorous types need a container a few inches wider. Fill the container one-third full with slightly damp, heavy, clay-based garden soil. Insert a water lily fertilizing tablet. Depending on the manufacturer, one fertilizer tablet may be required per 5 quarts of soil.

2. Fill the container to the top with soil and then add water until it seeps out the drainage hole.

3. Dig out a depression in the medium for the rhizome. Set it near the side of the container at a 45-degree angle, with the cut end at the side and the crown pointing up and oriented across the container. The rhizome should be deep enough to be covered with an inch of soil.

4. Fill the pot to within an inch or two of the rim. Let the growing tip protrude through the surface. Press the soil in, being careful around the crown.

5. Water the pot again. Top off the pot with pea gravel, leaving the growing point visible.

6. Place the pot in the water. Lower the pot slowly at an angle to allow any air bubbles to escape and to prevent the water from becoming clouded with mud.

7. The crowns of most hardy water lilies can be located 6 to 18 inches below the water surface. To keep them at this depth, place them on bricks or an empty overturned pot. To speed up their growth, place them on a pot 6 inches below the surface. As more leaves grow, move the plant gradually to deeper depths.

■ *Use a cold frame to harden off or acclimate seedlings to life outdoors. In late summer, use the cold frame for starting seedlings of cool-weather crops, such as lettuce and cabbage. A cold frame is also the perfect place to overwinter container-grown plants and summer-rooted cuttings of woody plants.*

CARE

ANNUALS

Tender annuals started indoors should gradually be "hardened off" before planting them in the garden. Hardening is a procedure that prepares indoor-grown plants for the rigors of the outdoors. Reduce watering and set them outdoors during the day. Bring them inside at night. Continue this for three to four days. If the temperature drops below 50 degrees Fahrenheit, take the plants inside. After four days, allow the plants to be outside all day and night. After about a week or two, the plants should be hardened off and ready to be transplanted with a minimum of shock. Alternatively, place plants in a cold frame for a week or two, monitoring the temperature and adjusting the coldframe cover accordingly. See November, Care.

Some annuals will produce hundreds of seedlings from last year's flowers. Look for "volunteers" of cosmos, cleome, impatiens, melampodium, silk flower, vinca, and others. Thin out the seedlings or transplant them to other parts of your garden.

As you remove cool-loving larkspurs, shake the plant over the soil to scatter seeds. Alternatively, shake the seeds over a sheet of newspaper, collect them, and sow them next fall.

In the Coastal Plain and warmer parts of the Piedmont, other cool-season annuals can be removed to make room for warm-season annuals.

Prune or shear alyssum and lobelia after blooming—this will make them look neater and encourage them to produce more flowers. Remove spent flowers from snapdragons for another crop of flowers. The blooms will not be as large, but they will provide garden color.

BULBS

When the flowers fade on your spring-flowering bulbs, cut them off to prevent seeds from developing. Don't cut or remove the leaves, which should be allowed to die naturally. Overcome the urge to braid the leaves or tie them into neat bundles.

EDIBLES

To keep the cauliflower curds pure white, loosely tie the long outside leaf onto the flat, open head when it is 1 to 2 inches across. Hold the leaves together with a rubber band until the head is ready for harvesting.

■ *Allow your onions to completely dry before curing or storing them. Squeeze the "neck" of the onion; if it does not slide back and forth between your thumb and forefinger, it's sufficiently dried.*

Continue to harvest asparagus in the Mountains until the spears become thinner than a pencil.

Root crops must be thinned, no matter how ruthless this practice seems. Thin beets, carrots, onions, Swiss chard, and turnips so you can get three fingers between individual plants.

Lavenders (*Lavandula stoechas* and *L. augustifolia*) and sage (*Salvia officinalis*) can be cut back in the spring as new growth begins. In both cases, do not cut below the point of new buds. With lavender this is usually 6 or 8 inches above the ground. Sage can be cut back lower still, provided you leave at least one pair of healthy green leaves on each stem from whose bases the new shoots will appear. Shearing lavender after the blossoms fade will also help keep the plants compact.

LAWNS

Mow cool-season lawns frequently, removing no more than one-third of the lawn height at a time. Leave the clippings on the lawn.

Before St. Augustinegrass comes out of dormancy, lower the mowing height to remove the tops of the dead grass blades.

PERENNIALS

Clean up plants and flowerbeds.

Pinched perennials produce more but smaller flowers than plants that have not been pinched. Pinching will stagger the bloom period of plants, particularly garden mums, and will prevent them from growing tall and straggly. Plants that respond well to pinching include aster, beebalm, garden mums, spotted Joe-pye weed (*Eupatorium purpureum* 'Gateway'), pink turtlehead (*Chelone lyonii*), spike speedwell (*Veronica spicata*), 'Autumn Joy' sedum, and others.

ROSES

Divide dormant miniature rosebushes that have produced a lot of woody, unproductive growth. Dig them up, then gently twist or cut apart the clumps. Trim any old woody growth and replant the divisions like new bushes.

Loosely tie climbing roses to trellises with broad strips of material such as soft twine or nylon. Use a figure-eight tie between the cane and the trellis so that the tie won't put pressure on or otherwise injure the cane. Do not use wires; they can damage canes.

Last year's mulch may contain fungal disease spores that can infect your rosebushes. If you haven't done so already, apply fresh mulch to blanket the old mulch. Keep the layer between 2 and 3 inches thick. If you prefer to remove the old mulch, apply it to other areas of the landscape not occupied by roses, or compost it.

Prune roses to buds that point outward. This encourages good air and sunlight penetration. Dark-colored canes indicate dead wood. Cut back an inch below these darkened areas. If the center of the cane is discolored, cut back further until your see white pith. If there are no live buds, remove the entire cane or branch.

SHRUBS

Do not be too quick to pull out shrubs that are damaged by cold. Cut back dead branches above the ground, but leave the roots in place until June. Sometimes it takes a few weeks of warm weather for the new shoots to be jumpstarted into growth. Check mulched areas and replace or replenish where needed.

If you aren't sure of the extent of winter injury, wait until growth begins before removing dead wood. Prune spring-flowering shrubs as their blossoms fade. Prune out dead, damaged, or pest-ridden branches first. Avoid using heading cuts to prune them into mushrooms or meatballs. Rather, use thinning cuts to remove renegade limbs and to accentuate their natural shapes.

To prune forsythia, quince, sweet mockorange, nandina, and other multistemmed shrubs, cut off a few of the older central stems at ground level so new ones can spring up and take over.

Prune azaleas only if they need it after they bloom. Thin wayward branches. Cut back branches that have just a ring of leaves at the top.

TREES

Avoid bumping into tree trunks with your lawn mower or whipping them with a nylon string trimmer. The resulting wounds can be colonized by fungal diseases or infested by borers, which can eventually kill the tree.

Repair the damaged or broken central leader of your fir, pine, or spruce to return the tree to its natural pyramidal shape. Begin by developing a new leader.

HERE'S HOW

TO FIX A DAMAGED OR MISSING CENTRAL LEADER ON YOUR SPRUCE

1. For Piedmont and Mountain gardeners, Norway spruce (*Picea abies*) is a conifer that typically grows to heights of 40 to 60 feet or more. When grown in full sun, it develops a dense, pyramidal habit without pruning. To return your spruces to their natural shape, begin by developing a leader in each tree. Select one of the topmost shoots growing from the whorl of branches and secure it upright to a wooden stick.

2. Shorten the remaining shoots to about two-thirds of their length, pruning each just above a bud to reduce competition with the leader.

3. Start at the top and begin pruning branches back to a lateral branch or bud. Work your way downward around the tree, pruning alternate branches on all sides. Avoid cutting back into the hardened older wood because new shoots will not grow and the form of the plant will be lost.

4. Once you've returned the trees to their natural shape, you can make them more compact in the future by heading back the terminal and side branches to lateral shoots or dormant buds in late winter or early spring before new growth resumes.

Broken central leader

Repaired central leader

Start training established trees and large shrubs with proper pruning cuts when they're young. Prune only small branches. If you didn't plant a high-quality tree with a strong trunk and well-spaced branches, you may have to prune regularly during its early years to improve its structure. Wait until they've had one full growing season before pruning them. Follow these proper pruning rules:

1. Cut the branch but not the branch collar. The collar is a swollen area at the base of a branch just before it enters the trunk. It acts as a natural barrier to decay-causing organisms.

2. Do not make "flush cuts" close to the trunk. These cuts create wounds to trunk tissue, which lead to decay.

3. Never leave a stub. Stubs usually die and are entry points for decay-causing fungi.

VINES & GROUNDCOVERS

If sweet peas are heavily mulched, their roots will be kept cooler and their season prolonged. Use rough plant litter or grass clippings for mulch. A little shade at midday will also help maintain the quality of the flowers and prolong the blooming season. Remove the pods, which inhibit flowering (unless you want to save the seed).

A few weeks after the last area freeze, bring your mandevilla outdoors. Before planting, set it in a shaded location for about a week or two; move it to a partially shaded location the following week. Then, plant it in a partially shaded location out of the hot afternoon sun. Fertilize every other month from spring through fall with a soluble houseplant fertilizer such as 20-20-20.

Prune wisterias, Carolina jessamine, and other spring-flowering vines after flowers have faded.

WATER GARDENS

If you didn't cut back the dead leaves from your marginal plants in the fall, now is a good time to remove them before or as the new growth emerges. Compost the trimmings or recycle them in the vegetable garden where they can be mixed into the soil.

Continue to remove fallen leaves and any floating organic debris from the surface of the pond.

WATER

ANNUALS
Keep transplants well watered and mulched to help them get settled in before summer's heat and humidity arrives.

BULBS
Spring is usually a wet time of year, so supplying supplemental water may not be necessary. If you have to water, keep leaves and flowers dry.

EDIBLES
The first few weeks after planting and transplanting and during the development of fruit or storage organs are times when plants may be adversely affected by shortages of water. Be sure they are watered well.

LAWNS
Newly seeded, plugged, or sodded lawns should be watered frequently. As the seedlings emerge and the sod "knits" into the soil, gradually water more deeply and less often.

Water established lawns as needed. One inch of water per week is adequate on clay soils. Apply ½ inch of water every third day on sandy soils.

PERENNIALS AND VINES & GROUNDCOVERS
Keep newly planted perennials well watered during the first few weeks to help them get quickly established.

Water any newly planted vines or groundcovers. Check the soil in the rootball regularly and water it when necessary.

ROSES, SHRUBS, AND TREES
To prevent water from running off, it is helpful to create a temporary berm, or dike, around newly planted roses in clay soil. Remove the berm when the roses become established. Whenever you irrigate, keep the leaves dry to reduce the growth and spread of diseases.

Sometimes it's necessary to create a temporary berm or dike around newly planted shrubs and trees in clay soil to prevent water from running off when watering. Remove the berm when the plants become established (see May, Water).

FERTILIZE

ANNUALS

If you fertilized at planting with a slow-release fertilizer, you may not have to fertilize until midsummer or later, depending on the fertilizer brand and formulation. Follow the label directions to learn the desired amount and frequency of application. Fast-release granular fertilizers can be applied every four to six weeks during the growing season. Plants can absorb liquid fertilizers through their leaves and roots, and they will have to be applied more frequently (typically every two weeks).

BULBS

Fertilize summer bulbs when new leaves emerge, using a single application of a slow-release nitrogen fertilizer. Instead of a slow-release fertilizer, you may use a balanced fast-release nitrogen fertilizer such as 8-8-8 or 10-10-10. An application every month or two during the growing season may be necessary to satisfy the needs of dahlias, gladiolus, and lilies. Avoid overfertilization, which can encourage the production of leaves at the expense of flowers. Let the appearance of the plant guide you. If plants look robust and are growing in a well-prepared, fertile bed, fertilizing may be unnecessary.

EDIBLES

Apply a nitrogen-containing fertilizer to asparagus to encourage the production of large ferny growth. Research has shown that the bigger the topgrowth, the better the yield. Sidedress young garlic plants when the new growth is 6 inches high. Sidedress Irish potatoes when the sprouts begin to break ground.

LAWNS

Do not fertilize established cool-season lawns at this time. Wait at least two or three weeks after your warm-season lawn has completely greened up before fertilizing according to soil test recommendations.

PERENNIALS

Apply a slow-release fertilizer when the new shoots emerge. Follow the label directions regarding the amount and frequency of application. Water afterward to make the minerals available to the roots.

ROSES

Fertilize once-blooming roses in early spring before growth begins. Repeat-blooming roses should be fertilized only if necessary. Evaluate the growth and appearance of the plant to decide if fertilizing is necessary. When using a fast-release fertilizer, time your application after each flush of bloom. Only one or two applications may be necessary during the season if you use a slow-release fertilizer. Refer to the fertilizer label for the rate and frequency of application. Water afterward to make the nutrients available to the rose.

SHRUBS

For blue flowers on your mophead and lacecap or French hydrangeas, maintain a soil pH between 5 and 5.5. An acidic soil increases the availability of aluminum, which turns the flowers blue. Apply aluminum sulfate or sulfur to reduce the pH to this ideal range when you see new growth emerging (wait until next month to do this in the Mountains).

TREES

Fertilize palms with a slow-release fertilizer having a 3:1:2 analysis such as 18-6-12 or 15-5-10. Apply according to label directions. Palms benefit from fertilizers that also contain magnesium and other micronutrients such as manganese. This is particularly true of palms growing on the outer Coastal Plain where micronutrient deficiencies are common. Broadcast or scatter the fertilizer under the canopy or over the bed area.

VINES & GROUNDCOVERS

Fertilize groundcovers and vines based on need. Vines may not need fertilizer if they look robust and are vigorously growing. Excessive fertilizer may

■ *If you maintain acidic soil conditions, you can intensify the blueness of the lace cap flowers of Bluebird mountain hydrangea (Hydrangea serrata 'Bluebird'), which will appear next month.*

encourage leafy growth at the expense of flowers, and vigorous vines may become unmanageable and require excessive pruning.

WATER GARDENS

Fertilize bog plants with aquatic plant fertilizer tablets when new growth emerges. Instead of the tablets, you can use a slow-release nitrogen granular fertilizer following the manufacturer's instructions. Avoid spilling any fertilizer into the pool.

Feed hardy water lilies once a month with the aquatic fertilizer tablets pushed into the soil when the water temperature goes above 70 degrees Fahrenheit. Keep the tablet about 2 inches away from the rhizome or tuber.

PROBLEM-SOLVE

ANNUALS

Watch out for aphids and whiteflies on China aster, impatiens, and other annuals.

Damping off can still be a problem on indoor seedlings. Use sterile seed-starting medium and avoid overwatering.

BULBS

Inspect the leaves of your bulbs for aphids and spider mites. Dislodge them with a strong spray of water in early morning, giving leaves plenty of time to dry before evening.

When iris leaves appear thin and limp, check for iris borers. These grublike insects can ruin an entire planting if not detected and eradicated early. Eggs overwinter in old, dried iris leaves and other debris. They hatch in mid- to late spring when the tiny larvae crawl up the young iris leaves and feed, producing telltale notches. Then they enter the leaves, producing pinpoint holes. As they slowly mine their way down toward the rhizomes, the borers leave a ragged, water-soaked tunnel in their wake. When you spot such a tunnel, squash the borer inside by pressing the leaf between your thumb and forefinger.

Alternatively, spray your plants with an insecticide when the leaves are 5 to 6 inches tall.

Handpull winter annuals such as common chickweed, henbit, and Carolina geranium to prevent them from reseeding. A shallow layer of mulch will suppress them.

EDIBLES

Mexican bean beetles—both adults and larvae—feed on bush, pole, and lima beans by skeletonizing the leaves from below. Handpick and destroy beetles and larvae on the leaves, or deposit them in a jar of soapy water. Parasitic wasps help control the beetles. Insecticides are also available.

Look for flea beetles on eggplant. They are about 1½ inches long, shiny black in color, and chew tiny holes in leaves. Control with the appropriate insecticides. Cutworms damage seedlings and transplants by cutting stems a few inches below or just above ground level. They feed mainly at night. See May, Problem-Solve for a description and controls.

Leaffooted bugs feed mostly on tomato, potato, bean, cowpea, and okra. Both nymphs and adults suck sap from pods, buds, blossoms, fruit, and seeds, causing distorted leaves and distorted or deformed fruit. Their life cycle lasts about forty days, with many generations per year. Plant early to avoid the first generation. Handpicking and destroying the eggs are time-consuming but effective measures. Insecticides are available.

Control weed seedlings when they are young because they grow rapidly and can be more difficult to remove later. A sharpened hoe is a good friend in the garden.

LAWNS

Rust attacks bluegrass and fescue, causing leaves to turn yellow before turning brown and dying. Look for red, orange, or brown spores. Many grass varieties have good-to-moderate levels of resistance, so this disease shouldn't be much of a problem. Collect infected grass clippings to prevent spores from spreading. Water in the early morning to avoid keeping the grass wet for long periods.

Dollar spot attacks bluegrass, fescue, bermuda, zoysia, and sometimes centipedegrass and St. Augustinegrass. It produces small circular areas of straw-colored grass from 1 to 6 inches across. Straw-colored lesions with reddish brown borders sometimes extend across the leaf blade while the tip remains green. Early in the morning a spider-web-like growth may extend over the area. Maintain adequate levels of fertility, especially nitrogen, because this disease favors "hungry" lawns. Fungicides are generally unnecessary.

Spring dead spot is a fungal disease that primarily attacks bermudagrass. In the spring, look for dead circular or doughnut-shaped patches, 2 or 3 feet across, as the bermudagrass comes out of dormancy. Cut out the patches and mix the soil or remove the soil and replace with clean soil. To manage this disease, avoid excessive nitrogen applications in late summer and fall and aerify lawns to reduce thatch (see September, Plan).

Florida betony (*Stachys floridana*) is a fast-spreading, cool-season perennial weed often called "rattlesnake weed" because it produces white, segmented tubers like a rattlesnake's tail. It emerges from seeds and tubers during the cool, moist months of fall. It grows and spreads rapidly throughout the winter months. From late spring to early summer Florida betony bears white to pink flowers. Growth stops at the onset of high temperatures and the plant becomes nearly dormant.

Pull or dig out all plant parts, especially the tubers, when the soil is moist. Hoe or cut the top-growth down to the soil level repeatedly to "starve" the plant. Spot-treat with a recommended herbicide.

PERENNIALS

Watch out for aphids and whiteflies on coreopsis, chrysanthemums, sedum, verbena, and others. Snails and slugs may be a problem on hosta, ligularia, bear's breeches (*Acanthus mollis*), and other perennials.

Look for columbine leaf miners. The larvae tunnel between the upper and lower leaf surfaces, producing telltale grayish white serpentine trails. There are several generations of larvae and adults per year. Control leaf miners by crushing the larvae inside the leaf before they become too disfigured or by cutting off the leaf altogether and removing it from the garden. For heavy infestations, cut columbines to the ground after flowering. New growth will soon emerge.

At the end of the growing season, remove any debris near the base of your plants to reduce next-year's overwintering offspring. Not all columbines are equally susceptible to this pest. The native columbine (*Aquilegia canadensis*), for example, is reported to be less susceptible to leaf miner attack.

Botrytis blight attacks peony buds, causing them to turn black and shrivel up. This fungal disease also attacks flowers' stalks, leaves, and leaf petioles. Remove and dispose of infected plant parts as soon as you spot them. If necessary, apply a fungicide in the spring as new shoots emerge.

Handpull bittercress, chickweed, henbit, and other annual winter weeds before they go to seed.

Pre-emergent herbicides are available for many of the more common perennials. These herbicides kill germinating weed seedlings before they appear. See March, Annuals for tips on selecting a pre-emergent herbicide.

ROSES

■ *Inspect your roses for rose aphids. See March, Problem-Solve for controls.*

SHRUBS

Watch for aphids, whiteflies, and spider mites. Azalea lace bugs suck sap from the undersides of azalea leaves, creating stippled or blanched areas. The underside of the leaf will be covered with splattered, brown or black, varnish-like patches of fecal material. The leaves will turn pale green or yellow and fall off. In the Carolinas expect two or three generations. Damage from this pest is most serious on azaleas growing in sunny locations. If yours are growing in full sun, try moving them to a location that receives only filtered sunlight or afternoon shade.

If you use an insecticide, start early in the season to destroy the first generation of nymphs. You can apply insecticidal soap or pyrethrin at three- to four-day intervals for a minimum of three applications, making sure to spray the undersides of the leaves. (If there is no rain to wash the leaves, don't exceed three applications or you may damage the plants.)

Look for tea scales on the undersides of camellia and holly leaves. They look like white waxy or cottony oval specks. Scale insects suck plant sap and exude a sticky honeydew that's often colonized by a sooty mold fungus. The young scale insects are called "crawlers" and are about the size of the period at the end of this sentence. They scurry about, then settle and produce a protective shell or cover. Heavy infestations cause leaf drop. Light infestations can be scraped off the plant. Control with summer horticultural oil sprays and other pesticides.

Azalea leaf gall is a fungal disease that infects newly emerging leaves and flowers of azaleas. The fleshy galls begin as light green to pink thickened areas on the leaves and turn chalky white as the spores are produced. Camellia leaf gall infects sasanqua camellias more than Japanese camellias. The gall containing the fungus eventually ruptures and disperses the spores to other plants. Handpick the galls and discard them. Fungicides are available.

Entomosporium leaf spot is a disease that attacks red tips (*Photinia* × *fraseri*) and Indian hawthorn (*Raphiolepis indica*), causing leaf drop. To manage this disease, see the Here's How box below.

For weeds, follow the guidelines described in March.

TREES

Watch out for the "cool-weather" mites: southern red mites that attack hollies and spruce, and spider mites, which feed on arborvitae, juniper, spruce, and other conifers. They attack in the spring and fall although at higher elevations they may be active all summer long.

Dogwood anthracnose is a devastating fungal disease of flowering dogwoods (*Cornus florida*). It produces leaf spots and cankers on the twigs and trunk, eventually killing the tree. Fungicides can control this disease. Dogwoods that are resistant to dogwood anthracnose include *Cornus kousa* 'Steeple' and the Stellar® hybrids, which are hybrids between flowering dogwood and kousa dogwood: *Cornus* × *rutgersensis* 'Rutfan' (Stardust®), 'Rutgan' (Stellar Pink®), and 'Rutdan' (Celestial™).

Many leaf diseases become active as the trees begin to leaf out. For example, apple scab attacks apples and crabapples as they come out of winter dormancy. Velvety brown to olive spots develop on the undersides of the leaves as they emerge in the spring. Eventually the spots turn black and the leaf dies. While apple scab will not kill your crabapple, severe leaf drop two or three years in a row can weaken your tree. As with all diseases, reduce future infections by collecting and disposing of fallen leaves. While fungicides are available, consider growing cultivars that are resistant to scab and other diseases such as fireblight, cedar-apple rust, and powdery mildew. A few of these cultivars are 'Autumn Treasure', 'Adirondack', 'Centurion', 'Callaway', 'Donald Wyman', 'Indian Summer', 'Molten Lava', and 'Tina'.

VINES & GROUNDCOVERS

Watch out for aphids, whiteflies, and spider mites. Evaluate the injury and decide if pest control measures are warranted.

Large-flowered clematis are highly susceptible to a notorious fungal disease called clematis wilt. See May, Problem-Solve for description and controls.

Handpull bittercress, chickweed, henbit, and other winter annuals before they go to seed. Weeds can be hoed out, but lightly, so as not to disturb the groundcovers. Grassy weeds can be controlled with a selective post-emergent grass herbicide.

WATER GARDENS

Any diseased leaves should be removed and discarded promptly.

HERE'S HOW

TO TREAT ENTOMOSPORIUM LEAF SPOT ON RED TIPS AND INDIAN HAWTHORNS

1. Prune only in the winter before growth begins. (Summer pruning encourages flushes of new growth, which are susceptible to attack.)

2. Remove infected twigs and leaves and rake up and discard fallen leaves.

3. Space plants far enough apart to encourage rapid drying of the leaves after rainfall; avoid wetting the leaves, because the fungus is spread by splashing water.

4. As a last resort, protect the new leaves with a fungicide. Because photinia produces several growth flushes a season, expect fungicide applications to be a regular gardening chore.

May

This must be the time for springtime flowers because my wife's allergies tell her so. She wonders aloud why plants have to bloom with such gusto. Alternatively, there are those who ask the age-old question, "Why don't my plants bloom?"

Has it ever flowered? How long has it been in the landscape? Is this the first year that it hasn't bloomed? Has the floral display declined over the years?

Answers to these questions provide clues to determine "what-dunnit." If a plant has never bloomed, it could be related to the age or maturity, climate, soils, light, or something else. Determine which one is missing or limiting and correct it. Here are a few factors that need to be evaluated.

1. **Plant maturity.** Some trees do not flower until they reach a certain age. Seedling dogwoods generally do not flower until they are seven years old. Seed-grown southern magnolias may take ten or twelve years before blooming.

2. **Climate.** Cold temperatures often kill flower buds while posing no harm to vegetative buds, leaves, and stems. Our temperature fluctuations in winter and spring plays havoc with our plants. When a plant breaks dormancy and starts growing in response to warm temperatures, it is more susceptible to injury when an uninvited cold air mass suddenly rolls in.

3. **Soils.** Inadequate soil preparation or overly wet or dry soils affect flowering. Could the soil pH be too acidic or is a nutrient lacking or unavailable? Overfertilizing with nitrogen will keep newly planted shrubs and trees in the business of making lots of leaves at the expense of flowers.

4. **Light.** Inadequate light may prevent flower bud set. If a plant had never flowered, it was probably planted in shade that was too dense at the start. If it used to flower, surrounding plants or new structures may have reduced sunlight to prevent it from flowering.

I hope this helps those readers who want to experience that rush of euphoria when their shrubs and trees burst into bloom. For those who wish that it would all go away—the flowers as well as the itchy eyes, runny noses, and scratchy throats—I share your pain. Or at least my wife does.

PLAN

ANNUALS

Too busy to enjoy your garden during the daylight hours? Then create an evening garden with annuals that look their best at twilight. These flowers open in the evening or release fragrances at night to attract night-flying pollinators such as moths. One of the more familiar night-blooming annuals is flowering tobacco (*Nicotiana alata*). Petunias open by day and release their scent at night. Try the varieties 'Celebrity White', 'Ultra White', or 'Apollo'.

Other night-blooming annuals to consider are the moonflower vine (*Ipomoea alba*), angel's trumpet (*Datura inoxia*), night phlox (*Zaluzianskya capensis*), and night-scented stock (*Matthiola longipetala*).

BULBS

As spring-flowering bulbs begin to fade, make plans to fill their voids with flowering annuals that are either direct-sown as seed or planted from transplants. Avoid injuring bulbs when planting over them.

Summer- and fall-flowering bulbs also make good fillers for a continuous floral display. Piedmont and Coastal gardeners can continue to plant summer bulbs; Mountain gardeners need to wait until the last expected freeze this month. When selecting bulbs for the summer and fall landscape, use your list of recommended types and cultivars. Pay particular attention to height and spread, bloom time, flower color, and fragrance. Finally, determine how many bulbs you'll need so you won't come home short-handed.

EDIBLES

If you lack the space for an herb and vegetable garden, consider growing them in containers. Remember these points:

1. Choose white or light-colored containers, which absorb less heat than dark-colored ones in full sun.

2. The container should be large enough to provide root-growing space. A 1-gallon container is suitable for beets, carrots, lettuces, onions, and radishes. A 2-gallon pot is fine for bush beans, mustard, and turnips. A minimum of 5 gallons would be necessary for bush squash, cabbage, and other cole crops, cucumbers, melons, and tomato.

3. Use a soil-less potting mix for small containers. Because the expense of prepackaged or soil-less mixes can be high for large-container gardens, prepare your own soil by mixing equal parts of peat moss, potting soil, and clean coarse builder's sand or perlite.

4. Container-grown vegetables and herbs have the same requirements for light, moisture, and nutrients as garden-grown plants. Being confined to containers, however, means they require more-frequent watering, which leaches out nutrients, so they also require more-frequent fertilizing. Use a slow-release fertilizer to make fewer applications.

■ *Purchase wide, shallow pots to plant a salad bowl and fill the bowl about halfway with potting soil.*

■ *Fill in around the plants with potting soil and water the plants. On hot days, move the bowl into some shade. On cool days, move the bowl into the sun. If temperatures are forecast to drop below freezing, bring the bowl into the garage.*

HERE'S HOW

TO RAISE A SUMMER-TOUGH LAWN

1. Encourage the development of a deep root system by watering only when the need arises. Look for signs of moisture stress: folded or curled leaves, a dull bluish gray color, and footprints that remain in the grass long after you've walked over it. Water areas that exhibit these symptoms first. Irrigate only those areas that are important to your landscape.

■ *Short frequent waterings lead to shallow roots (left) while deeper, infrequent waterings encourage the production of deeper-growing roots.*

2. Water late at night or early in the morning when dew has formed, which will not encourage disease. It will also save you money. At midday, in hot, dry, windy weather, 30 percent or more of the water evaporates. Watering at night or in early morning cuts evaporation in half, to 15 to 20 percent. Because it takes 640 gallons of water to irrigate 1,000 square feet with 1 inch of water, late night and early morning watering provides substantial savings.

3. Gradually raise the mowing height by one-quarter to one-half as the temperature climbs. A higher mowing height encourages deeper root growth and reduces heat stress.

4. Make sure that your mower blade is sharp. Grasses that are cut cleanly lose less water and heal more rapidly than leaves shredded by a dull mower blade.

5. Avoid a fast-food diet by using a slow-release fertilizer that contains one-fourth to one-half of its nitrogen in a "water-insoluble" or "slowly available" form.

LAWNS

See the "Here's How" for a few techniques to help you toughen up your lawn while reducing your water bill.

PERENNIALS & ORNAMENTAL GRASSES

If you're serious about growing perennials well, start a journal this month, perhaps even a blog. Document your observations, thoughts, and plans for the future. Take note of some of the following items:

- Blooming dates for each variety

- Condition of the flowers, leaves, and overall health of your perennials

- Pest problems such as insects, diseases, and weeds

- Kinds of pesticides used and when they were applied

- Plants that need to be moved or replaced because they grew larger than you expected or were more demanding than you had planned

Your journal can become a teaching tool, especially when you need the assistance of a county Extension agent, Master Gardener, or a garden center staff person to help you diagnose a particular problem. The notes you took about weather conditions, fertilizing, watering, and any pest control applications are important clues that can help reveal the answer. So start writing.

■ *Drip irrigation systems offer many different types of fittings to suit your particular needs.*

SHRUBS

With summer around the corner, take some time this month to consider the irrigation method best suited to your situation.

If you're going to water by hand, find a nozzle that breaks the water into rain-size droplets that won't wash the soil away. If you choose to automate, consider an irrigation system.

Some install-it-yourself systems allow you to turn the water on and off yourself or automatically, in various patterns and for any length of time. The simplest is a soaker hose, a fibrous tube that "sweats" or allows water to seep out along its length. It is suitable for dense plantings.

Some systems have nozzles that deliver the water in a low, horizontal pattern that wets the root zone but keeps the plants dry.

The most efficient watering method is drip or trickle irrigation. Such systems use short tubes, called emitters, which come off a main water-supply hose and go directly to the base of the plant. This is generally the most expensive form of irrigation and the most complex to set up, but it has advantages. The weeds in the area are not watered, and evaporation from the soil is minimized. Drip systems can have problems with clogging from soil particles and/or mineral salts suspended in water taken from springs or wells. New designs address this problem: some include filters and self-flushing emitters. All these systems can work on a timer.

TREES

Update your gardening journal, noting spring-flowering trees, their peak bloom periods, and pest problems. Use this information to add trees, rearrange or replace, and correct any problems. Keep a record of the varieties you grow. By knowing the specific names, you can ask for that variety next season if you like it, or avoid it if it wasn't up to par.

VINES & GROUNDCOVERS

This month, keep an eye out for troubling spots in the landscape. If you've been struggling to grow turfgrass in an area that receives less than four hours of sunlight and you choose not to thin out the tree canopy to admit more sunlight, consider evergreen shade-loving groundcovers. Some shade-loving groundcovers that can be used in place of turf are English ivy, liriope, pachysandra, periwinkle (*Vinca minor*), wintercreeper euonymus, and carpet bugleweed (*Ajuga*).

WATER GARDENS

Consider expanding your pool to include a bog garden. Creating a bog will be easy if you have a naturally low, poorly drained area that collects water.

If you're going to install a bog garden, you can dig a shallow depression outside of the water garden that can catch any overflow. Extend the flexible liner over this basin and fill it with soil.

Visit The Bog Garden in Greensboro and the University of North Carolina at Charlotte Botanical Gardens to see the beauty and diversity of bog plants.

1. Dig a hole 2 to 2½ feet deep and as wide as you like. Twelve to 15 square feet is the minimum size.

2. Lay a thin liner over the hole and press it in. Weigh the ends down with bricks or stones to keep it in place.

3. Fill in the hole with soil to within 3 or 4 inches of the top.

4. Trim the edges of the liner and fold them back into the hole. Add the remaining soil to hide the edges.

5. Wet the soil heavily and then let it settle for a day or two before planting it.

6. Water your bog garden whenever the surface feels dry. Stop watering when water starts to come up to the surface.

PLANT

ANNUALS

Plant warm-season annuals for summer color. Set out those you started indoors. Continue to plant zinnia seed at intervals to have cut flowers until frost.

Overplant bulb beds with annuals using seeds or transplants. Take care to avoid injuring the bulbs when planting.

Although cool-season annuals such as pansies and violas may still be flowering, the heat will make them stretch and get leggy. Pull them out and replace them with heat-loving summer annuals such as African daisy, ageratum, celosia, cockscomb, marigold, pentas, vinca or Madagascar periwinkle, petunia, portulaca, salvia, and zinnia for sunny areas. Geraniums and New Guinea impatiens are excellent if you have afternoon shade. For shady areas, use begonias, coleus, and impatiens.

Grow your own dried flowers. Start seeds of statice, globe amaranth, strawflowers, and other everlastings for this year's arrangements.

BULBS

After the last freeze, plant tender summer bulbs such as cannas, dahlias, ginger lilies, and tuberoses that have been stored over the winter or purchased from mail-order companies or garden centers. In the Mountains, plant tuberous begonias, but don't set the pots out until after the last expected freeze. Plant caladium bulbs when soil temperature goes above 70 degrees Fahrenheit. Caladiums prefer shade to partial shade; however, there are fancy-leaved selections that do well and tolerate sun such as 'Aaron', 'Carolyn Whorton', 'Fire Chief', 'Florida Elise', 'Florida Sweetheart', 'Red Flash', 'Scarlet Beauty', and 'White Queen'. A few sun-tolerant lance-leaved types include 'Gingerland', 'Miss Muffet', and 'Red Frill'.

EDIBLES

Sow warm-weather vegetables such as beans, cucumber, okra, and southern peas.

Extend your sweet corn harvest by planting successive crops when the previous crop has three to four leaves, or plant early-, mid-, and late-maturing varieties all at the same time.

Set out herb transplants. Continue setting out transplants of warm-weather vegetables such as eggplant, muskmelon, New Zealand spinach, peppers, summer squash, sweet potato slips, tomatoes, and watermelon. French tarragon doesn't like the heat and wet weather in the warmer areas of the Coastal Plain; a heat-tolerant substitute is Mexican mint marigold (*Tagetes lucida*).

LAWNS

Think twice before starting a cool-season lawn now from seed. The seedlings won't have time to get settled before the onset of hot weather. Consider installing sod, provided you're willing to keep it watered during its establishment and droughty periods this summer.

For warm-season lawns, see April.

PERENNIALS & ORNAMENTAL GRASSES

It's not too late to plant perennials as long as you're willing to pamper them, helping with regular watering to speed up their establishment before hot summer weather arrives.

ROSES

A potted rose makes a great gift for Mother's Day. Refer to the how-to plant instructions in March.

SHRUBS AND TREES

Although shrubs are best planted in the fall, container-grown plants can be planted throughout the summer as long as you pay careful attention to watering. When the flowers fade on your Mother's Day hydrangeas, don't throw them out. Plant them in the garden where they'll get morning sun and afternoon shade.

Trees are best planted during cooler seasons when the top-growth has little demand for moisture. Container-grown plants, however, can be successfully transplanted on the heels of summer if you water them regularly during their establishment period.

Palms transplant best in spring and summer when they're actively growing. (When it's time to plant tomatoes, it's time to plant palms.) They prefer a well-drained, fertile, slightly acidic to neutral soil. Cold-sensitive palms should be placed within 8 to

■ *Mountain and Piedmont gardeners can grow Japanese pachysandra in very shady areas.*

10 feet of the warm, southwest side of a brick wall for a few extra degrees of protection in the winter. Tender palms should not be planted in exposed areas where they can be harmed by dry, cold winter winds.

VINES & GROUNDCOVERS

It's a good time to dig and divide those crowded liriope borders. You may be able to find enough neighbors to share the bounty.

Plant container-grown vines and groundcovers, but be careful—they'll need attention after planting until they get established. Make sure you're familiar with the plant's site preferences prior to planting.

Plant seeds or seedlings of annual vines like morning glory, moonflower, and scarlet runner bean.

■ *Now is a good time to transplant a palm tree.*

HERE'S HOW

TO PLANT A TROPICAL WATER LILY

1. Select a roomy container with a drainage hole. Tropical water lilies grow from a tuber, so a deep 5-gallon pot that allows for more vertical growth than horizontal growth would be fine. Fill the container one-third full with slightly damp heavy, clay-based garden soil. Insert a water lily fertilizing tablet. Depending on the manufacturer, one fertilizer tablet may be required for 5 quarts of soil.

2. Fill the container to the top with soil and then add water until it seeps out of the drainage hole.

3. Plant the tuber in the center of the pot. Look for a white line on the tuber. This is where the soil level should be once you refill the pot.

4. Fill the pot to within an inch or two of the rim. Let the growing tip protrude through the surface. Press the soil in and be careful around the crown.

5. Water the pot again. Top off the pot with pea gravel, leaving the growing point visible to prevent soil from washing away. (Though experts feel that pea gravel is unsightly and is not necessary if you lower the pot slowly into the water.)

6. Place the pot in the water. Lower it slowly and at a slight angle allowing any air bubbles to escape. This will prevent it from muddying the water.

7. The depth for tropical water lilies should be between 6 and 12 inches from the crown to the water's surface.

Plant the summer annuals you sowed indoors into the garden after the last freeze in your area.

WATER GARDENS

Time the planting of your tropical water lilies with the planting of your tender vegetables and warm-season annuals after the last expected freeze. They can be planted in your water garden when the water temperature stays above 70 degrees Fahrenheit.

Tropical water lilies are sold dormant and bare root or nondormant with a few leaves, roots, and perhaps buds. It's important that you prevent the tuber from drying out. Put it in a bowl of water before planting.

CARE

ANNUALS

Thin direct-seeded annuals to the correct spacing. To make room for warm-season annuals,

Mountain gardeners can remove cool-season annuals when they begin to decline.

Although plant breeders have developed compact, sturdy varieties that require no support, other

■ *Get mums to bloom in the fall by pinching off the flower buds during the summer.*

tall-growing types need support for protection from buffeting winds and rain. See May, Care for techniques.

To promote bushy growth, pinch back annuals when they're 4 to 6 inches in height. Specific plant tips include:

- Pinch out the shoot tips of marigolds, petunias, salvias, and zinnias.

- Pinch the shoot tips of cosmos to encourage branching. If unpinched, the stems may require staking to keep them upright.

- Shear alyssum and lobelia after flowering.

- Remove the spent flowers of sweet William.

- Remove the yellow flowers of dusty miller to keep the leaves looking good throughout the growing season. If the plant gets leggy, cut it back to about half its height to encourage branching and denser growth.

BULBS

After blooming, cut off spent flowers and stalks from bearded irises.

Cut flower stalks back to the ground on daffodils and other spring-flowering bulbs as flowers fade. Do not cut the leaves until they die naturally. (Leaves are necessary for producing strong bulbs

capable of reflowering.) If you have to hide the dying leaves, consider these tips:

- Interplant with perennials that will grow above and hide the bulb leaves.

- Plant taller flower bulbs behind lower-growing shrubs.

- Intersperse clump-forming plants such as ornamental grasses, liriopes, and daylilies.

- Underplant with low-growing, sprawling groundcovers like junipers and some cotoneasters, which allow you to tuck the leaves beneath the branches.

EDIBLES

Harvest broccoli when the florets are still tight and green. After harvesting the main head, broccoli will put out smaller-sized heads from the side shoots. Pick cauliflower before the curds begin to separate, and cabbage before it bolts (blooms). Pick green, sugar snap, and snow peas every couple of days to keep more coming. Stop harvesting asparagus spears when they get close to pencil size. Fasten indeterminate tomatoes to a stake. This will keep their fruit off the ground to avoid disease problems. Determinate tomatoes, which branch more and ripen their fruit all at once, are best enclosed in a reinforced wire tomato cage. Wind their branches around the inside of the cage as they grow.

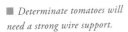

■ *Determinate tomatoes will need a strong wire support.*

■ *Mow your lawn at the appropriate height for your grass, and use a sharp mower blade to cut the grass cleanly.*

With your fingers, pinch out the "suckers" of indeterminate tomatoes to harvest larger tomatoes. Suckers are shoots that develop in the "U" between the main stem and a branch. If left in place, they will eventually become larger branches. Your plant will produce smaller tomatoes, but lots of them.

LAWNS

Maintain a sharp mower blade and recycle the grass clippings by leaving them on the lawn.

Mow your warm-season lawn at the recommended height with a sharp blade. Avoid cutting more than one-third of the height or the plant may be stressed, exposing it to a weed invasion.

PERENNIALS

Begin staking tall-growing plants when they reach one-third of their mature height. Place the stakes close to the plant, but take care to avoid damaging the root system. Secure the stems of the plants to stakes in several places with materials that will not cut into the stem. Tie the twine into a figure eight to avoid binding the stem. Summer- and fall-flowering perennials often require support. Some plants, however, can simply be pruned back lightly in midsummer to reduce their height and encourage branching and sturdiness. Swamp sunflower (*Helianthus angustifolius*) can be handled this way. See June, Care for more information about this technique.

In the spring, when new shoots in a clump of garden phlox reach 8 to 10 inches tall, thin out all but four or five of the well-spaced healthy ones to allow good air circulation. Thinning helps prevent disease (especially powdery mildew), improves the appearance of the plants, and produces sturdier stems.

Some spring-flowering perennials should be sheared after flowering, cutting them back by one-half. Among them are cheddar pinks (*Dianthus gratianopolitanus* 'Bath's Pink' and 'Firewitch'), evergreen candytuft (*Iberis sempervirens*), and moss phlox (*Phlox subulata*). Garden chrysanthemums can be sheared when the new growth reaches 4 to 6 inches in length. Shearing an inch off the top will delay flowering and encourage bushiness and the production of a lot of flower buds.

■ *Cut back cheddar pinks by one-half after flowering to encourage bushiness.*

HERE'S HOW

TO STAKE TALL, FLOPPY PLANTS

1. Place several stakes in and around the plant clump to serve as a framework and as individual supports. If one branch is particularly large and floppy, put one of the stakes next to it, about an inch away from the plant stem.

2. Start creating a web of string between the stakes. Try to pull the string as taut as possible between stakes, without bending the stakes. You can create as many crisscrossing strings as you'd like. The more string, the more support for the plants growing through the web.

3. You can tie individual stems to stakes with longer pieces of twine. This lets the stems "lean" as if they're naturally growing but still gives them individual support.

4. When you're finished creating your web of string and tying heavy individual stems to the stakes, your plants will be standing upright. As the plants grow, their foliage will hide the stakes and string. If the stakes are much taller than the projected size of the plant, you can cut them shorter with hand pruners.

ROSES

Old garden roses, species, and shrub roses come in a wide range of sizes and shapes. Generally, allow the natural shape of the plant to guide your pruning cuts. Hold off on pruning them until they've achieved a decent size, perhaps after the second or third growing season. Here are a few pruning tips:

- Shorten long, vigorous canes by up to one-third to encourage production of flower-bearing side shoots.

- Tip-prune last year's lateral or side shoots to 6 inches in length.

- On established plants, remove one or two of the oldest canes that produce few, if any, flowers, maintaining a balance between old and new growths.

To avoid pruning flower buds, remember that one-time bloomers or roses that produce their heaviest flush on old wood should be pruned after flowering in the spring. For shrub roses that produce attractive hips, or rose fruits, such as hybrid rugosa roses, prune only some of the shoots, preserving some of the hip-bearing branches.

SHRUBS AND TREES

To prevent damage to shrubs and trees while mowing, surround them with a 2- to 3-inch ring of mulch. Keep the mulch a hand's width from the trunk. Apply the mulch as far as the dripline or outermost branches.

SHRUBS

As French or lacecap hydrangeas age, renew the plants to encourage new shoots. Remove no more than one-third of the oldest shoots at the base immediately after flowering. They will be replaced by more-vigorous younger shoots, which will flower the following season. Alternatively, grow reblooming (called remontant) mophead cultivars that produce flowers on current season's growth. They include 'Bailmer' (Endless Summer™), 'David Ramsey', 'Decatur Blue', 'Luvumama', 'Madame Emile Mouillere', 'Oak Hill', 'Penny Mac', and the lacecap 'Lilacina'. In addition to these remontant mopheads, select other hydrangeas that produce flowers on the current season's growth including

panicle hydrangea (*H. paniculata*) and smooth hydrangea (*H. arborescens*).

Continue pruning spring-flowering shrubs as their flowers fade. The new growth that develops will mature over the summer and fall and produce flowers next spring.

Not all azaleas have to be pruned. If they've overgrown their location or have dead branches, they will benefit from careful trimming. Take out individual branches with thinning cuts, removing the oldest branches at the base.

Prune rhododendrons immediately after flowering. Snap off old flower trusses. Remove them carefully so you won't damage next year's flower buds.

TREES

Remove dead or diseased wood at any time. If you cut into diseased wood, disinfect your pruning shears with Lysol®, which is less corrosive than the traditional mixture of water and household bleach (sodium hypochlorite) at 4 parts water to 1 part bleach. This can prevent the spread of disease to other branches.

Palm leaves die naturally and new leaves are produced from the growing point or "head" of the palm. Prune old, dead palm fronds to tidy up the tree. Leave the leaf base attached to the trunk so the fibers of the trunk won't be torn away. Do not injure the growing point or the entire tree will die.

VINES & GROUNDCOVERS

Mulch vines and groundcovers to suppress weeds and to conserve moisture. Organic mulches will break down and enrich the soil with nutrients. Create supports for annual vines before they become a tangled mess. Use strings, trellises, or other supports, making sure that they will be strong enough to support the weight of the vines. Train newly planted vines onto their vertical supports by securing one end of the string to the support and the other end to a rock or a stick driven next to the vine. As the vine grows, use soft twine or nylon to tie the vine to the support until it begins to twine or cling.

Limit pruning to plants that have already finished flowering.

WATER GARDENS

Remove faded, dying, or dead leaves from water lilies, lotuses, and bog plants.

FERTILIZE

ANNUALS

Continue to make applications of a fast-release fertilizer every four to six weeks if necessary. Follow the label instructions. Water the fertilizer in to make it available to the plants.

When reworking flowerbeds, use a slow-release fertilizer, especially in sandy soils. The nutrients are released over an extended period, perhaps three or four months, depending on the product. Use as recommended on the label.

BULBS

Lightly fertilize summer bulbs when their shoots emerge, using a slow-release fertilizer. Follow the manufacturer's instructions regarding the amount and frequency. Water thoroughly afterward.

There is no benefit to fertilizing spring-flowering bulbs during or after bloom. In fact, as the soil warms up after flowering, nitrogen in the fertilizer can encourage the development of the fungal disease Fusarium. Rotting bulbs infected with Fusarium have a sour smell.

EDIBLES

Sidedress sweet corn when it is 8 to 12 inches high and again when the tassel is just beginning to show. Use a nitrogen fertilizer such as calcium nitrate, bloodmeal, or cottonseed meal.

LAWNS

Wait until fall to fertilize your cool-season lawn. St. Augustinegrass can be fertilized this month with a slow-release nitrogen fertilizer, which will help reduce chinch bug and gray leaf spot problems.

PERENNIALS & ORNAMENTAL GRASSES

Evaluate your perennials for color and growth to determine the need for fertilizer. To encourage more growth, apply a slow-release fertilizer.

ROSES

See April.

SHRUBS, TREES, AND VINES & GROUNDCOVERS

Look for these signs of plants that are deficient in minerals: stunted growth, smaller-than-normal leaves, poor leaf color, and early leaf drop.

Evaluate your shrubs and trees for color and growth to determine the need for fertilizer. To encourage more growth, fertilize with a slow-release fertilizer. Water well immediately afterward. Avoid excessive fertilization. High levels of nutrients, particularly nitrogen, will encourage leafy shoot growth at the expense of flower buds.

WATER GARDENS

When the water temperature stays above 70 degrees Fahrenheit, fertilize all water lilies at least once a month (or follow label instructions) with a tablet form of fertilizer especially formulated for aquatics. It should contain both slow- and fast-release nitrogen. Follow the manufacturer's instructions regarding the amounts and frequency of application.

WATER

ANNUALS

Newly set transplants should not be allowed to dry out. But keep the leaves dry—extended periods of wetness on the leaves promote the growth and spread of diseases.

BULBS

Water newly planted bulbs to settle them in. Apply a shallow 2- to 3-inch layer of mulch to conserve moisture, suppress weeds, and keep the soil cool.

EDIBLES

Water deeply, keeping the leaves of your vegetables dry. Invest in soaker hoses or drip irrigation. "Seep-irrigate" with plastic milk jugs. Punch holes in the sides of a jug with a large nail, spacing them about 2 inches apart. Bury the jug, leaving the neck above the soil. Fill the jug with water (solutions of liquid fertilizer may be used to fertilize at the same time) and screw the cap on firmly.

Identify weeds after they emerge to select an appropriate post-emergent herbicide labeled for your lawn. Grassy summer annuals to watch out for include crabgrass, goosegrass, and sandbur. Dallisgrass and bahiagrass are perennial grasses that may be present.

"Centipedegrass decline" usually occurs in spring when parts of the lawn fail to come out of dormancy, or start to green up then die in late spring and summer. Several factors cause centipedegrass decline—high soil pH, high amounts of nitrogen and phosphorus applied the previous year, heavy thatch buildup, nematodes, and diseases. Follow the renovation steps described in April, Plant.

PERENNIALS & ORNAMENTAL GRASSES

Aphids, spider mites, and whiteflies can be a problem. Spider mites are especially fond of chrysanthemums, coneflowers, daylilies, and phlox.

Avoid leaf spot diseases by watering your perennials from below and limiting water on the leaves. Proper spacing with plenty of air movement will reduce fungal infections.

ROSES

Be on the lookout for damage caused by rose aphids, spider mites, and flower thrips. Take necessary action if their feeding is more than you or your roses will tolerate.

Leaves attacked by blackspot and powdery mildew should be picked up and discarded. To improve the effectiveness of fungicide sprays, practice good sanitation: Clean up any fallen leaves and faded blooms, prune out dead, damaged, and diseased canes, and replace mulch each spring.

SHRUBS

Be on the lookout for damage caused by aphids and spider mites. Blast these critters off with a strong spray of water from the hose. Get underneath the leaves to dislodge spider mites.

Boxwood leafminer is the most serious pest of boxwoods, with heaviest infestations occurring on common box (*Buxus sempervirens*), littleleaf boxwood (*B. microphylla*), and Harland boxwood

(*B. harlandii*). The larvae feed inside the leaves, resulting in splotchy, yellow, puckered, or blistered areas on the undersides of the leaves. Heavily infested leaves often drop prematurely. Severe attacks can weaken the plant, resulting in twig dieback and exposing the plant to diseases and winterkill in colder regions.

Apply a systemic insecticide to kill the young larvae inside the leaves. Alternatively, replace your susceptible boxwood hedge with common box cultivars such as 'Suffruticosa' (English boxwood) and 'Argenteovariegata', that escape serious attacks, or the Japanese boxwood (*B. microphylla* var. *japonica*) cultivars 'Morris Midget' and 'Morris Dwarf'.

■ *Fireblight is a bacterial disease that causes new shoots to suddenly wilt; turn brown, then black; and then die, as on this Kieffer pear.*

Watch for Japanese beetles in the eastern Carolinas.

During long, wet springs, azaleas and camellias may be attacked by the leaf gall fungus, which causes the new leaves to become thick and fleshy. See April, Problem-Solve.

Fireblight is a bacterial disease that attacks cotoneaster, flowering quince, and pyracantha. The new shoots suddenly wilt, turn brown, turn black, and die. Prune out the diseased branches several inches below the infection. Grow fireblight-resistant pyracantha cultivars such as 'Apache', 'Fiery Cascade', 'Mohave', 'Navaho', 'Pueblo', 'Rutgers', 'Shawnee', and 'Teton'.

TREES

Aphids are soft-bodied insects often found clustered at the ends of tender new growth. They suck plant sap with their piercing-sucking mouthparts, causing the leaves to curl and become malformed. Aphids have many natural predators including ladybird beetles, lacewings, and syrphid fly larvae. Crapemyrtle aphids can be controlled with summer horticultural oil, insecticidal soap, and other insecticides. Specialized equipment may be required to treat large crapemyrtles. The *faurei* hybrids (hybrids between the Chinese, *Lagerstroemia indica*, and the Japanese, *L. fauriei*) have moderate resistance to aphids. A few of these hybrids are 'Acoma', 'Biloxi', 'Caddo', 'Choctaw', 'Natchez', 'Muskogee', and 'Tuscarora'.

The adult dogwood borer is a clearwing moth that resembles a slender bee. The moth is attracted to weakened, stressed trees where it lays eggs on wounds, cankers, or pruning cuts. When the eggs hatch, the caterpillars bore into the bark and begin tunneling.

Dogwoods can be protected from attack with a pesticide application in late spring or early summer. As with all borers, timing is very important. The insecticide must be in the tree (systemic) or on the bark to intercept the newly hatched larvae before they burrow into the tree. Only wounded and cankered areas on the bark should be treated. There's no need to spray the healthy portions of the tree.

Watch for bagworms on arborvitae, blue spruce, juniper, hemlock, and Leyland cypress. Bagworms also feed on many broadleaf shrubs and trees including rose, sycamore, maple, elm, and black locust. See page 129 for a description and controls.

Look for powdery mildew on flowering dogwoods (*Cornus florida*), a white powdery growth on infected leaves that may cause them to drop. Most powdery mildews of landscape trees occur in late summer and do not pose any harm because they will be shedding their leaves shortly; dogwoods, however, become infected in early summer. Fungicides can control this disease. Powdery mildew-resistant dogwoods include the Kousa dogwood cultivars 'Big Apple', 'China Girl', 'Gay Head', 'Greensleeves', 'Julian', 'Milky Way Select', and 'Temple Jewel'. The Stellar® hybrids—*Cornus* × *rutgersensis* 'Rutfan' (Stardust®), 'Rutgan' (Stellar Pink®), and 'Rutdan' (Celestial™)—are also resistant to powdery mildew.

VINES & GROUNDCOVERS

Poison ivy is dangerous year-round. Expect irritation from the leaves, roots, berries, and even smoke when burning the vines. Learn to identify this deciduous vine with compound leaves comprised of three leaflets, hairy aerial roots along its stem, and clusters of white waxy fruit in late summer. Don't confuse it with Virginia creeper (*Parthenocissus quinquefolia*), which has five leaflets and climbs by tendrils with adhesive disks at its tips. If you think you contacted poison ivy, wash immediately with soap and water and remove any clothes that may have the oil on them.

Aphids, Japanese beetles, and spider mites can be a problem. Look for spider mites on junipers, pachysandra, and other groundcovers.

Watch for snails and slugs on your groundcovers.

Several fungi cause leaf spots on English, Algerian, and other ivies. A bacterial disease called bacterial spot and canker is more serious because it attacks the leaves and produces cankers—discolored areas of dead tissue—on the stems, which result in dieback. Clip off infected leaves. Prune out and discard dead or dying plants. Identify the particular disease before seeking control with a fungicide.

Leaf and stem blight is a serious pest of pachysandra—brown blotches appear on the leaves and spread to the stems. Remove and discard infected plants. To avoid this blight, rake up and compost any leaves in the fall. Fallen leaves create moist conditions that favor the growth and spread of disease.

Scale insects are often associated with leaf and stem blight. Control them with a horticultural oil or other insecticide.

Large-flowered clematis are highly susceptible to clematis wilt, often when plants are on the verge of flowering. Although wilted leaves and stems that droop and turn black are the first signs, the fungus initially attacks the stem close to the soil line, invading cracked, damaged, or weak tissue.

Fortunately, clematis wilt is rarely fatal. Even when all topgrowth is killed, new healthy shoots can emerge from basal buds below the soil surface. This is the reason for the recommendation that clematis be planted with the crown at a depth of 2½ inches below soil level.

Prune back infected stems to healthy tissue and discard the trimmings. Fertilize and water to encourage regrowth. Smaller-flowered clematis such as *C. alpina, C. macropetala, C. viticella,* and their hybrids are less susceptible to clematis wilt.

Juniper tip blight, caused by a fungus called phomopsis, attacks the tips of shore and creeping junipers and others in the spring. The dead branches gradually turn gray. Tiny black dots on recently killed needles are the fruiting bodies of the fungus. Prune out infected plant parts and discard them, because this fungus survives in dead and decaying plant material.

WATER GARDENS

Trim off any diseased leaves from your water lilies and marginal plants and discard them.

For some, summer is the season for vacations. Fine, but that doesn't mean that your landscape has to go on vacation too. Extend the springtime pageantry of colors, flowers, and fragrances throughout the summer with bulbs. Some bulbs require a little attention, while others thrive on neglect. Here are a few of my favorite summer bulbs.

Dahlias come in nearly every color but blue, on stems that range from a foot high to over 5 feet. Their head-turning flowers range from soft peony shapes to spiky "cactus" shapes. Competitive gardeners should grow the mammoth "dinner plate" dahlias with 6- to 9-inch-wide flowers, such as 'Thomas Edison' (purple), 'Kelvin Floodlight' (golden yellow), or 'Garden Wonder' (red).

For looks and fragrance I turn to lilies with flowers that come in several colors: red, yellow, orange, pink, lavender, cream, white, and purple. For starters I recommend Asiatic lilies, Easter lilies (you planted your potted Easter lilies outside, didn't you?), and the late summer- to early fall-flowering Formosa lilies that bear fragrant, white funnel-shaped flowers in a candelabra-like display.

Pineapple lilies, particularly 'Sparkling Burgundy' with its intense reddish purple leaves, has been a reliable performer for me. With anticipation I look forward to the miniature purple pineapple flower bud rising a foot or two high and watch it open gradually to reveal a spike of white flowers.

Crinums or swamp lilies are the quintessential summer bulb for Southern gardens. In the spring, bold green leaves sprout from underground bulbs (some attain the size of grapefruits) to create a fountainlike haystack of straplike leaves. In the summer clusters of lilylike flowers appear on 3-foot-tall stalks in colors that range from white, pink, or striped ("milk and wine lilies"). Several common varieties include 'Ellen Bosanquet', 'Cecil Houdyshel', and *C. × powellii* 'Album'. The Orange River lily (*C. bulbispermum*) is well-suited for wet areas ("hog wallows"); it blooms in the spring and sporadically through the summer and fall. More hard-to-find cultivars worth seeking include the purple-leaved 'Sangria' and 'Regina's Disco Lounge'.

These are just a few of the many summer bulbs that will invigorate you and your landscape this summer without having to take a vacation.

PLAN

ANNUALS

This is a good month to visit public gardens to view the tremendous variety of annuals on display. Of special note are the All-America Selections (AAS) display gardens that exhibit the most recent All-America Selections Winners. Visit their website for a list of AAS display gardens in the Carolinas.

BULBS, SHRUBS, AND TREES

Witness the splendor of public gardens throughout the Carolinas. Refer to Public Gardens (pages 228 to 230) for a list of gardens and their addresses.

EDIBLES

If you've planted more than you can use, share your bounty with friends and neighbors. What about your community? Make plans to share your vegetables and herbs with your community soup kitchen or food bank. Herbs are especially welcome because they provide nutrients as well as flavor. Get the address of the nearest food pantry or soup kitchen that needs fresh produce from a church organization that helps the needy or from the social services department at your town hall.

LAWNS

The best way to determine the fertilizer requirements of your lawn is by having your soil tested at least every three years through your local county Cooperative Extension Service office. Plan to have your soil tested this month or next so you can be ready for fall.

■ *It's not too late to plant cosmos, an easy-to-grow annual for sunny areas. Deadhead the spent flowers to keep them flowering.*

HERE'S HOW

TO GATHER SOIL FOR TESTING

Clean a thin garden trowel and gallon bucket with a mild soap mixture. Allow them to dry before gathering the soil.

Use a garden trowel to collect twelve or more samples that will be combined into one composite sample. Lawn samples should be taken from a depth of only 2 to 3 inches.

Place the samples in a clean bucket and mix them thoroughly. Bring a minimum of 2 cups of soil per sample to your County Extension Office.

PERENNIALS & ORNAMENTAL GRASSES

When you planned your garden, you probably chose perennials for their flowers, bloom time, and other features. But have you thought about selecting perennials for their ability to attract beneficial insects? Beneficial insect predators and parasites such as lady beetles, lacewings, syrphid flies, and tachinid flies prey on harmful insects including aphids, caterpillars, and mites. In general, the larvae feed on insects and mites while the adults feed on nectar and pollen—either exclusively or to supplement their diet when insects, or mites are in short supply. Some of the perennials found by researchers to attract beneficial insects include fernleaf yarrow (*Achillea filipendulina*), basket-of-gold (*Aurinia saxatilis*), feverfew (*Tanacetum parthenium*), stonecrop (*Sedum kamtschaticum*), goldenrod (*Solidago 'Peter Pan'*), and spike speedwell (*Veronica spicata*).

To keep beneficial insects in your landscape, plan to have flowering perennials in bloom all season long to provide them with a ready supply of nectar and pollen.

ROSES

Visit private and public gardens that feature roses. Seeing those extraordinary roses that you've glimpsed only from photos can be inspiring. Some notable rose gardens are the All-America Rose Selections Public Gardens. These accredited gardens—seven in the Carolinas—showcase those three or four exceptional roses selected from thousands each year.

VINES & GROUNDCOVERS

Note bloom times, ornamental features, growth rates, and pest problems. Begin making plans to correct any problems or to make arrangements to replace some of the poorly performing plants.

WATER GARDENS

For water lilies (*Nymphaea* spp.) in containers, choose a watertight one that's at least 18 inches in diameter and 1 foot deep. Fill the container with water and let it sit for about twenty-four hours to allow any chlorine to evaporate and for the water to come to air temperature. They will need at least six hours of direct sun. Some hardy

■ *Fernleaf yarrow attracts and supports a menagerie of beneficial insects.*

■ *Lacewings may look dainty, but their larvae are voracious predators that consume a wide variety of pests, including aphids, scale insects, spider mites, and thrips.*

water lilies that do well in aboveground containers that remain above freezing in winter are yellow-flowering 'Chromatella' and *Nymphaea* × 'Helvola'; white 'Hermine'; deep red 'Froebelii'; and orange-red 'Graziella'.

PLANT

ANNUALS

It's not too late to plant annuals. If your needs are great or your budget small, consider sowing seeds directly into prepared garden beds. Cosmos, cleome, marigold, Mexican sunflower, portulaca, sunflower, and zinnia are good choices for direct sowing. Just remember to keep the seedbed moist during the first few weeks after establishment.

Stagger the plantings of sunflowers and zinnias a couple of weeks apart so you can enjoy fresh blooms longer.

BULBS

Bearded irises can be planted now while in bloom. Wait until late summer or early fall to divide or transplant existing clumps. Bearded irises form the beginnings of next year's flowers in the six or eight weeks after blooming. Disturbing the plants at that time risks next year's flowers.

Plant autumn crocuses (*Colchicum autumnale*) now, as soon as you purchase them. These unusual bulbs flower on bare stems in fall and produce leaves the following spring. Use golf tees to mark their position so you can plant something that will fill the void left when their leaves die down next summer.

Dahlia tubers may still be planted for fall bloom. Place them 6 to 8 inches deep and 3 to 4 feet apart.

Because the leaves of most spring bulbs have finished maturing by now or have died back, they can be cut back to ground level. Dig up any crowded bulbs that have declined and produced few, if any, flowers. Replant larger bulbs and discard smaller ones, unless you are willing to wait for them to reach blooming size, which may take two years or more. The spaces vacated by spring-flowering bulbs can be seeded or planted with annual transplants to provide summer and fall color.

Divide overcrowded daffodil bulbs after the foliage has ripened and died down. Use a flat-tined garden fork to unearth the bulbs. Carefully pry out a clump of bulbs. Handle them gently to avoid bruising them. Brush off the excess soil with your fingers, and separate the bulbs as you remove the soil. Carefully break apart the bulbs that are loosely connected to one another, but leave the offsets or small bulbs that are firmly attached to the mother bulb. Any damaged, soft, or rotten bulbs should be discarded. Plant the bulbs immediately or store them for planting in the fall. If you choose to

store them, let the bulbs cure by putting them on an old window screen in a well-ventilated shady spot. After a few days of curing, put the bulbs into paper bags and store them in a cool, dark, well-ventilated place.

Replant the bulbs, saving the largest ones for planting where you want the showiest display. The smaller offsets will not flower for the first few years, so you can use them in a naturalized area where a few bulbs that haven't flowered won't be obvious. Select a well-drained location that receives full sun or part shade. Loosen the soil 8 to 12 inches deep and mix in several inches of compost. After watering, cover the bulbs with an inch or two of mulch such as shredded leaves or compost to conserve moisture and suppress weeds.

EDIBLES

Sow another batch of sweet basil seeds for late summer. Mountain gardeners can sow seeds of summer crops such as beans, cucumbers, okra, pumpkins, southern peas, and squash, and a last planting of sweet corn. Also, set out transplants of pepper, tomatoes, and sweet potato slips.

LAWNS

If you need to plant a cool-season lawn, install Kentucky bluegrass or tall fescue sod. Make sure you have plenty of water to help it get established and survive the summer.

■ *Rolling out and installing sod is a quick way of creating an instant lawn.*

TO PROPAGATE PERENNIALS BY SOFTWOOD CUTTINGS

1. Use a sharp knife or razor blade to take 3- to 6-inch-long cuttings of terminal growth (top of stem). Make an angled cut just below a node—the point where the leaf joins the stem. Remove the lowest leaf or two.

2. Dip the cut end into a rooting hormone suited for herbaceous plants.

3. Fill a small pot with equal parts of peat moss and perlite. Use a pencil to poke a hole in the medium before inserting the cutting. This prevents the rooting powder from being scraped off.

4. When you have inserted all the cuttings, water them well, and place the pots in a plastic bag closed at the top with a twist-tie.

5. Set the pots in a bright location but not in direct sunlight. When the cuttings have produced small new leaves, move them to the garden. Instead of transplanting them to their permanent homes, plant them in a "halfway house"—a makeshift nursery where they won't be neglected. After a few weeks, when they've grown large enough to hold their own, move them to their permanent spots.

Install sod or plant plugs or sprigs of warm-season grasses. There's still time to renovate warm-season lawns. If possible determine what led to the lawn's demise and correct any mistakes. See April, Plant.

PERENNIALS & ORNAMENTAL GRASSES

Many perennials can be propagated by rooting softwood stem cuttings, including balloon flower, beebalm, chrysanthemum, penstemon, phlox, salvia, and veronica. (Softwood stems are mature and firm but not yet hardened and woody.)

Continue planting perennials; with the onset of hot, dry weather, however, be prepared to provide adequate water throughout their establishment period. Continue to move perennials outdoors that you grew from seed. Depending on their size, it may be better to transplant them to your home nursery. Better yet, transplant them in the fall when the weather becomes cooler and less stressful.

Plant Shasta daisy, coreopsis, and coneflower from seed. Sow them directly in the garden or in trays or pots. Seeds will take two to three weeks to emerge. When seedlings are 2 to 3 inches high, thin the plants to about 6 inches apart, or transplant them into individual containers.

ROSES, SHRUBS, TREES, AND VINES & GROUNDCOVERS

With the availability of container-grown plants, the planting season is limited only by extremely hot weather, frozen soil in winter, and your ability to water regularly. With the onset of hot, dry weather be prepared to be on call with adequate water throughout their establishment period. Unless you're willing to put in the time, wait until fall when the odds of successful establishment are in your favor.

June and July are ideal times to take semi-hardwood cuttings when the new green growth begins to harden and turn brown. When you snap the twig, the bark often clings to the stem. Some of the plants that can be rooted now include broadleaf evergreens such as camellias, banana shrub (*Magnolia figo*), azaleas, osmanthus, magnolia, nandina, coniferous evergeens like Japanese plum yew (*Cephalotaxus* spp.), podocarpus, and many others.

WATER GARDENING

Grow bog plants such as umbrella palm, water canna, and Japanese iris in containers of ordinary garden soil placed on ledges in the pool or on inverted pots at their required depths. Marginal plants provide shelter for wildlife and shade and protection for fish. Some marginals can handle either shallow or deep water levels, even dry areas, while others need a certain depth of water above their crowns. If your pond doesn't have shelves, raise or lower the plant by using inverted pots, bricks, or weathered cinder blocks.

Submerged plants are essential for releasing oxygen into the water and competing with algae for nutrients to keep the water clear. Some of the most popular are Canadian elodea (*Elodea canadensis*), cabomba (*Cabomba caroliniana*), coontail (*Ceratophyllum demersum*), and tape grass (*Vallisneria americana*).

Plant hardy water lilies now. Mountain gardeners should be able to plant tropical water lilies safely when the water temperature has reached 70 degrees Fahrenheit and is not expected to go lower.

CARE

ANNUALS

Pull up and discard pansies as the heat causes them to look ratty. Replace them with transplants or seeds of warm-season annuals.

Look for a crop of self-sown seedlings or "volunteers" from last year's impatiens, cleome, annual vinca, and other annuals. Look around for them and transplant them as you like.

Some annuals need to be jump-started either now or next month. Trim back petunias toward the end of the month to keep them bushy and encourage the formation of new flowers. After watering and fertilizing, they'll soon be full and attractive again. Remove spent blossoms on annual flowering plants as often as possible. This encourages further flowering rather than seed production. Seed collectors and those who want the dried seedpods for arrangements might ignore this rule. In most cases, however, seed collectors should delay until the end of the blooming season. Then the last few blooms may be kept for seed. Seeds of hybrids will not reproduce true from the parent plant.

Cosmos reseeds readily. Shear the spent blooms, leaving some to germinate and grow during the warm summer weather.

BULBS

Loosely tie gladioli to stakes, or mound soil around the base of the plants to prevent them from toppling over.

Remove spent tuberous begonia blooms. They may be infected by the fungus disease gray

■ *Harvest onions when the tops flop over and start to yellow.*

mold. Clip off amaryllis and iris blooms after they've faded.

EDIBLES

The best time to harvest most herbs is just before flowering when the leaves contain the maximum essential oils.

Harvest beans, cucumbers, okra, and squash daily to keep the plants producing. Pick cucumbers when the fruits are small and before they turn yellow.

Harvest okra pods when they are 2 to 4 inches long. Wait much longer and the pods become tough and fibrous and the plant stops producing—an exception is 'Burgundy', whose pods can stay tender even when 6 to 8 inches long. Pick yellow squash when the fruit is 4 to 6 inches long, zucchini when it is 6 to 8 inches long, and patty pan squash when it is 3 to 5 inches wide.

Pick eggplant after the fruit reaches 3 to 5 inches in length. The skin should be glossy and fully colored. Dull skin indicates it's overripe. Dig onions when about half the tops begin to turn yellow and fall over. Brush the soil off and cure them in a dark, warm (80 to 85 degrees Fahrenheit), well-ventilated space for two to three weeks. Store them in a mesh bag in a dry, dark, cool place.

Harvest Irish potatoes when the vines have died back about halfway. Save some of the small potatoes, refrigerate them, and plant them whole in the fall.

Watch out for blossom end rot, a disorder that causes tomatoes to turn black on the blossom end. It occurs when there are extremes in soil moisture, which result in a calcium deficiency in the fruit. When rain or irrigation follows a dry spell, the roots cannot take up calcium fast enough to keep up with the rapid fruit growth. Blossom end rot also occurs if the delicate feeder roots are damaged during transplanting or by deep cultivation near the plants.

LAWNS

If the lawn grew so high that mowing it at the correct height would remove more than one-third its ideal height, raise the mower height so you will remove no more than one-third of the lawn height. Gradually reduce the mower height, with one or two days between mowings, until you reach the correct height.

For the most attractive look, mow bermudagrass and zoysiagrass with a reel-type mower. Allow the clippings to lie on the lawn.

PERENNIALS & ORNAMENTAL GRASSES

Pinch out the terminal growth of fall-blooming garden mums. Repeat the pinching each time a lateral bud sends out a shoot—pinch as soon as the new shoot has about three sets of leaves. This will increase the number of blooms and produce bushier plants. To produce fewer

HERE'S HOW

TO COMBAT BLOSSOM END ROT

- Keep moisture levels uniform by regular watering and by maintaining a mulch layer around the base of the plants.

- Maintain a pH between 6 and 6.5 and an adequate calcium level by liming or applying gypsum.

- Finally, avoid overfertilizing, which inhibits calcium uptake.

- Remove the flowers and fruits from late-season tomato transplants before setting them out.

■ *Pinch your garden mums to make them bushier and to delay flowering.*

but larger blooms, disbud chrysanthemum flowers—see August.

Sedum 'Autumn Joy' tends to flop over in midseason, especially when sited in partial shade. Pinch out the growing tips or cut back the stems to a foot to encourage branching and the production of lots of flowers.

Deadhead achillea, bellflower, baby's breath (*Gypsophila paniculata*), columbine, pincushion flower (*Scabiosa* 'Butterfly Blue'), spike speedwell (*Veronica spicata*), and salvia to lateral or side buds. After the side buds finish flowering, cut the stems down to the basal leaves at the crown.

To avoid staking late-flowering plants such as asters, Joe-Pye weed, or heliopsis (*Heliopsis helianthoides* 'Summer Sun'), prune them back to one-third their height. This will give them a fuller and more compact growth habit.

Pinch out the growing tips of other late-summer and fall-flowering plants such as boltonia, Swamp sunflower (*Helianthus angustifolius*), and sneezeweed (*Helenium autumnale*). They will produce many smaller flowers without any noticeable loss in height.

Cut back amsonia and baptisia after flowering by one-third to one-half their height; otherwise, they will continue to grow with abandon and will splay apart in late summer.

ROSES

Climbing roses may not produce canes near the base after a period of years. If removing some of the oldest canes doesn't spark any growth, try notching. Make a cut above a bud near the base of the plant by slicing one-third of the way through a stem. This tends to force that bud into growth.

Cut few if any flowers during the first blooming season. By removing only flowers and not stems, you will encourage plants to develop into large bushes by fall, at which time some flowers and stems may be cut. Deadhead flowers as soon as they have passed their peak. If allowed to remain on the plant, the flower heads will develop

seedpods (also called hips) that draw heavily on the plant's food supply. Always use sharp pruning shears and cut on a downward slant from the bud.

Remove any spindly shoots or suckers originating below the graft union, or any damaged, diseased, or dead canes. To produce specimen flowers on hybrid tea or garden roses, remove flower buds that have developed on shoots other than the main one. Allow only one flower bud to develop and mature on each main shoot.

Prune once-flowering climbers and ramblers that bloom on last year's growth. Thin out any of the oldest canes to make room for new ones from the base. Long canes that have to be removed should be cut out in a piecemeal manner. Cut the cane into 8- to 12-inch sections and remove them one at a time. It's far easier to deal with the cane in short bites than to wrestle all of its length out at once. Head back any wayward canes to keep them confined to their support. Refer to May, Care for more details.

SHRUBS AND TREES

If mulch doesn't protect the bark of young trees from mower damage, resort to putting up stakes or guards.

Prune out dead, damaged, or pest-ridden branches immediately. When shearing your hedges, shape the plants so the base of the hedge is wider than the top. See March.

If you shear your boxwoods, thin out some of the interior branches to admit sunlight and air movement. Light encourages growth on the inner stems, and air circulation reduces the occurrence of fungal diseases.

When you find dead or damaged branches on shade trees, prune them out immediately. Storm-damaged trees should be repaired when needed, rather than waiting for the dormant season. Hire certified arborists to remove large damaged limbs.

VINES & GROUNDCOVERS

Train the new growth of clematis, Confederate jasmine, swamp jessamine, trumpet honeysuckle, and other twining vines to guide them onto the trellis. Use soft twine to give the new shoots a start. Keep the "feet" of your clematis cool by creating shade with shrubs or planting a ground cover or perennial that will not be invasive. Some good clematis companions are candytuft, creeping phlox, hardy geraniums (*Geranium*), coralbells, silvermound artemisia, and most veronicas.

Limit your pruning to vines that have already flowered on last year's growth. Shear off the flower buds of silver-leaved lavender-cotton (*Santolina chamaecyparissus*). These ground-hugging plants tend to decline after flowering, so diverting the plants' energy to the leaves will prevent them from deteriorating.

WATER GARDENS

Deadhead water lilies to encourage more flowers. The difference between hardy and tropical water lilies is most tropical water lilies hold their flowers above the water. Leave the spent flowers on lotus because the ornamental pods that develop will look terrific in flower arrangements.

Remove any leaves that are yellow or damaged by insects or diseases. Continue to remove organic debris—grass clippings, fallen leaves, needles, and so forth—from the pond.

Keep an eye on invasive plants and trim or remove them so they won't crowd out more restrained growers. Some of the plants that float free on the surface may grow with abandon. Pond lily (*Nuphar* spp.) can become a pest if left unchecked.

Keep track of water pH, ammonia, and nitrate levels, especially if you have fish. If you don't stock your aboveground half-barrel or other water container with fish to consume mosquito eggs and larvae, mosquitoes can become a problem. Buy a few briquettes of mosquito larvae killer sold as Mosquito Dunks® (which contains a bacterial insecticide called *Bacillus thuringiensis* var. *israelensis*). One briquette can treat 100 square feet of water regardless of its depth. Break them up into four pieces and put them out at the start of each month to float on the surface of the water.

WATER

ANNUALS

A crusty surface on the walls of clay pots or over the potting medium indicates a salt problem. Leach containers occasionally to remove any mineral salt deposits that accumulate from fertilizer and hard water. To leach the container, allow the water to run until it drains freely from the bottom holes. Wait a few minutes, then repeat.

When watering, apply sufficient moisture to soak the soil deeply to the root zone.

BULBS

Be prepared to water summer bulbs if little rain occurs this month. Keep water off the leaves.

EDIBLES

Corn needs water at two crucial times: when the tassels at the top are beginning to show, and when the silk is beginning to show on the ear. If rainfall is scarce at these times, water.

LAWNS

Water your lawn when it show signs of stress: bluish gray color; footprints that remain in the lawn after walking on it; wilted, folded, or curled leaves. During long, dry, hot spells, you have two choices when it comes to watering an established lawn:

1. Don't water. Let the lawn turn brown.

2. Water the grass to keep it green.

When a Kentucky bluegrass lawn turns brown during a drought, it's a sign of dormancy. The leaves and shoots die, but buds in the crown and rhizomes (underground stems) generally remain alive and grow when more favorable conditions return. Tall fescue has no means of escape; three weeks or more without rain in the summer can injure or kill tall fescue.

If your lawn is experiencing drought stress, apply about an inch of water per week in clay soils and ½ inch in sandy soils every three days. Set your irrigation system to apply the correct amount of water; too much will be wasteful and too little produces shallow-rooted plants.

Whatever option you choose—to water or not to water—stick with it. Flip-flopping between the two can weaken your lawn.

PERENNIALS & ORNAMENTAL GRASSES

Water recently planted perennials, which are especially vulnerable to heat and drought stress. Water thoroughly to encourage deep rooting.

ROSES

Keep the following "ground rules" in mind when watering your roses this summer:

- Newly planted roses need to be watered often enough to prevent the soil from drying out

■ *Follow label directions on the package when preparing a liquid fertilizer.*

as they settle into their new surrounding. Reduce the frequency of watering gradually, but continue to water deeply to encourage the development of a deep, extensive root system.

- Roses in sandy soils will require more-frequent watering than roses in clay soils.

- Roses will need more water when the temperatures are high than when they're cool.

- Water deeply and infrequently, wetting as much of the root zone as possible. Roots may extend to a depth of 6 to 12 inches. The goal is to produce deeply rooted plants. Shallow, frequent sprinklings on established plants encourage shallow roots.

- Keep the leaves dry by applying water to the soil surface. Fungal diseases such as blackspot rely on moisture to infect and spread.

- Mulch your roses with a 2- to 3-inch layer. Organic mulches—compost, pine needles ("pine straw"), shredded leaves, and wood chips—conserve moisture, suppress weeds, and supply nutrients as they decompose. Keep the mulch a few inches away from the crown.

SHRUBS, TREES, AND VINES & GROUNDCOVERS

Water recent plantings, which are especially vulnerable to heat and drought stress. Water thoroughly to encourage deep rooting. Avoid irrigating shrubs with an overhead sprinkler. Besides wasting water and watering weeds, wetting the leaves encourages disease outbreaks. Use soaker hoses to water groundcovers on slopes; this will reduce water runoff and soil erosion.

FERTILIZE

ANNUALS

Annual beds can use a boost, especially where the soil is sandy or the season has been rainy. Apply slow-release fertilizer for maximum benefit with minimum effort. For a quick but brief response, water plants with a liquid fertilizer such as 20-20-20.

Do not overfertilize cosmos or nasturtiums or you will run the risk of having a lot of leaves and few, if any, flowers.

BULBS

If summer-flowering bulbs were not fertilized when their shoots emerged, it may be necessary to fertilize them now. Follow the manufacturer's instructions regarding the rate and frequency of application. Avoid overfertilization, which can encourage the production of leaves at the expense of flowers. Let the appearance of the plant guide you. If the dahlias, gladioli, and lilies look robust and are growing in a well-prepared, fertile bed, fertilization may be unnecessary.

Stop cutting asparagus when the spears become thin. Fertilize the bed and allow the "ferns" to grow during the summer to store food in the roots for next year's crop. After they have set their first fruit, sidedress eggplants, peppers, and tomatoes with a nitrogen fertilizer such as bloodmeal, calcium nitrate, or cottonseed meal; sidedress sweet potatoes six weeks after planting.

LAWNS

Do not fertilize cool-season lawns at this time. Fertilize bermudagrass and zoysiagrass this month with a nitrogen fertilizer. Remember, this application will encourage growth, which translates into higher maintenance.

PERENNIALS

If you used a slow-release fertilizer early in the season, check the label and evaluate the growth and appearance of your perennials to see if a second application is warranted.

ROSES

Avoid excessive fertilization. It produces the soft, succulent growth favored by pests. Try to grow your roses on the "lean and mean" side. Evaluate the quality and quantity of flowers and shoots produced by your roses, and decide if a boost of fertilizer is warranted. Never skimp on building up the natural fertility of the soil with applications of organic mulches such as compost. If you used a slow-release fertilizer early in the year, check the label and evaluate the growth and appearance of your everblooming roses to see if a second

■ *Certain French and lacecap hydrangea cultivars will bear pink flowers when grown in soil with a pH between 6.0 and 6.5 and blue flowers at a pH of 5.0 to 5.5.*

application is warranted. Supplement mulch with well-rotted horse or cow manure to add nutrients.

SHRUBS AND TREES

If necessary, fertilize your palms with a slow-release nitrogen fertilizer as described in April. The goal is to maintain growth. If the soil is low in magnesium as determined by a soil test, apply the recommended amount of Epsom salts.

Pink flowers occur on French and lacecap hydrangeas with a soil pH between 6.0 and 6.5. In this pH range, aluminum becomes "tied up" or rendered unavailable in the soil and so is absent from the flowers. Use lime to increase the soil pH to this desirable range. To avoid having to maintain this pH, grow pink-flowering cultivars such as 'Forever Pink' and 'Pia'.

Fertilize trees based on need. If the trees are growing in a fertilized lawn, fertilizing may not be necessary. Time the application for the appropriate time for the grass. This is especially important for warm-season grasses, which may be subject to winterkill if they're fertilized late in the fall or early in the spring. Because most of a tree's roots can be found in the top 12 inches of soil, the simplest way to fertilize them is with a rotary or cyclone spreader according to soil-test results.

VINES & GROUNDCOVERS

Follow soil-test results when fertilizing your vines and groundcovers. Supplement mulch with well-rotted horse or cow manure to add nutrients.

WATER GARDENS

Fertilize water lilies with aquatic fertilizer tablets, using the amount prescribed by the manufacturer. Bog plants can be fertilized based on their growth rate and appearance. To play it safe, fertilize them at half the rate of your water lilies.

PROBLEM-SOLVE

ANNUALS

Be on the lookout for aphids, spider mites, snails, and slugs.

Allow beneficial insects such as lady beetles to reduce aphid numbers. Aphids can sometimes be washed from plants with a strong stream of water. Many safe insecticides are available, including insecticidal soaps, horticultural oils, or Neem. Apply according to label directions.

Avoid overhead watering, and remove spent flowers and dead or dying leaves. Keeping plants clean will reduce the chance of infection.

Look for signs of powdery mildew on your garden zinnias. Infected leaves have a whitish gray powder on both sides. Heavy infestations can cause the leaves to become curled and eventually yellow and die. Remove any infected plants and discard them. Thin out the bed to improve air movement. In the future, select varieties that are resistant to powdery mildew.

■ *For repellants to be effective, especially on hostas (otherwise known as "deer candy"), they will have to be reapplied after rain or heavy dew, and quite often to new growth.*

Rabbits and deer can be a problem. Commercially available mammal repellents can be applied on or near your flowers. To make your own repellent, see October, Problem-Solve.

BULBS

Pests to watch for include aphids, spider mites, thrips, and Japanese beetles. Handpick Japanese beetles and discard them into a jar of soapy water. Neem can be applied to the leaves to reduce feeding by the adults. Use other insecticides for heavy infestations. If the rhizomes of your bearded irises are riddled with holes, they could be infested with iris borers. See April, Problem-Solve for a description and controls.

Watch out for fungal leaf spot diseases during wet spring and summer seasons. To control leaf spot diseases, remove blighted leaves during the season. Remove and discard any infected foliage in the fall. Fungicides can be applied to control certain leaf spot diseases.

Powdery mildew may be a problem on dahlias. This fungal disease commonly occurs during the spring and fall seasons, when the days are warm and humid and the nights are cool. This fungus is more severe on plants that are shaded or crowded. To reduce the chance of infection, improve air movement by siting them in an open location and by selectively pruning out interior growth to eliminate congestion. Pick off and destroy infected leaves.

EDIBLES

Corn earworm caterpillars chew on corn ears, gaining entry through the cornsilks. Avoid this pest by planting corn earlier in the season, or apply mineral oil on the cornsilks five days after they emerge from the husk. Insecticides are also available. Watch out for leaffooted bugs. See April, Problem-Solve.

Mites feed on nearly all vegetable crops, but are a common problem on beans, tomatoes, and eggplant. Whiteflies are tiny insects that attack tomatoes, peppers, beans, cucumbers, squashes, melons, and okra.

Pickleworms mostly attack cantaloupe, cucumber, and squash. The young larvae usually feed on leaves and flowers. The older larvae bore into the sides of the fruit and continue to feed. Grow resistant varieties and plant early to harvest before the insects arrive.

Squash vine borers are the larvae of a wasp-like clearwing moth that lays oval, flat brown eggs on the stems and leaf stalks of squash and gourds. Upon hatching they bore into the stem, causing the vine to wilt and die. Squash vine borers are difficult to control with pesticides. Once inside the stem, they cannot be reached. The best control is prevention. Here's how:

- Cover seedlings or transplants with a layer of spun-bonded row cover to keep the adult

moths at bay. This will have to be removed to allow pollination.

- To find stems attacked by borers, look for an entry hole near the base and some fine, brown sawdust-like frass (insect feces). Carefully split the stem lengthwise with a penknife and remove the borers or kill them with a long pin or needle.

Pinch or prune out any diseased leaves or stems on herbs. Watch out for bacterial wilt on tomatoes. See July, Problem-Solve for information about this disease.

In most gardens, annual weeds can be controlled by mulching and handweeding. Using a herbicide in a herb and vegetable garden is difficult because there are few herbicides that can be safely applied to the wide range of plant species grown in the garden.

LAWNS

Beginning late this month, sample areas where you previously observed damage from mole crickets in the spring. Early in the morning or late in the afternoon, mix 2 tablespoons of liquid detergent in 1 gallon of water and pour it over a 1- to 2-foot-square area. The detergent solution irritates the mole crickets, forcing them to the surface. Newly hatched mole crickets are only about ¼ inch long and tend to disappear quickly after coming to the surface, so watch very closely for two to three minutes. If small mole crickets appear, apply an insecticide according to the label directions. Irrigating dry soil twenty-four hours before applying the pesticide will cause mole crickets to move into the moist soil, making them easier targets.

Be on the lookout for nematodes, which are microscopic, soil-inhabiting, eel-like worms that feed on turfgrass roots. They are more commonly found in coarse-textured sandy soils than fine-textured clay soils. Nematode-infested roots cannot take up water or fertilizer as well as healthy ones. The infested lawn grass wilts easily and lacks normal green color. High nematode populations result in severe yellowing. The damage usually occurs in irregularly shaped or circular areas. Centipedegrass is especially susceptible to damage by ring nematodes. Lance nematodes are often found on St. Augustinegrass. See July, Problem-Solve for information on acquiring a nematode assay. The best defense is to keep your lawn healthy. The healthier a plant, the less susceptible it will be to light or moderate nematode attacks.

Brown patch is a devastating disease that attacks most fescue and bluegrass. It's favored by high temperatures and high humidity. Look for circular, tan-colored dead patches several feet in diameter. Sometimes there's a tuft of green grass in the center creating a "doughnut." This disease is most severe on grasses receiving high levels of nitrogen in late spring or summer. Collect and compost clippings from infected areas. Fungicides can be used to protect healthy grass from attack. Wait until fall to rake up dead areas and seed or sod.

Look for gray leaf spot on St. Augustinegrass. Infected leaves and stems have oblong tan lesions with purple borders. The gray spores can sometimes be seen during warm, wet weather. When severe, the entire lawn may look scorched. Collect the infected clippings while mowing, and compost them. Gray leaf spot can be controlled with fungicides. During the growing season use moderate amounts of nitrogen fertilizer, preferably one that contains ¼ to ½ of the nitrogen in a slow-release form.

Apply post-emergent herbicides as needed to control summer annual and perennial broadleaf weeds such as knotweed, lespedeza, and spurge. Do not apply post-emergent herbicides unless weeds are present, grass is actively growing, and the lawn is not suffering from drought stress.

PERENNIALS & ORNAMENTAL GRASSES

Be on the lookout for aphids, slugs and snails, spider mites, and thrips. Handpick Japanese beetles and discard them in a jar of soapy water. Neem can be applied to the leaves to reduce feeding by the adults. Use other insecticides for heavy infestations.

Avoid overhead watering and remove spent flowers and dead or dying leaves. Look for signs of powdery mildew on garden phlox and beebalm. Infected leaves have a grayish white powder on both sides. Heavy infestations can cause the leaves to curl and eventually yellow and die.

Remove infected plants and discard them. Thin out the plants to improve air movement. Fungicides can be applied when the symptoms appear and until they're gone. In the future, select varieties resistant to powdery mildew (see September, Problem-Solve).

ROSES

Pests to watch for include rose aphids, spider mites, thrips, and Japanese beetles. Handpick Japanese beetles and discard them in a jar of soapy water. Neem can be applied to the leaves to reduce feeding by adults. Use other insecticides for heavy infestations.

Be on the watch for blackspot and powdery mildew. To avoid resistance to controls by the disease organisms, when using synthetic fungicides, switch back and forth between different kinds.

SHRUBS

Pests to watch for include aphids, spider mites, and Japanese beetles.

Two-spotted spider mites (pale yellow, sometimes green, brown, or red) are "hot-weather" mites, becoming active during the heat of summer. They attack a wide variety of shrubs. Evaluate the extent of injury and decide if pest-control measures are warranted.

Gardenia and whiteflies go together like peanut butter and jelly. These tiny mothlike insects are a common pest. Whiteflies feed by sucking plant sap from the leaves. Lightly infested leaves develop a mottled appearance while higher populations cause leaves to yellow, shrivel, and die prematurely. Heavy infestations result in sticky leaves covered with a thin black film of sooty mold, a fungus that feeds on the honeydew excreted by the whiteflies.

Azalea stem borers infest azalea, rhododendron, blueberry, and mountain laurel. Prune out the wilted twigs and discard them. Plants attacked year after year can be protected with an insecticide.

See July, Problem-Solve for a description and controls of nematodes.

Be on the lookout for root rot caused by the fungus Phytophthora, which means "plant destroyer." See July for a description and controls.

Handpull, or use a herbicide to spot-treat water- and nutrient-stealing weeds from your shrub beds and borders. A makeshift cardboard shield can be used to protect your shrubs from accidental contact with the herbicide. Suppress their emergence with a layer of mulch.

TREES
Be on the lookout for aphids, scale insects, spider mites, and dogwood borers. Monitor trees for Japanese beetles. Adults lay eggs in July and

August and continually migrate to susceptible hosts. If only a few are present, pick them off by hand and discard them in a jar of soapy water. Neem can be applied to the leaves to reduce feeding by the adults. Use other insecticides for heavy infestations.

Keep bagworms at bay by applying the bacterial insecticide *B.t.* (*Bacillus thuringiensis*) as the larvae begin to feed and construct their bags. Heavy infestations may require an application of a systemic insecticide later in the season. Light infestations of bagworms can also be controlled by handpicking. Remove the bags with scissors or a knife, and dispose of them by dropping them into a container of soapy water. Birds and parasitic wasps will work in concert with your efforts, and low winter temperatures can damage overwintering insect pest eggs.

Fireblight is a bacterial disease that attacks apple, loquat, pear, and other trees. Prune out the diseased branches several inches below the

■ *Bagworms* (Thyridopteryx ephemeraeformis), *the larvae or caterpillars of a moth that is rarely seen in its adult stage, are particularly damaging to conifers like arborvitae, spruce, hemlock, Leyland cypress, and juniper, which can experience branch dieback or be killed within one or two seasons of complete defoliation. You can recognize bagworms by their spindle-shaped bags, which the larvae lug around as they feed. Each larva constructs a bag of silk and bits of leaves and twigs from the host plant, so its appearance will vary from plant to plant.*

HERE'S HOW

TO GIVE YOUR TREES A THREE-STEP "SEVEN-POINT CHECK-UP"

First step: Stand far enough away from your tree so you can look up into its canopy.

1. **Dead, hanging, or broken branches.** Branches larger than 2 inches may cause damage if they fall and should be removed immediately.

2. **Leaning tree.** See if your tree leans to one side or appears off-kilter. If you see exposed roots or a mound of soil near its base, this tree may be an imminent hazard that requires immediate action.

Second step: Walk up to the tree and closely examine the branches and trunk for defects.

3. **Multiple trunks.** Look for cracks or splits in codominant stems. Wishbone-like trunks of equal diameter may separate during wind- and ice storms. Also, closely examine trees with several branches that arise from the same point on the trunk; these branches may be weakly attached and tend to separate away from the trunk.

4. **Weak branch unions.** Inspect large branches greater than 3 inches in diameter at a point where they attach to the trunk.

■ *Tree trunks or branches with conks, bracket fungi, or mushrooms indicate dead, decaying wood that is susceptible to breakage.*

infection. If you cut into a diseased branch, disinfect your pruning shears with Lysol®, which is less corrosive than the traditional mixture of water and household bleach (sodium hypochlorite) at 4 parts water to 1 part bleach). This can prevent the spread of fireblight to other branches or trees.

Powdery mildew is a grayish white fungal disease that attacks the leaves, flowers, and shoots of older cultivars of crapemyrtle. Prune out heavily infested shoots. Fungicides are available; however, specialized equipment may be required to treat large crapemyrtles. Instead, grow the *faurei* hybrids, which are resistant to powdery mildew. They are crosses between the Chinese *Lagerstroemia indica* and the Japanese *L. faurei*, developed by Dr. Donald Egolf of the U.S. National Arboretum.

While trees provide significant benefits to our homes and communities, they may also become liabilities when they fall or break apart, causing property damage, personal injuries, and power

A crack or split at the union indicates a high probability of failure and warrants action. It's best for you to remove the branch rather than a storm.

5. **Trunk and branch cracks.** If you find cracks in the trunk or branches, measure its depth with a pencil or similar object. If the crack extends beyond the bark and into the wood, contact an arborist to have it inspected.

6. **Decayed wood.** Inspect the trunk and large branches for cavities, cankers, mushrooms, and conks. Look for mushrooms and conks along the trunk and on exposed roots. These signs and symptoms are evidence of decay. A trained arborist should be contacted to conduct a risk assessment to evaluate the tree's condition and its potential as a hazardous tree.

Third step: Finally, look down and inspect the base of the tree.

7. **Root problems.** Examine the base of the trunk for damage from rodents, string trimmers, and so forth. Look for a soil mound, soil cracking near the root collar, or broken roots sticking out of the soil. Remove any soil or mulch away from the root collar and see if there is a flat side to the trunk. If you find any encircling, constricting roots, consult a certified arborist (see www.isa-arbor.com) to address this problem.

This seven-point checklist takes less than thirty minutes to complete. Conduct it twice a year and this hour-long investment of time will benefit your trees and everyone who dwells with them.

■ *Encircling and girdling should be addressed by a professional certified arborist, who may suggest a root flare inspection.*

outages. Inspect your trees for common structural defects once or twice a year to help you find and correct potential failures before they cause damage or injury.

VINES & GROUNDCOVERS

Look for the telltale signs of Japanese beetles, aphids, spider mites, and thrips. See July, Problem-Solve.

Avoid overhead watering and remove spent flowers and dead or dying leaves.

WATER GARDENS

Black water lily aphids can disfigure leaves and flowers. Remove them with a strong spray of water or submerge plants and give them a shake. Spider mites can appear on the undersides of water lily leaves and lotus. Clip off heavily infested leaves and dislodge the mites with a strong spray of water from the hose.

Handpick brown snails from iris leaves. Continue to trim away any dead, damaged, or diseased leaves.

July

After experiencing many brutally hot and dry summers, I finally stopped grieving for my drought-damaged and withered plants. Instead, I look at these losses as learning opportunities.

Here's my short list of seven lessons that I gleaned over several summers.

1. **Select plants that match the conditions in your landscape.** Besides meeting a plant's requirements for sunlight, be mindful of dry and wet areas in the landscape. Select plants that will thrive in those conditions. Also, group plants together according to their requirements for water. Divide your landscape into "hydrozones," which allow you to water more efficiently. Plants in the low-water use zone receive less frequent—if any—water than those in the high-water use zone.

2. **Install a drip or microsprinkler irrigation system.** They are simple to install and use less water than conventional irrigation systems.

3. **Mulch.** A 2- to 4-inch layer of mulch conserves moisture, suppresses weeds, and enhances plant growth.

4. **Avoid heavy applications of fertilizer to your plantings.** Heavy applications of fertilizer will result in a lot of soft, lush top growth that will have to be supported by regular applications of water. Keep your plants "lean, green, and mean" to help them deal with summertime stresses.

5. **Add organic matter to the planting area.** It improves air and water movement in clay soil and acts like a sponge to retain moisture and minerals in sandy soils.

6. **Water new plantings regularly until they become established.** Spring and summer plantings are especially vulnerable to perishing from a lack of water during their "growing-in" period. During the first few weeks, water often enough to keep the soil moist. Then, start cutting back on watering to every few days or longer. Eventually, water on a weekly or as needed basis by testing the soil and rootball for moisture until the plants become established.

7. **Go on vacation next summer and forget about it.** Heed the advice of the world-famous American horticulturist Liberty Hyde Bailey (1858–1954) who said, "I stayed home from a vacation one summer that I might keep my plants from dying. I have since learned that if the plants in my borders cannot take care of themselves for a few weeks, they are of little comfort to me."

PLAN

ANNUALS AND VINES & GROUNDCOVERS

If you're going on vacation, make plans to have someone take care of your plants. Not only does this keep up the appearance of the plants, it also makes it look as if someone is home. To make things easier for the caregiver, group plants in containers near a water source and out of the after-noon sun. There may be some pots that need more attention than others; use colorful flags to mark those pots, or tie a bright ribbon around a few of the plants to remind your caregiver that these pots or beds need to be inspected more often. Before you leave, water everything thoroughly, weed, and deadhead any spent flowers.

BULBS

Your summer bulbs can be enjoyed outdoors or indoors as cut flowers. Create a cutting garden where you won't have to worry about color combinations and other design features. A cutting garden produces lots of flowers for tables, picnics, or sharing with friends. The following list of cut flowers have sturdy stems, interesting flowers with color that doesn't fade, and lots of fragrant blossoms: African corn lily (*Ixia*), calla lily (*Zantedeschia*), crinum, fragrant gladiolus (*Acidanthera*), gladiolus, pineapple plant (*Eucomis*), liatris, Asiatic lily, oriental lily, summer hyacinth (*Galtonia*), and tuberose (*Polianthes*).

EDIBLES

Start planning your fall garden. Choose early-maturing vegetables when you can. Sow beans, cucumbers, or even short-season corn. They will be ready to pick before freezing weather comes. Note the dates to remind you when to plant them—allow adequate time to mature before the first expected freeze.

LAWNS

Apply the correct amount of water each time you irrigate. To do this, calibrate your irrigation system so you'll know how much water you apply per hour and exactly when to stop watering.

PERENNIALS & ORNAMENTAL GRASSES

Record your observations of the performance of your plants, pest problems, control measures, and what needs to be done as summer closes and gives way to fall. Write down the plants that need to be composted or given away. Finally, find some good books about perennials and learn more about the design of perennial borders.

ROSES

This is the perfect month to find a comfort-able chair, a cool drink, and another good book (besides this one). Kick back and enjoy the fruits of your labors. You might select a book about the lore of roses. The beautiful flowers, the exquisite fragrances, the nutritious rose hips, all set among vicious thorns, is the stuff of poetry.

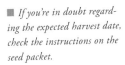

■ *If you're in doubt regarding the expected harvest date, check the instructions on the seed packet.*

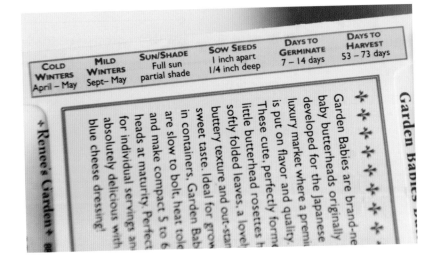

■ *A small pond and fountain not only add the illusion of luxury to your landscape, but they also add the sound and sparkle of moving water and invite birds to join the party.*

Much has been written since roses were first cultivated during the Shen Nung dynasty in China (2737–2697 B.C.).

SHRUBS AND TREES

In some front yards you'll see the same handful of shrubs used over and over. It reminds me of an eight-pack of Crayola crayons. Although there are so many wonderful colors available, the same eight crayons are always used. Take some time this month to look at the big box of 64 crayons. Increase your shrub vocabulary to learn about the tremendous diversity that can be cultivated in your Carolina landscape. Take it from your children: once you use burnt sienna, salmon, or aquamarine, you won't want to go back to using the red, yellow, and blue in the box of eight.

Don't forget native "American-made" shrubs that deserve a place in the landscape. These plants were growing in North America when the Europeans first arrived and are still here, which is proof of their longevity and ability to adapt readily to our Carolina climate, soils, and pests. Besides, they make terrific plants for attracting songbirds, butterflies, beneficial insects, and other wildlife. Look for cultivars of native plants ("nativars") that will fit perfectly into your landscape.

WATER GARDENS

Plan to improve your water garden next year. Did the tropical water lilies look as good as the pictures in the catalog? Have some of the aquatic plants turned out to be thugs in disguise by taking more space than you allotted to them? Perhaps you heard some recommendations from friends and other water gardening enthusiasts regarding some aspect of pond care. Compile your notes and plan to act on them next season.

PLANT

ANNUALS

Indoors: Seeds of hardy annuals that will bloom in the fall and winter can be started this month. They include alyssum, calendula, and ornamental cabbage and kale. Biennials that can be planted for transplanting later include foxglove, money plant, and sweet William. Coastal gardeners can wait until next month to start these seeds.

Outdoors: Look for empty spaces in the landscape and fill them with warm-season annuals. If you're planting among bulbs or perennials that have gone dormant such as bleeding hearts, inspect the area carefully before planting to avoid damaging the perennial's crown.

Cleome, cosmos, marigolds, sunflowers, and zinnias can still be planted or sown for bloom until frost. When the seedlings are about 2 inches tall, thin them where they're too crowded, or transplant them to other parts of the garden. Some quick-growing and flowering annuals that can be planted now from seed include cosmos, gomphrena, Klondyke marigolds, Mexican sunflowers, dwarf sunflowers, and zinnia. For the price of a few seeds, they will make a spectacular late-summer show in five to six weeks.

BULBS

Plant reblooming irises. Those that have performed well in the South Carolina Botanical Garden in the Piedmont include 'Autumn Tryst', 'Clarence', 'Harvest of Memories', 'Raven's Return', and 'Violet Music'. They require a little more attention to fertilizing and watering, but their two seasons of flowering in late spring and early fall are well worth the effort.

Lift and divide overgrown clumps of bearded irises after they have bloomed in the Mountains. See next month's Plant section for step-by step instructions. Gardeners in the Piedmont and Coastal Plain can wait until the next month or early fall when the temperatures are cooler.

EDIBLES

Sow another round of basil, cucumbers, squash, and southern peas. Consider varieties that offer disease resistance, earlier yields, or better flavor.

Sow pumpkin seeds for Halloween.

Mountain and Piedmont gardeners can start seeds of Brussels sprouts, cabbage, and cauliflower for the fall garden. Sow seed indoors or in a partly shaded area outdoors.

■ *Trim, divide, and replant your bearded irises this month.*

Make a first planting of seeds for some fall crops including broccoli, Brussels sprouts, cabbage, carrots, collards, and cauliflower. Also plant transplants of eggplant, pepper, and tomato for a fall crop. Attention to watering will be needed to get these up and growing. Wait until next month in the Coastal Plain.

LAWNS

Sod can be installed during hot weather as long as you provide sufficient water to keep the soil moist. Before laying the sod, moisten the soil to prevent the roots from coming into contact with excessively hot and dry soil. Water immediately afterward to wet the soil below to a depth of 3 or 4 inches. See March for more details.

TO CALIBRATE AN IN-GROUND IRRIGATION SYSTEM

Use cans to determine sprinkler rates for either an inground system or a portable sprinkler.

1. Place several equal-sized coffee cans or other straight-sided, flat-bottomed containers randomly throughout the area to be irrigated. For aboveground, portable, hose-end sprinklers, containers should be arranged in a straight line away from the sprinklers to the edge of the water pattern.

2. Turn on the irrigation for 15 minutes.

3. Turn off the water, collect the cans, and pour all the water into one of the cans.

4. Measure the depth of water you collected.

5. Calculate the average depth of water by dividing the total amount of water in inches by the number of cans. For instance, if the total depth was 3 inches, and you used six containers, then the average depth would be ⅜, or 0.5 inches.

6. Multiply the average depth by four to determine the application rate in inches per hour. For example, ½ inch multiplied by four equals 2 inches per hour. If you run the system for one hour, it will apply 2 inches of water; run it for half an hour, and it will apply 1 inch.

easily down to 2 to 4 inches is enough to know that it's dry. Look at your roses. If the leaves are grayish green in color and slightly wilted, moisture could be lacking. Waiting until the roses are completely wilted before watering can affect their health and survival.

SHRUBS AND TREES

Water recently planted shrubs and trees, which are especially vulnerable to heat and drought. Water thoroughly to encourage deep rooting. Check the rootball and soil before watering instead of relying on the calendar. Avoid overwatering, which can suffocate the plant roots, causing the leaves to wilt. It can also expose the shrub/tree to attack from root rot, a deadly fungal disease that prevails in waterlogged conditions and attacks susceptible plants (see September).

Established, drought-tolerant shrubs and trees may not require water; other shrubs, however, may need to be watered during prolonged dry periods. These shrubs will benefit from an application of 1 inch of water per week.

VINES & GROUNDCOVERS

See June.

WATER GARDENING

Check the water level of your pool to see if it has dropped. Tap water shouldn't be added directly to a water garden containing fish because the chlorine is toxic to them. If you add less than an inch of tap water to your pool, a dechlorinating agent won't be necessary. For larger amounts, a dechlorinating chemical will have to be added.

Chloramine is another water treatment agent that's used to treat tap water. Unlike chlorine, it doesn't escape naturally from the water, and a special water conditioner needs to be added to remove it. Contact your local public water department to find out which chlorinating product is used in your water supply, and use a de-chlorinating agent designed for that product.

ANNUALS

If you use a slow-release fertilizer, now is the time to make your second application (your first application should have been incorporated into the bed at planting time). Fast-release fertilizers should be applied every month or six weeks throughout the growing season. Water afterward to make the nutrients available to your plants.

BULBS

Evaluate the growth rate and appearance of your summer-flowering bulbs prior to fertilizing them with a fast-release fertilizer. If they look robust, fertilizer won't be necessary. To enrich the soil, topdress the beds lightly with composted manure. Mountain gardeners can lightly fertilize bearded irises, Louisiana irises, and Siberian irises with a low-nitrogen fertilizer such as 5-10-10. Avoid getting fertilizer on the rhizomes. Water in the fertilizer afterward so that the nutrients can be absorbed by the roots.

EDIBLES

Restore soil fertility before planting your fall crops by working in fertilizer or manure. Do not fertilize drought-stressed plants. Wait until after watering or rainfall and the plants' leaves have dried off.

LAWNS

See May.

PERENNIALS

After pinching or pruning your perennials, fertilize them to speed up their recovery. If you use a slow-release fertilizer, now is the time to make your second application of the season according to the label directions (your first application should have been applied in the spring at planting or when the new shoots emerged). Water afterward to make the nutrients available to your plants.

ROSES, SHRUBS, TREES, AND VINES & GROUNDCOVERS

Don't fertilize unless you're willing to irrigate regularly afterward. Water is necessary to make the fertilizer available to the plant roots, and also to keep the new growth healthy and alive. If your healthy-looking shrubs already fit into their allotted space, there's no reason to encourage any further growth with fertilizer. If your plants are experiencing drought stress, water is what they need most. Wait until late fall to fertilize them when they'll be more receptive.

In the hotter parts of the Carolinas, rest your roses this month. When the cooler fall temperatures arrive, resume feeding and water them for a fabulous fall display.

■ *Even if you don't catch adult Japanese beetles in the act of devouring your plants, their calling card is obvious: ragged flowers and "skeletonized" leaves that are nothing but a lacy network of veins.*

WATER GARDENS

Fertilize floating-leaved plants with slow-release aquatic plant tablets available from water garden suppliers. Bury the tablets in the soil so the fertilizer will be available to the roots and not leach out into the water (which can stimulate the growth of algae).

PROBLEM-SOLVE

ANNUALS

Aphids, spider mites, and whiteflies continue to be on the prowl this month. They can be washed from plants with a strong stream of water. Insecticidal soap, insecticides, and miticides will keep their numbers in check.

Watch out for Japanese beetles. The adults eat flowers and foliage.

Watch out for powdery mildew on zinnias. Pull out and discard infected plants. Reseed the vacant areas. In the future, select zinnias that are resistant to powdery mildew.

BULBS

Japanese beetles skeletonize leaves and feed on buds and flowers. Aphids occur in clusters near the tips of shoots and their feeding causes leaves to become wrinkled, sticky, and sometimes coated with black sooty mold. Spider mites cause yellow or bronze stippling on the leaf surface. Thrips damage flower buds, creating streaks or spots on the open blooms and brown edges on flower buds that fail to bloom.

Watch out for the lesser canna leaf roller. It attacks young growth, causing leaves to become frayed, tattered, and shot full of holes. Some will appear sealed together with webbing. The adult brown moths with 1-inch wingspans emerge in March and April, and the females lay yellowish white eggs in small patches on the emerging foliage. When the tiny caterpillars hatch, they tunnel into the canna leaves, as many as six invading a single rolled leaf. The larvae, which eventually grow to nearly an inch in length, have cream to greenish bodies and yellow heads.

The caterpillars typically feed only on the upper surface of the leaf but will sometimes bore through the furled leaf, creating a series of holes when the leaf unfurls. To shelter themselves, the caterpillars often fasten the edges of leaves with silk to prevent them from unrolling, and older larvae can reroll opened leaves and hold them closed with silk. When fully grown, the caterpillars pupate inside a filmy cocoon. There are usually two generations per year. The easiest way to control the lesser canna leaf roller is with early applications of *Bacillus thuringiensis* (*B.t.*). Direct the spray into the center of furled leaves, where the caterpillars are feeding. Cleaning up and discarding aboveground portions of cannas after the first freeze will also remove overwintering caterpillars.

EDIBLES

Squash bugs feed on pumpkin and squash plants. Early planting for an early harvest can usually beat them. Capture them by placing a shingle on the ground. Bugs will gather under it during the heat of the day and can be destroyed.

If your vegetables looked stunted, poorly colored, and wilted, check the roots for signs of a nematode infestation. These microscopic roundworms are commonly found in coarse-textured sandy soils and feed on plant roots. The root knot nematode produces knots or galls in the roots. Have the soil analyzed through your County Extension Center. If the findings reveal damaging levels of nematodes, the course of action includes rotating vegetables away from this site, and planting nematode-resistant vegetables such as 'Carolina Wonder' and 'Charleston Belle' bell peppers; 'Colossus' southern pea; 'Better Boy', 'Celebrity', or 'OG 50' tomatoes; and 'Jewel' sweet potato. Soil solarization as described below will also reduce their numbers.

See June, Problem-Solve for help in controlling leaffooted bugs, pickleworms, and spider mites.

Bacterial wilt attacks tomatoes, Irish potatoes, eggplants, and peppers. It causes an entire fruiting plant suddenly to wither and die. To control this disease, remove and dispose of infected plants, roots and all. Rotate susceptible vegetables to different locations in your garden every year. Currently, no chemicals or totally resistant tomato plants are available. Two cultivars show promise, and you may want to try 'Tropic Boy' or 'Neptune' tomatoes.

Handpull or hoe out any weeds to prevent them from stealing water and nutrients. Suppress their emergence with a layer of mulch over any bare ground. Sheets of newspaper camouflaged with grass clippings or other organic matter will suppress subsequent weed seed sprouting.

To suppress soil pest problems such as nematodes, bacteria, fungi, weeds, and insects, solarize the soil. Solarizing uses clear plastic or polyethylene to intensify sunlight, which raises soil temperatures and kills soilborne pests. The best time to solarize the soil is during the hottest part of summer.

LAWNS

Sample areas where you observed damage from mole crickets in the spring and treat accordingly.

See June, Problem-Solve. Brown patch attacks fescues and bluegrass and is encouraged by overwatering and overfertilizing with nitrogen. Collect and compost clippings from infected areas. Fungicides can be used to protect healthy grass from attack. Wait until fall to rake dead areas and seed or sod.

Pythium blight is a hot-weather (80 to 95 degrees Fahrenheit) fungal disease that rapidly gobbles up lawns. Infected leaves look water-soaked; are copper-colored, dark brown, or black; and feel greasy. Look for fungal strands during the evening or early morning. Avoid spreading this disease when mowing. Collect the infected clippings and compost them. Fungicides are available.

To avoid pythium blight, postpone seeding until the arrival of cool temperatures in the fall. Water before dew forms at night or in the morning after sunrise. Do not fertilize cool-season lawns in the summer months.

HERE'S HOW

TO USE THE SUN TO SUPPRESS SOIL PEST PROBLEMS

1. Cultivate the soil to a depth of 6 to 8 inches. Level the soil. Remove weeds, plants, and crop debris, and break up large clods of soil so the plastic will come in close contact with the soil.

2. Moisten the soil to conduct heat more deeply into it.

3. Dig a shallow trench around the plot to hold the edges of the plastic shut.

4. Stretch a clear plastic sheet that is 1 to 4 mil thick over the bed. A plastic that contains ultraviolet inhibitors will prevent it from deteriorating too quickly. Tuck it into the trench and bury the edges with soil to secure it in place.

5. Leave the plastic in place for four to six weeks in full summer sun.

■ *Solarization uses clear plastic sheeting and the sun's heat to raise the soil temperature to kill soilborne pests naturally.*

Watch for gray leaf spot on St. Augustinegrass. Collect infected clippings and compost them. Use a slow-release nitrogen fertilizer to reduce gray leaf spot problems.

During this time of the year it may seem as if the weeds are healthier and growing more vigorously than the lawn grass. Look out for southern sandspur or sandbur. This upright-growing, tufted summer annual produces a spike of spiny burs from midsummer to fall. The burs cling to skin, clothing, socks and shoes, and can be carried by water. Although southern sandspur is killed by a heavy frost, the burs can persist during the winter months and into the following summer. Handpull this shallow-rooted weed. Alternatively, apply a pre-emergence herbicide in early spring next year when the soil temperature reaches 50 degrees Fahrenheit. Emerged weeds can be treated with a post-emergence herbicide when the weeds are young and immature.

PERENNIALS

Aphids, spider mites, and whiteflies continue to be on the prowl this month. They can be washed from plants with a strong stream of water. Insecticidal soap, insecticides, and miticides will keep their numbers in check.

Watch for Japanese beetles this month. Adults emerge as early as mid-May in the Coastal Plains. Their highest numbers occur this month. Thankfully, there's only one generation a year.

Southern blight may attack a number of perennials, especially artemisia, columbine, aster, coralbells, liatris, phlox, salvia, and Shasta daisy. This soilborne disease occurs during periods of high temperatures (80 to 90 degrees Fahrenheit) and in moist soils. The fungus attacks the stem at soil level and moves up rapidly, killing the tissues as it ascends. The leaves turn yellow and wilt, and eventually the entire plant collapses. Look on the infected stem for dozens of brown, mustard seed-sized sclerotia—the "seeds" of the fungus. Remove and discard infected plants. Leave the area fallow for six months or longer. Fungicidal soil drenches can be used to treat the soil when a shorter fallow period is used.

Leaf diseases may show up during wet weather. Trim away heavily infected leaves and compost them.

Continue handpulling weeds out of the flower beds. With proper spacing, your perennials should be able to shade out the soil naturally and keep the weeds at bay.

ROSES

Several insects are active now. Japanese beetles skeletonize leaves and feed on flower buds and flowers; rose aphids occur in clusters near the tips of shoots, and their feeding causes leaves to become wrinkled, sticky, and sometimes coated with a black sooty mold; spider mites cause yellow or bronze stippling on the leaf surface; thrips damage flower buds, creating streaks or spots on the open blooms and brown edges on flower buds that fail to open.

Nematodes are microscopic organisms that live in the soil and attack roots. They are more commonly found in coarse-textured sandy soils than in fine-textured clay soils. One type, the root knot nematode, produces small galls or swellings on the roots. Nematode-infested roots cannot take up water or fertilizer as well as healthy ones. The plants may be weak looking, stunted, and wilted. Their leaves turn yellow or off-color and drop off earlier than normal.

If you suspect nematodes, have your soil assayed by the North Carolina Department of Agriculture, Agronomic Division. South Carolina residents can submit soil samples to the Agricultural Service Laboratory at Clemson University. Submit samples through your County Extension Office. If nematodes are a threat, the best defense is to keep the plants healthy. Add organic matter such as compost, composted pine bark, or peat moss to improve soil structure and moisture retention in sandy soils. This not only makes a better growing environment for the plant but also creates a favorable environment for the growth of natural predators of the nematode.

SHRUBS

Be on the lookout for damage caused by aphids and spider mites. Take necessary action if their feeding is more than you or your shrubs can tolerate. Blast these critters off with a strong spray of water from the hose. Get underneath the leaves to dislodge spider mites.

The second generation of azalea lace bugs occurs in late July through September. The adults and nymphs have piercing-sucking mouthparts for sucking sap from the undersides of the leaves. Injury by their feeding results in stippled or blanched areas on the upper leaf surface. They also deposit black, tarlike feces (frass) and the skins of molting nymphs on the undersides of the leaves. Heavy infestations cause the leaves to turn pale green or yellow and fall off.

Damage from this pest is most serious on azaleas growing in sunny locations. If yours are growing in full sun, try moving them to a location that receives only filtered sunlight or afternoon shade. This tactic should reduce the lace bug populations.

Apply an insecticidal soap at three- to four-day intervals for a minimum of three applications, making sure to spray the undersides of the leaves. If there is no rain to wash off the leaves, then do not exceed three applications or you may damage the plants. Other insecticides are available.

Consider replacing them with lace bug–resistant azaleas such as 'Cavalier', 'Dawn', 'Dream', 'Elsie Lee', 'Eureka', 'Macrantha', 'Marilee', 'Pink Fancy', 'Pink Star', 'Red Wing', 'Salmon Pink', 'Seigai', and 'Sunglow'. Recent work by USDA scientists has shown resistance in '4th of July' (*Rhododendron oldhamii*) azalea and three Encore Azaleas®: 'Conlee' (Autumn Amethyst™), 'Conlec' (Autumn Royalty™), and 'Conlep' (Autumn Twist™).

Watch for Japanese beetles this month. These big slow-flying bugs, metallic green with bronze wing covers, skeletonize leaves, leaving only a lacy network of leaf veins after their feeding. They also feed on flowers. Pick them off and discard them into a jar of soapy water. Neem can be applied to the leaves to reduce feeding by the adults. Other insecticides can be used for heavy infestations. If you choose to use Japanese beetle traps, place them far away from your susceptible shrubs. Thankfully, there's only one generation a year.

Look for shoot blight on rhododendrons. The terminal bud and leaves turn brown, roll up, and

drop. Prune out affected branches. Fungicides can be applied at the first sign of disease. There is no cure for infested plants.

Inspect your plants for Phytophthora root rot, a devastating fungal disease that attacks a wide variety of plants. Look for wilted, dying plants. Scrape the bark near the crown and look for a reddish brown discoloration where the fungus has moved into the stem. Examine the roots as well. The "outer skin" or cortex of the root can be slipped off easily like the paper covering from a straw. When you slice it open, a root rot–infected root is reddish brown inside instead of a healthy white in color. When symptoms are evident, chemical fungicides are often ineffective in controlling this disease. Remove the infected plant. If you want to replant in this area, select root rot–resistant plants.

Control weeds by handpulling and maintaining a shallow layer of mulch. Prevent the weeds from going to seed by removing the flowers.

TREES

Japanese beetles are highly attracted to some trees. A long-term solution is to substitute Japanese beetle-prone trees with less palatable ones. Here are a few attractive ornamentals from a long list of resistant trees: arborvitae, ash, balsam fir, butternut, Chinese redbud, cryptomeria, dogwood, ginkgo, hazelnut, hemlock, hickory, Japanese pagodatree, hollies, magnolia, maples other than Norway, oaks other than chestnut and pin, smoketree, spruce, sweetgum, tamarisk, tuliptree, and yew.

Spines of sawdust an inch or more long sticking out of the trunk are a sign of the Asian ambrosia beetle. This aggressive pest first appeared in this country in 1974 in Summerville, South Carolina, and has now spread to other southeastern states where it attacks more than 100 species of trees. The 1/8-inch-long reddish brown beetles typically invade young trees less than a foot in diameter. Because nearly the entire life cycle of the beetle is spent inside the wood, ambrosia beetles are difficult to control with insecticides. There are typically two generations per year, and for trees younger than three years old, infestations are likely to be fatal. Spraying trunks and limbs with an insecticide in late February or March will help reduce infestations, but the only guaranteed way to kill all of the beetles is to dig up and destroy an infested tree. Older trees are likely to survive an attack, however, particularly if they are growing vigorously.

Remove bagworms with scissors or a sharp knife. Bagworms are parasitized by several kinds of parasitic wasps and insecticides are effective, if applied when the bagworms are small.

Powdery mildew attacks the leaves and shoots of the older crapemyrtle cultivars. See June, Problem-Solve.

When some gardeners find lichens growing on their shrubs, they often panic, thinking their plants are under siege. Relax. Lichens are ominous-looking but harmless organisms that consist of a fungus and a green or blue-green alga that live in association with each other, looking like a single plant. Their presence on failing trees is a sign, but never the cause, of poor plant health—the reduction of plant vigor has resulted in a more open canopy, which increases sunlight penetration and subsequent lichen growth.

VINES & GROUNDCOVERS

Aphids and spider mites can be washed from plants with a strong stream of water. Use insecticidal soap and insecticides for aphids and miticides to keep mites in check.

Kabatina blight is a disease that attacks the tips of shore and creeping junipers and others in the summer. Prune out infected plant parts and discard them, because this fungus survives in dead and decaying plant material.

Start pulling weeds out of groundcover beds. Maintain a shallow layer of mulch to suppress them. Eventually the groundcovers will fill in and shade the soil, naturally preventing weed seeds from germinating.

WATER GARDENS

Water lilies and some marginal plants may be attacked by aphids. Dislodge them and knock them into the water where they can be eaten by fish. Holes in water lily leaves may be caused by

■ *Lichens on a tree may look sinister, but they actually cause no harm.*

water lily beetles or midges. Simply pick off the infested leaves to destroy the insect eggs or larvae.

Several diseases may occur while hot and humid conditions prevail. Trim off and discard any diseased leaves.

they become too crowded. Water as needed, give them plenty of sun, and fertilize weekly with a liquid fertilizer.

The seeds of cabbage and kale should be sown about eight weeks before the first freeze. Keep them cool after they sprout and move them outside when night temperatures begin to cool down in early fall.

Take cuttings of favorite annuals or sow seeds in pots for winter flowering indoors.

BULBS

Plant or move summer-flowering bulbs that have already bloomed, such as amaryllis, crocosmia, iris, and lily.

Divide bearded irises so the plants will have plenty of time to become established before cooler weather arrives. Gardeners in the warmer parts of the Carolinas can wait until September, which will allow the divisions to settle in after the heat of summer has passed.

■ *Raise lettuce seeds indoors or in a shaded location outdoors where the soil temperatures are cool. (Lettuce seed experiences thermoinhibition and will not germinate when the soil temperature exceeds 85 degrees Fahrenheit.) Allow 3 to 4 weeks for the seedlings to reach a size at which they can be transplanted to the main garden. Consider growing heat-resistant varieties, such as 'Buttercrunch' (Bibb type), 'Ermosa' (butterhead), 'Red Sails' (leaf), and 'Apollo' (romaine).*

EDIBLES

Set out cloves of garlic for a harvest early next summer. In the Piedmont and Coastal Plain, sow beans, beets, Brussels sprouts, cabbage, carrots, broccoli, cauliflower, lettuce, rutabaga, and squash. Plant greens, such as kale, mustard, and turnips, in intervals now and next month to lengthen the harvest season. In the Mountains, plant the last fall garden vegetables. For hardy crops like cabbage, cauliflower, and collards, count back from your average first frost date the number of days the particular variety requires to mature; plant at the appropriate time. For half-hardy crops like beets and carrots, allow an additional week. Lettuce, radishes, beets, spinach, mustard, turnips, and peas can be started from seed. Set out transplants of kale, lettuce, broccoli, cabbage, cauliflower, and collards.

LAWNS

Avoid seeding or sprigging warm-season grasses in late summer or early fall because they may be killed by cold weather. If you have to plant now, sod early this month to get the plants settled before they go dormant with the first frost.

■ *Marigolds are fast-growing annuals that can be planted from leftover seed and expected to bloom shortly thereafter.*

HERE'S HOW

TO DIVIDE IRISES

1. Loosen the soil around the rhizomes (horizontally creeping stems) with a spading fork. Watering the bed the day before will make digging easier.

2. Dig up the clumps and separate the rhizomes. Divide each rhizome into sections with a sharp knife, making sure that each section has at least one bud or fan of leaves. The young rhizomes will be growing from the sides of the older, spongy rhizomes.

3. Cut the young rhizomes away from the older sections with a sharp knife. Discard the older pieces and any sections that are undersized or diseased. (Don't think twice about throwing away the old rhizomes. They bloom only once and then become a flowerless food reservoir). The rhizomes may be infested with borers. Discard heavily infested rhizomes. Salvage others by digging out the pinkish larvae with a pocketknife and trimming away any damaged tissue. Because the larvae's feeding creates opportunities for bacterial soft rot, soak the damaged rhizomes for half an hour in a 10 percent solution of household bleach and water. Then dust them with powdered sulfur and allow the cut surfaces to air-dry in a shady place for several hours before replanting. Before you replant the irises in their original location, comb the soil carefully for signs of brown pupal cases. Collect and destroy them to prevent the dusky brown adult moths from emerging in the fall and laying eggs on or near your plants.

4. Trim leaves to about one-third to one-half their height to reduce moisture loss. Make sure that each division consists of a firm rhizome with a fan of healthy leaves.

5. To help prevent infection, dust the cut ends with powdered sulfur. Lay the trimmed plants in a shady spot for a few hours to allow the cut ends to dry and heal.

6. Replant the bearded irises in a sunny, well-drained location. Dig the hole 8 to 12 inches deep, then form a cone of soil in the center, making it high enough so the rhizome will be planted just above ground level in heavy clay soils. For lighter sandy soils, the top of the rhizome may be ½ inch or less below ground level. Spread the roots around the top of the cone, pressing them firmly into the soil. Space the divisions about 12 to 18 inches apart. Plant them in groups of three to form a natural-looking clump.

7. Cover the freshly planted rhizomes lightly with soil. Use about ½ inch of soil—less for very small rhizomes.

8. Water the young plants to settle soil around the roots. Mulch in the Mountains to prevent freezing and thawing of the soil, which can heave the plants out of the ground. Remove the mulch in early spring, or too much moisture may remain around the rhizomes.

PERENNIALS & ORNAMENTAL GRASSES

Any planting done now should be followed with regular watering, keeping the soil moist in order to speed up establishment. Mountain gardeners can divide or move perennials to other parts of the garden, paying attention to watering and mulching after planting.

ROSES, SHRUBS AND TREES

Potted roses, container-grown shrubs and trees can be planted in the Mountains. They ought to have plenty of time to get established before cold weather arrives. Pay attention to regular watering during the first few weeks after planting. Water is the most important "soil amendment" when establishing plants.

Gardeners in the milder areas of the Carolinas can plant now or wait until cooler weather arrives.

VINES & GROUNDCOVERS

Plant container-grown vines and groundcovers. This is a very stressful time, however, and unless there is sufficient water available, you may want to wait until September or October when the temperatures are more favorable for planting.

WATER GARDENING

American lotus (*Nelumbo lutea*), commonly known as water chinquapin, is native to the eastern half of the United States. It is closely related to the water lily and produces a large, round arrangement of floating leaves joined by stalks to a thick, below-ground stem or rhizome.

As new growth emerges over the course of a season, aerial leaves shaped like shallow bowls are produced on stems that rise high above the pad, sometimes 5 feet or more. Magnificent flowers are borne high over the water on a thick stalk above the aerial leaves. The flowers may be white, pale yellow, pink, or deep rose, depending on the species, and range from 4 to 12 inches across. In the center of each flower is a yellow receptacle with tiny holes that looks like a showerhead. This "seed-pod" enlarges as it matures, changing to green and then to brown. By that point the individual seeds are held loosely in depressions on the pod's face. Because of their decorative value, these seedpods are often dried, bronzed, or silvered and used in floral arrangements.

To root a seed, scarify or abrade the impervious seed coat with sandpaper or a file prior to sowing. Sow the seed in a mix of two parts heavy garden soil and one part coarse sand, in a non-draining container. Plant the seed at a depth twice its diameter and fill the container with water so that the mix is submerged by 2 inches. Set the container in a window with a southern exposure where the air temperature is above 75 degrees Fahrenheit and the water temperature above 65 degrees. The seed should germinate in two to three weeks. When three leaves have appeared, the seedlings can be transplanted to larger pots filled with heavy garden soil. These pots can then be set in a larger container of water.

■ *Unlike hardy water lilies that rest their flowers on the surface, tropical water lilies hold their flower high above the water.*

AUGUST

Transplant again whenever a seedling has filled its pot. Allow the delicate root tips to protrude from the soil and make sure there is enough water to support the developing leaf pad.

When water temperatures outside have reached at least 70 degrees Fahrenheit, young lotuses can be moved outdoors. Each plant should then be given a container at least 9 to 10 inches deep and 16 to 20 inches in diameter.

Use ½-pound commercial aquatic plant fertilizer per bushel of soil. Add a 1-inch layer of pea gravel on the surface. Before submersing the container, water it thoroughly; then place it in the pool. The gravel layer should be 3 or 4 inches below the water surface. As growth continues, the lotus plants can be moved to deeper water, 6 to 12 inches below the water surface.

Choose the site carefully: Lotus is a very invasive plant. In a few growing seasons it can spread rapidly and overtake a shallow pond. Keep the surface of the pond covered so that one-half to three-quarters of its surface is covered with leaves.

CARE

ANNUALS

Do not disturb the soil in your flowerbeds during hot, dry August days. Loosening the soil can damage surface roots and increase water loss from the soil.

Inspect the mulch in flowerbeds. If wind, rain, and natural decay have reduced its thickness to an inch or less, apply more mulch to raise the level to 2 to 3 inches, but only about ½ inch around the bases of the plants. Use compost, pine straw, pine bark, or hardwood mulch.

If the cutting garden looks bedraggled, clear out the annuals that have finished blooming or are overgrown.

Many plants in the flower border will make excellent houseplants this winter.

Early this month, pinch back fall-planted snapdragons to produce bushier plants. Deadhead any faded flowers or seedpods from snapdragons that survived the summer; this will encourage another round of flowers this fall.

BULBS

The leaves of your summer-flowering bulbs may look tattered and unattractive, but don't remove them until the foliage and shoots turn yellow. Cut them off a few inches above the ground.

Remove spent flowers as they fade. If the weather is hot and the flowers are in afternoon sun, blooms will not last very long. Cut the flowers and use them in arrangements.

EDIBLES

Dry herbs. Gather bundles of each type of herb and spread on cheesecloth or hang upside-down in a warm, dark, dry place. Harvest garlic when the leaves turn yellow. Lift the entire plant and dry it in a well-ventilated, covered space. Save some for replanting and eat the rest. To protect pumpkins from rot, slip a shingle under ripening fruits to lift them off the soil. Winter squash is ready to harvest when the rind is hard and cannot be punctured with your thumbnail. Pull out plants that have stopped producing, including bush beans, early cucumbers, and summer squash. High temperatures slow tomato production. There is nothing to do but wait for the weather to cool. Then they will start producing again. The same goes for bell peppers. Too much fertilizer can cause pepper blossoms to fall off. Peppers are moderate feeders, needing only a little fertilizer at planting and a light sidedressing after the first fruits have set.

LAWNS

Continue to mow your lawn regularly, removing no more than one-third of the grass height at each mowing.

PERENNIALS & ORNAMENTAL GRASSES

If you're going on vacation this month, have someone take care of your flowerbeds while you're away. See July, Plan for some helpful suggestions.

■ *Microwave drying is a quick and easy way to dry small amounts of herbs. Lay a single layer of clean, dry leaves between paper towels and place in the microwave for 1 to 2 minutes on high power. Allow the leaves to cool. If they are not completely dry, reheat for 30 seconds and retest. Repeat as needed until herbs are completely dry.*

Deadhead phlox to prevent the flowers from going to seed. The seedlings do not come true to the color of the parent, and often their sheer numbers overtake a planting, giving you the impression that the flowers from the parents have magically changed color.

Disbud chrysanthemums to produce fewer but larger blooms. Most mums, except spray types, respond well to disbudding. To disbud, pinch off the side buds that form in the angles of the leaves along the main stems. Leave only the large top bud. The plant will channel its energy into this bud, which will develop into impressive proportions.

SHRUBS & TREES
Remember the "3 Ds" when visiting the garden: damaged, diseased, or dead twigs must go. Hold off on major pruning until late winter. Major pruning now will only stimulate tender, new growth, which can be killed by our first freeze.

Remove any suckers from the rootstocks of grafted roses. The leaves on these shoots will look different from the grafted variety.

ROSES
If you rested your roses last month, Mountain and Piedmont gardeners can jump-start ever-bloomers into growth for a fall-flowering display. Coastal Plain gardeners can wait until later this month or early next month.

VINES & GROUNDCOVERS
Collect seeds from annual vines and store them for planting next year. Actively growing vines may need to be secured to their moorings. Vines that do not have tendrils will have to be tied with soft twine. Check the fastenings on other shoots to see that the stems aren't being girdled.

WATER GARDENS
Inspect the submerged plants in your pool and thin them out if necessary. Compost them or recycle them in the vegetable garden as mulch.

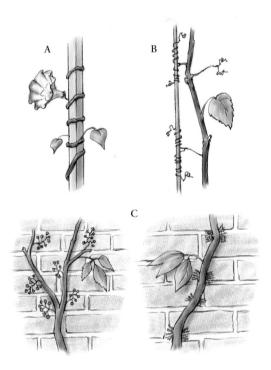

■ *Vines cling to supports in any of three ways: flexible stems that wrap around structures (A); tendrils, slender modified leaves, that grasp and curl (clematis has coiling, tendril-like leaf petioles) (B); rootlets or tendrils tipped with adhesive disks that act like suction cups to allow vines to cling to walls, trees, and other rough-textured surfaces (C). Construct an appropriate structure that matches the climbing abilities of the vine.*

Trim off spent flowers and clip away any leaves that may be in the water. The leaves and other organic matter can break down in the water, especially in hot weather, and can harm plants and fish. Clean the surface of the pond of debris to prevent it from sinking to the bottom and fouling the water.

WATER

ANNUALS

Check the soil in flowerbeds to determine if you need to water. Water deeply to wet the entire root zone of the plants.

Container-grown flowers can dry out quickly, especially when located in full sun. Feel the soil in containers at least once a day to check for moisture. When water is necessary, apply it long enough so that it runs out of the drainage holes. Keep in mind that clay pots will need to be watered more often than plastic pots. Also, small pots will dry out faster than large planters.

Check hanging baskets daily in the summer. Wind and sun dry them much more quickly than plants in other kinds of containers.

BULBS

Water regularly and thoroughly. During hot, dry, August days, avoid deep cultivation in your

■ *Plants in containers may need to be watered daily.*

flowerbeds. Loosening the soil under these conditions reduces water uptake by increasing loss of soil water and damaging surface roots.

EDIBLES

Watering properly is critical in the heat of summer. Slow, deep soakings are best done with trickle irrigation or soaker hoses.

LAWNS

Water dormant lawns every three weeks in the absence of rain, or take your chances knowing that reseeding may be necessary in the fall. Water only those areas that really need it.

PERENNIALS

During periods of low or no rainfall, water plants—especially new plantings—when they need it, and not by the calendar. When you do water, do a thorough job so water penetrates the soil deeply. Wait until the soil becomes dry in the upper inch or so before watering again.

Avoid irrigating your perennials with an overhead sprinkler. In addition to wasting water and watering weeds, wetting the leaves will encourage diseases.

Mulch to decrease weeds and conserve moisture. Inspect the mulch in flower beds. If wind, rain, and natural decay have reduced its thickness to an inch or less, apply more mulch to raise the level to 2 to 3 inches. Mulch conserves moisture, suppresses weed growth, and makes those weeds that do grow easier to pull out.

ROSES

See May, Plan.

SHRUBS, TREES, AND VINES & GROUNDCOVERS

If the soil is dry near the rootballs of newly planted shrubs, give them a good, thorough soaking. Check the soil before watering and look at the plant to see if water is necessary. When you water, water deeply, and thoroughly wet the soil.

Coastal gardeners who have saline water will benefit from drip-irrigation systems. They use less water to moisten the root zones of your plants, thus putting less salt in the soil. Planting your shrubs in raised beds will also make it easier to flush out accumulated salts with irrigation water and rainfall.

WATER GARDENS

Check the level of your pond to see if it has dropped. Tapwater shouldn't be added directly to a water garden containing fish because the chlorine is toxic to them. If you add less than an inch of tap water to your pool, a dechlorinating agent won't be necessary. For larger amounts, a de-chlorinating chemical will have to be added.

FERTILIZE

ANNUALS

If they haven't been fertilized in over six weeks, leggy plants that were cut back will benefit from a light feeding with a fast-release fertilizer. Apply a water-soluble fertilizer, such as 20-20-20, to container-grown annuals, according to label directions. Water the soil first, and then apply the fertilizer.

BULBS

Piedmont and Coastal Plain gardeners can lightly fertilize bearded irises, Louisiana irises, and Siberian irises early this month with a low-nitrogen fertilizer such as 5-10-10. Water the fertilizer in afterward.

EDIBLES

Feed basil with a liquid fertilizer to keep it productive into fall. Trim off seedheads and flowers so the plants will spend their energy on flavorful foliage.

LAWNS

See April. Avoid overfertilizing centipedegrass, which can lead to "centipede decline" as a result of excessive thatch.

PERENNIALS & ORNAMENTAL GRASSES

Be cautious about fertilizing. Unless the leaves look pale or off-color, fertilizing won't be necessary. Avoid excessive fertilization. It produces the soft, succulent growth favored by pests.

Never skimp on building up the natural fertility of the soil with applications of organic mulches such as compost.

ROSES

Depending on the fertility of your soil, ever-blooming roses may require a little boost from a fast-release fertilizer. Follow label directions to determine the amount to apply.

SHRUBS, TREES, AND VINES &GROUNDCOVERS

If you established a need for fertilizing and you're willing to provide adequate moisture, for roots to grow and absorb the applied minerals, use a slow-release fertilizer. Otherwise, wait until next spring when new growth begins.

WATER GARDENING

Fertilize floating-leaved plants with slow-release aquatic plant tablets available from water garden suppliers. Bury the tablets in the soil so the fertilizer will be available to the roots and not leach out into the water, which can stimulate the growth of algae. Bog plants can be fertilized based on their growth rate and appearance. To play it safe, fertilize them at half the rate of your water lilies.

PROBLEM-SOLVE

ANNUALS

Be on the lookout for aphids and spider mites. Plants infested by spider mites have faded, stippled leaves. Remove these pests with a strong spray of

■ *Heavy, out-of-control spider mite infestations cover leaves and shoots with fine webbing.*

water. Resort to a pesticide if their numbers are high and damage is great. If these plants are going to be removed and replaced by cool-season annuals, spraying with a pesticide may be unnecessary.

Nematodes may threaten your plants as well. See July, Problem-Solve.

Fungal leaf spots, powdery mildew, and other diseases could be afflicting your warm-season annuals. Evaluate the extent of damage to determine if a fungicide application is necessary. Heavily infested plants should be removed and discarded. Avoid wetting the leaves when watering to limit the spread of diseases.

Control weeds by handpulling and maintaining a layer of mulch. Keeping the beds weed-free will also remove overwintering sites for spider mites.

BULBS

Spider mites are especially troublesome during the hot, dry weather of this month. See April, Problem-Solve for controls.

Watch out for powdery mildew. Warm, humid days and cool night temperatures in the milder areas of the Carolinas favor the growth of this grayish white foliar disease.

Handpull any weeds and suppress their growth with a layer of mulch. Watch out for particularly aggressive weeds such as ground ivy and Indian mock strawberry.

EDIBLES

Pests reach record numbers in the fall months. Remove old plants that have stopped producing to eliminate shelters for insects and disease organisms. Nematodes can be a problem with vegetables. Remove and discard infected plants. Watch for signs of leaffooted bugs and spider mites. See April, Problem-Solve.

Gummy stem blight is a fungal disease that mostly infects cantaloupes, cucumbers, and watermelons in the Coastal Plain. Look for brown lesions on leaves and stems. If the stem is infected, the vine beyond the lesion will wither and die. Pull out and destroy infected vines. Remove and discard crop debris at the end of the growing season. Rotate with other vegetables other than vine crops or melons for two years. Avoid wetting the leaves when watering. Fungicides are available.

LAWNS

If your lawn looks wilted, even after watering; if it's been torn up by skunks, birds, and moles; or if parts have turned brown and feel spongy, check for a white grub infestation. White grubs are the larvae of scarab beetles, including Japanese beetles, masked chafers, and May and June beetles. They have plump, cream-colored, C-shaped bodies and distinctive yellow to brown heads. Most have life cycles lasting from several months to three years.

The Japanese beetle is the most common. Adult females lay their eggs in the soil around July. Two weeks later the grubs hatch and begin feeding on grass roots. The most serious damage occurs in September and October before hibernation and during April and May before the larvae pupate to become adults.

Make cuts on three sides of a 12-inch square of damaged area. Pry this flap back and examine the roots and upper 3 inches of soil. Count the number of grubs. Move on to another patch. After several samples, determine the average number of grubs. Most healthy lawns can tolerate ten Japanese beetle grubs per square foot. If your count is higher, an insecticide may be needed.

Look for brown patch disease on tall fescue.

Check for gray leaf spot disease on St. Augustinegrass. Collect infected clippings and compost them. Use a slow-release nitrogen fertilizer to reduce gray leaf spot problems.

Apply herbicides to your lawn for winter annual or perennial weeds that germinate or form rosettes in fall. Check herbicide labels before using.

If annual bluegrass and other winter weeds are a problem in spring, control them now.

Apply a pre-emergence herbicide to prevent them from appearing this fall.

TO MANAGE RED IMPORTED FIRE ANTS

1. Broadcast a fresh-bait insecticide over the entire landscape. While it can be used on individual mounds, it's best to distribute it widely. It's less expensive than individual mound treatments and controls colonies even when mounds aren't visible. Apply the bait when the workers are foraging for food. In the spring and fall, this is during the warmer daylight hours. In the summer, apply the bait in late afternoon or evening. Distribute the bait with a handheld seed spreader. Make one or two passes over the area at a normal walking speed. Most mounds that receive this slow-acting treatment will eventually be eliminated.

2. No sooner than seven days after applying the bait, treat only those mounds that pose a threat, located near walkways, play equipment, and other high-traffic areas. Use an approved fire ant insecticide following label directions. If you use a soluble powder, distribute it evenly over the mound. Liquid concentrates—chemical products diluted with water and then applied to the mound—must be used in sufficient volumes to penetrate the entire nest. Before using any of these pesticides, read and follow the label directions carefully. Alternatively, granular insecticides are available. These products are not baits, but can be broadcast over the entire area that is infested. They only control fire ants in the treated area.

The red imported fire ant was introduced into the United States as early as 1918. Because it's not native to this country, fire ants have no competitors, parasites, or predators. They produce unsightly mounds and their painful stings pose a health threat, particularly to young children and older people. If fire ants are in your landscape, control them with the "two-step method."

PERENNIALS & ORNAMENTAL GRASSES

Trim any dead, damaged, diseased, or insect-infested leaves. To improve their appearance, deadhead the spent flowers from garden phlox, obedient plant (*Physostegia virginiana*), perennial salvia, pincushion flower, purple coneflower, and sneezeweed. See July, Problem-Solve for more information.

Be on the lookout for aphids and spider mites. Remove these pests with a strong spray of water from the hose. Resort to a pesticide if their numbers are high and damage is great.

Fungal leaf spots, powdery mildew, and other diseases could be afflicting your perennials. Evaluate the extent of damage to determine if a fungicide application is necessary. Remove and discard heavily infested plants.

Control weeds by handpulling and maintaining a shallow layer of mulch. Prevent the weeds from going to seed by removing the flowers. Any seeds that can be eliminated now will not have to be dealt with next year.

ROSES

Inspect your roses for Japanese beetles, rose aphids, and spider mites. Evaluate the extent of injury and decide on the level of control. Should you resort to handpicking Japanese beetles? Or is the infestation bad enough that you should cover the roses with cheesecloth or netting? Are they present in such high numbers that chemical control is the best course of action?

Coastal Plain gardeners confronted with root-knot nematodes (see July, Problem-Solve for more information) should plant roses grafted onto *Rosa fortuniana*, a rootstock highly recommended for sandy

■ *Black spot, the Achilles' heel of roses, is characterized by black spots ⅛ to ¾ inch in diameter that develop on the upper leaf surface. While fungicides are available to control this disease, your best bet is to grow disease-resistant roses.*

southeastern soils. This heat-tolerant rootstock is resistant to root-knot nematodes. Unfortunately, roses on these rootstocks can be difficult to find. Your best bet is to buy them from companies that specify the rootstock used.

Watch out for blackspot and powdery mildew. Warm, humid days and cool night temperatures favor the growth of powdery mildew.

Rose mosaic virus is the most common viral disease of roses. Symptoms usually occur on new growth; look for crinkly deformed leaves, misshapen buds and flowers, leaves with blotches of yellow, ring patterns of light green, yellow lines, or a mottling of different shades of green. Rose mosaic virus makes a rose less vigorous, reduces the size and number of flowers, and sometimes deforms them. The plant is stunted and the bud graft may fail, killing the top variety and leaving the rootstock.

Rose mosaic is systemic, meaning that it can be found in all parts of the plant except the few cells at the tips of the growing points. Infected plants may decline in vigor and become stunted, so your only course of action is to remove them. Pruning away the afflicted parts will not remove the virus from your rose. There are no chemicals that cure a virus-infected plant or any that protect plants from

becoming infected. This particular virus spreads through the propagation of infected plants, as when virus-infected plant material is budded or grafted to a healthy plant. Because there is little natural spread of rose mosaic viruses, plants that develop mosaic symptoms in the rose garden do not need to be replaced as long as their growth is acceptable.

The only control for viruses is prevention so avoid purchasing plants showing mosaic symptoms. The industry is taking steps to rid rose cultivars of viruses. The plants are extensively tested to be sure that the virus is not detected in the treated material. Plants that pass the test are used to propagate virus-free stock.

Handpull grassy and broadleaf weeds from your rose beds. Maintain a shallow mulch layer to suppress their growth.

SHRUBS

Spider mites are very active during hot, dry weather. Their feeding injury results in discolored, bronze-colored leaves. Check for mites by tapping a branch onto a white sheet of paper and looking for moving specks. Natural predators can control spider mite populations. You can also wash off mites with a strong stream of water.

Redheaded azalea caterpillars devour entire leaves and completely defoliate branches. Identify this caterpillar by its red head and yellow stripes. When disturbed, it curls backward in a defensive posture. Handpick the caterpillars and discard them in a jar of soapy water. *Bacillus thuringiensis* is a biological insecticide that will control young caterpillars. Other insecticides are available and can be applied to control heavy infestations.

Remove the silken needle-covered bags of bagworms on pines, junipers, hemlocks, arborvitae, and other evergreens.

Weak-looking, stunted plants may be infested with nematodes. Determine the identity of the nematodes attacking your plants and consider outsmarting them by growing resistant shrubs. See July, Problem-Solve for a description and controls.

Wilted, dying plants may be a symptom of Phytophthora root rot. See last month's Problem-Solve for a description and controls. Although this fungal disease is often found in wet or poorly drained sites, it will attack plants in fairly dry sites if they are planted too deeply. Overwatering plants also favors attacks by this disease.

TREES

Spider mites are very active during hot, dry weather, especially on junipers, hollies, and many other ornamentals. Feeding injury results in discolored, bronzy leaves. Check for mites by tapping a branch onto a white sheet of paper and looking for moving specks. Natural predators can control spider mite populations. A strong spray of water from the hose applied to the undersides of the leaves will dislodge the adults during the growing season. An insecticidal soap, Neem oil, or a miticide will also be effective, although repeated applications may be necessary.

The leaves on deciduous trees will be falling in the next few months, so infected leaves may not require attention at this time because they're going to be shed soon.

Powdery mildew diseases attack a great many ornamentals, most often in late summer when the days are warm and nights are cool. Prevention is the first defense.

1. Grow powdery mildew-resistant varieties.

2. Prune plant to improve air circulation and sunlight penetration.

3. Reduce fertilizer applications to avoid excessive, late-season growth.

Cercospora leaf spot is a common disease of crapemyrtles that becomes noticeable this month and next. Diseased leaves have brown lesions that eventually turn yellow to red in color and then are quickly shed. The following cultivars are resistant to powdery mildew and Cercospora leaf spot: 'Tuscarora', 'Tuskegee', 'Tonto', and 'Fantasy' Japanese crapemyrtle.

VINES & GROUNDCOVERS

Inspect your vines and groundcovers for aphids and spider mites. Evaluate the extent of injury and take action if the health of the vine or groundcover is in jeopardy. See July, Problem-Solve for more information.

Watch out for leaf spot diseases. Infected leaves can be trimmed out and discarded. Severe infections can be treated with a fungicide. If fungicides are required on a regular basis, plan on replacing the vine.

See July, Problem-Solve for more details about controlling weeds.

WATER GARDENS

Your aquatic plants may be attacked by insects. Cut off any infested plant parts. Remove the offenders by submerging them in the water and giving them a shake. Handpick brown snails from iris leaves. Trim away any dead, damaged, or diseased leaves.

HERE HOW

TO AVOID ROOT ROT IN SHRUBS AND TREES

1. Avoid planting in poorly drained sites.

2. Improve drainage in heavy clay soil by planting in slightly raised beds, or add organic matter such as composted pine bark to as large of a planting area as possible.

3. Use plants that are highly resistant to root rot. Azaleas resistant to Phytophthora root rot include 'Corrine', 'Fakir', 'Fred Cochran', 'Glacier', 'Hampton Beauty', 'Higasa', 'Merlin', 'Polar Seas', and 'Rose Greely'. Grafting can also be used to thwart Phytophthora root rot. For example, susceptible Japanese camellia cultivars can be grafted onto rot-resistant sasanqua camellia rootstock.

September

With the onset of fall, you're probably preparing your garden and landscape for winter: sowing cover crops, tidying up flower beds, and winterizing equipment. Wait a second, my gardening friend. This is the South, where fall is a season for celebrating the end of summer. It's the time to escape from the confines of air-conditioned homes and shake off the chills of summer cabin fever. It's also the best time of year to plant, so don't put your shovels and trowels away. The shorter days and cooler temperatures will help the plants settle comfortably into their new surroundings. When spring arrives next year, they'll be ready to face the difficult months of summer.

It's also the time of year to appreciate late-season flowering plants, especially those that grow along our roadsides. Yes, these roadside beauties grow neglected and unnoticed all season long, coping with the punishing heat and humidity of summer. Then, toward the end of the season they burst forth onto center stage. Many of them are flowering right now in eye-popping displays of purples, yellows, reds, and whites.

In the Mountains and Piedmont look for the purple and lavender flowers of asters—Curtis aster, late purple, and wavy leaf aster. Across the Carolinas you'll find the bright yellow flowers of goldenrods, which are mistakenly accused of causing hay fever. The drab-looking, wind-pollinated ragweed is really the culprit.

Other yellow flowers include tickseed or beggar's ticks, naked stem sunflower, and narrowleaf sunflower. The spectacular display of whites and purples could be boneset, Joe-pye weed, and New York ironweed. Space is not a problem with these big, meaty plants.

Our roadsides wouldn't be complete without our native grasses and their fluffy plumes of flowers and shimmering leaves. Some attractive native grasses include little and big bluestems, plumegrass, and Indiangrass, the official state grass of South Carolina.

Avoid the temptation to dig them up. Fortunately, nurseries and garden centers carry nursery-propagated native species along with their more refined cousins, such as 'Fireworks' goldenrod or 'Purple Dome' aster. Often, cultivated varieties are more spectacular than their kin, bearing larger and more plentiful flowers. Like their roadside relatives, however, these domesticated types can be grown with relative ease.

These are just a few late season lovelies that have earned my admiration . . . and respect.

PLAN

ANNUALS

Plan to obtain seeds or transplants early this month for fall planting. Let your journal be your guide. It should document the annuals that performed well in your garden, or those that you've admired during your travels. Try your hand at annuals mentioned in conversation with friends and acquaintances.

Be adventurous: experiment with colorful vegetables that include purple mustard (*Brassica juncea* var. *rugosa* 'Red Giant'), mizuna (*Brassica rapa* var. *nipposinica*), Japanese mustard-spinach (*Brassica rapa* var. *perviridis*), tatsoi or flat pak choi (*Brassica rapa* var. *rosularis*), and arugula or roquette (*Eruca vesicaria* ssp. *sativa*). These minimum-care greens can be terrific fall and winter bedding plants that make a great foil for pansies and calendulas.

BULBS

When you consider buying spring-flowering bulbs, look at color, bloom period, and height. Check the merchandise carefully. Remember that "bigger is better" when it comes to bulbs. Bigger bulbs produce bigger blossoms. Stay away from soft, mushy, moldy, or heavily bruised bulbs. It doesn't matter if the tunic (the dry, papery, onion-skinlike covering) is loose or torn, but it should not harbor any insects or diseases.

Do not dismiss bargain bulbs that are smaller in size and less expensive than the larger ones. They may not give you the big impact you are looking for next year, but they will bring some color to large areas of the landscape (by the backyard fence, along the driveway, and so forth) for the right price. In a few seasons they will bulk-up sufficiently so no one will know they were bargain bulbs.

Finally, plan to try something new. It may be a bulb that has screaming pink flowers, or one that has a botanical name that's difficult to pronounce, but produces extraordinary blooms.

EDIBLES

Whether you garden year-round or hang up your hoe at summer's end, start tidying up the garden

■ *Prepare your garden for a fall vegetable garden, or plant cover crops to protect the soil from erosion and improve its structure for next year's garden.*

and take steps to build up the soil for next spring. Certain insects and diseases overwinter in plant debris. Time spent now burying plant stalks, debris, and mulch will eliminate winter havens for pests.

Consider the steps you will take to build the soil for next season. Planting a cover crop or "green manure" this fall that you will turn under in the spring is a great way to improve soil fertility and structure, hold valuable topsoil in place, improve water and nutrient retention in sandy soils, facilitate water and air movement in clay soils, attract earthworms and other beneficial critters, and suppress winter weeds. The most useful cover crop for home gardeners is one of these legumes: crimson clover; Austrian winter pea; rough pea; or common, smooth, or hairy vetch. They can be planted at least a month before the first killing frost, adding nitrogen as well as organic matter to the soil, and they are relatively inexpensive. Non-legume cover crops provide less nitrogen but more organic matter. These are mainly grasses like oats, buckwheat, rye, and barley, which are planted in late summer. In the spring, turn under your cover crop three weeks before planting your garden.

LAWNS

Lawns need air to breathe. When clay soil becomes compacted, closing up the air-filled spaces, the lawn declines. Compacted soil also reduces the movement of water and nutrients. Soon the grass weakens, making it less able to compete with weeds and slow to recuperate from injury. Eventually the lawn thins out, giving rise to goosegrass and prostrate knotweed—two notorious weeds that thrive in compacted soils. Make plans to help your lawn breathe easier this fall by aerifying your lawn.

The simplest and cheapest way is with a spading fork. Push the tines into the soil at least 4 inches and rock the fork back and forth, loosening the soil and making room for new grass roots. The only limitation is that as you are making a hole, you may be forcing soil particles around the hole closer together, causing more compaction.

■ *Aerating your lawn with a power-driven, hollow-tine core aerator removes plugs of soil from the lawn. The "pores," or holes, in the lawn increase the amount of air, water, and nutrients available to the roots.*

Larger lawns require a power-driven core aerator or aerifier, which can be rented at lawn-and-garden supply centers. These have spoon-shaped tines or hollow tubes. As the tubes are driven into the lawn, cores of soil are removed and strewn across the lawn. The holes that result increase air, water, and nutrient availability to roots.

Cool-season lawns should be aerified in the fall when there is less heat stress and danger of invasion by weedy annuals. Allow at least four weeks of good growing weather to help the plants recover. Warm-season lawns can be aerified in the spring.

PERENNIALS & ORNAMENTAL GRASSES

As late summer approaches and you feel as bedraggled as your garden, gain inspiration from fall-flowering perennials. Garden mums have long been the mainstay of the fall garden and are available in a wide array of heights, flower forms, and colors. But there's more than mums. Consider asters such as aster (*Aster* × *frikartii* 'Monch'), *Sedum* 'Autumn Fire', ironweed (*Vernonia noveboracensis*), Confederate hibiscus

■ *Asters make a colorful late-season addition to the garden.*

(*Hibiscus mutabilis*), Joe-pye weed (*Eupatorium purpureum*), goldenrod (*Solidago* 'Golden Thumb' and 'Peter Pan'), swamp sunflower (*Helianthus angustifolius*), Japanese anemone (*Anemone hupehensis*), *Salvia guaranitica*, and the tender Mexican sage (*Salvia leucantha*).

Ornamental grasses also make great choices for the fall and winter garden with their plumes of flowers and shimmering leaves. Some great choices include maidenhair grass (*Miscanthus sinensis* 'Morning Light'), pink muhly grass (*Muhlenbergia capillaris*), feather reed grass (*Calamagrostis × acutiflora* 'Karl Foerster'), and switch grass (*Panicum virgatum* 'Heavy Metal'). Learn more about these and other late-season flowering plants that will thrive in your corner of the Carolinas. Look for them in your garden center or mail-order/online catalogs, and plan to weave them into your landscape.

■ *Shredded leaves provide an excellent source of carbon, or "browns," in compost piles.*

ROSES

Order roses for delivery in December on the Coast, and early next year elsewhere. Select roses for their flowers, fragrance, and ability to withstand the rigors of summer heat and humidity. Disease resistance should be as important as the appearance of the plant.

SHRUBS

As summer's heat and humidity finally yield to the shorter, cooler days of autumn, visit those far corners of the garden that haven't seen a gardener's eye since the Fourth of July. Begin a wholesale evaluation of your landscape and make notes about tasks that need to be completed this month. Look for plants that may be in decline and will have to be replaced.

If you need some ideas for plants, look at the North Carolina Association of Nurserymen Plant Introduction Program. Along with the JC Raulston Arboretum, these plants have been selected for their outstanding landscape attributes and their adaptability to the southeast. Coastal Gardeners should consider the Lowcountry Gold Medal Plant Award Winners selected by the Charleston Horticultural Society. These plants are evaluated and chosen for their flowers, colorful leaves, pest resistance, and durability.

TREES

This fall recycle your fallen leaves into mulch or compost. For a fine-textured mulch, shred the leaves with a lawn mower or a leaf shredder. Finely cut leaves look more attractive and tend to stay where you put them.

To compost leaves, researchers recommend building piles at least 4 feet in diameter and 3 feet in height. To keep them manageable, make the piles no larger than 5 feet high and 10 feet wide. Compost leaves separately or add fresh vegetable peelings, grass clippings, or other kitchen or yard trimmings.

To speed up the composting process, shred the leaves before putting them into the pile. Avoid adding meat or grease, which may cause odors and attract pests. Pay particular attention to moisture and air. Keep the ingredients moist enough that you can squeeze water droplets from a handful of leaves. Aerate or supply air to the pile by turning the materials. During warm weather, turn the pile once a month; in cool weather, turn it less frequently to prevent too much heat from escaping. To convert the leaves to compost fairly quickly, add nitrogen to the pile. Add a nitrogen-containing fertilizer such as 10-10-10 or a natural substitute such as horse or cow manure, bloodmeal, or cottonseed meal. Mix this crumbly, earthy-smelling "black gold" into heavy clay soil to improve drainage and make the soil easier to cultivate. Compost helps sandy soils retain water and nutrients.

VINES & GROUNDCOVERS

For something completely different, grow well-behaved vines on some of your shrubs and trees. Draping vines on other plants allows you to create eye-catching combinations. Use flowers and leaves to create contrasting colors and textures, extending the flowering display of a tree with flowering vines, and dressing up otherwise boring plants with a feather boa of vines. Annual vines good for this purpose include black-eyed-Susan vine, love-in-a-puff, and moonvine. Some choice perennial vines are clematis, 'Tangerine Beauty' cross vine, potato vine (*Solanum jasminoides*), and hairy Virginia creeper (*Parthenocissus quinquefolia* var. *hirsuta*).

WATER GARDENS

Your water garden should blend harmoniously with the rest of your terrestrial plantings of trees, shrubs, perennials, annuals, groundcovers, and bulbs. Plan to grow some woody or perennial groundcovers about 3 to 4 feet from the edge of the water garden. As they grow and fill in, they'll create a natural look on the edge of the pool. Think about picking up some of the variegated colors of the aquatic plants and repeating the colors in a nearby flowerbed.

PLANT

ANNUALS

Plant seeds of California, Iceland, and Shirley poppies. Mountain gardeners can set out calendulas, pansies, and violas when they become available at local nurseries. Start setting out ornamental kale and cabbage for winter color. You will have to pull out some robust-looking annuals now or early next

month to make room for them. In the warmer areas of Zone 8, petunias, especially the species petunia (*P. integrifolia*) and those in the Wave series, can generally be left in place. They usually bounce back unperturbed after cold snaps and continue flowering.

Sowing seeds of hardy annuals (such as calendula, calliopsis, sweet alyssum, larkspur, and pinks) now will give the seedlings time to get established and develop good root systems before the coldest part of winter. This gives them a head start on growth and flowering next spring.

BULBS

Plant fall-blooming bulbs such as autumn crocus, autumn daffodil (*Sternbergia lutea*), fall-blooming crocus (*Crocus speciosus*), and nerine lily as soon as you receive them.

■ *Iceland poppy seeds can be planted now for a showy display in a month or two.*

HERE'S HOW

TO PLANT INDIVIDUAL BULBS

■ *Plant larger bulbs (bulbs the size of your closed fist) in individual holes. Use a trowel or soil knife to dig a hole that is four times as deep as the height of the bulb.*

■ *Place the bulb in the hole with the pointed end up. You don't need to put bonemeal or bloodmeal in the hole. In fact, bonemeal acts like a homing beacon to squirrels that would like nothing better than to dig up the bulbs, so skip it.*

■ *If you have several bulbs to plant, you'll be done faster (and you won't forget where you've already planted) if you set the bulbs out first, then plant each one. Don't be afraid to really pack the bulbs into the planting area. Dig the holes, plant them, cover the holes with soil, and top with mulch.*

■ *After planting all of the bulbs, water them in. Additional watering may be unnecessary unless the soil is extremely dry. We usually receive enough rain in late fall and winter to satisfy the bulbs' moisture requirements.*

Plant the summer-flowering madonna lily now or in early spring with no more than 1 inch of soil covering the "nose" of the bulb.

Plant lily bulbs soon after you receive them because they do not have a truly dormant period.

Prepare beds for spring-flowering bulbs as soon as possible. Cultivate the soil and add generous amounts of organic matter to improve drainage. Bulbs will rot without proper drainage.

EDIBLES

Pot up chives, parsley, and other herbs and bring them into the house to extend the growing season.

Take cuttings or buy small plants of rosemary, oregano, sage, and other herbs. Grow them in 6-inch containers in a sunny window. Keep well watered; if possible, set them in a shallow tray containing pebbles and water to increase humidity. Opening the window on mild days can help.

In the mild winter areas of the Piedmont and Coastal Plain, plant cilantro, a winter annual whose seeds are called coriander.

Plant beets, carrots, kale, lettuce, spinach, turnips, and radishes. Soak seed furrows well before sowing seed, and mulch lightly. Water daily to promote germination and growth.

All sorts of fall vegetables can go in right away, including transplants of leaf lettuce, Swiss chard, broccoli, Brussels sprouts, cauliflower, and cabbage.

Mountain gardeners can plant onion sets anytime this month. Gardeners in the Piedmont and Coastal Plain should wait until the next month or two when cooler weather prevails. Choose small, firm sets that are less than ¾ inch in diameter for bulb onions. Larger sets can be used for green onions, because they tend to "bolt" and produce a seedstalk instead of a bulb.

Sow onion seeds or set out transplants. Use short-day onions in South Carolina and intermediate and long-day types in North Carolina.

Contact your County Extension Center for recommended varieties.

Plant parsley and perennial herbs such as sage, thyme, and rosemary, and annual herbs like dill and coriander.

LAWNS

In the Piedmont and Mountains, seed thin, bare areas in cool-season lawns with a blend of at least two grass varieties.

Overseed warm-season lawns with cool-season perennial ryegrass (*Lolium perenne*) or annual ryegrass (*Lolium multiflorum*) to provide green color during the winter months after warm-season grasses are brown and dormant. Perennial ryegrass is more expensive but offers a higher-quality look. It's also more tolerant of cold, disease, and drought than annual ryegrass. These strengths allow perennial ryegrass to live longer than annual ryegrass, making it a burden in the spring when you want the warm-season lawn to overtake the ryegrass.

Never overseed turfgrasses in moderate to heavy shade—the ryegrass will survive and linger into

■ *Curly-leaf parsley is one of many herbs that can be planted in the fall. Its foliage contrasts well when interplanted with pansies and other violas.*

HERE'S HOW

TO OVERSEED A LAWN

1. Mow the lawn closely.

2. Use a power rake to remove excess thatch and open up the lawn for good seed-to-soil contact.

3. Use a rotary or drop-type spreader to apply 5 to 10 pounds of ryegrass seed per 1,000 square feet. Sow half the seed in one direction, the other half at right angles to the first.

4. After seeding, rake the ground with a stiff broom or rake to make sure the seed is in contact with the soil. Follow up by "topdressing" (applying a shallow layer) with compost.

5. Water the lawn lightly two or three times a day until the seeds germinate.

6. When the lawn becomes established, water only when necessary.

7. After the second mowing, fertilize with 1 pound of nitrogen per 1,000 square feet, using a complete fertilizer, such as 16-4-8.

■ *Drag a leaf rake upside down over the surface to rake in the seeds.*

summer, competing with the turf awakening from dormancy, resulting in a thinned-out lawn easily invaded by weeds.

Overseeding is best done on a lush, healthy lawn. The best time is two or three weeks before the expected first frost or when the soil temperature drops below 75 degrees Fahrenheit. Bermudagrass lawns tolerate overseeding better than centipedegrass, St. Augustinegrass, or zoysiagrass.

PERENNIALS & ORNAMENTAL GRASSES

Establish new perennial flowerbeds: dig, divide, and replant overcrowded beds of beebalm, daylilies, cheddar pinks, Shasta daisies, and threadleaf coreopsis. Spread a liberal amount of organic matter over the area and mix it into the soil at least 6 to 8 inches deep. Space divisions at least 1 foot apart in all directions so that root competition will not be a problem for several years.

■ *Use lime, chalk, or flour to outline your new garden bed.*

■ *Once you have determined the space for your new garden bed, the next step is to remove the existing turf with a sod cutter.*

Plant cool-season ornamental grasses now to take advantage of the cool temperatures, allowing the roots to become established before spring's burst of growth.

Astilbe is not a long-lived perennial, so divide it every three or four years to maintain its vigor. When replanting divisions, leave three or four "eyes" in each section, and replant so the eyes are about ½ inch below the soil surface.

Now is the time to move perennial plants started from seed in midsummer to the home nursery row or to their permanent spot in the garden. Follow these general guidelines for spacing plants. Small plants under 1 foot tall or front-of-the-border plants should be spaced about 12 to 18 inches apart; plants of intermediate size (1 to 2½ feet tall) should be placed at least 18 to 24 inches apart (three or four plants per 10 square feet); and larger plants should be spaced roughly 3 feet apart.

ROSES

It is a good time to plant roses. Look for roses that you can purchase as replacements, or other good roses that deserve to be in your garden.

Continue tying up the canes of climbing roses, securing them sideways to encourage horizontal growth.

SHRUBS, TREES, AND VINES & GROUNDCOVERS

Fall is the prime-time planting season. Select healthy container-grown or balled-and-burlapped shrubs and plant them properly in the right location in your landscape.

Mountain gardeners can also plant container-grown vines and groundcovers this month. Water the plants well following planting and until they become established. It's a good time to transplant groundcovers to fill in bare areas. Some groundcovers such as euonymus and English ivy already have visible roots. Prune a stem and bury the shoots. Roots will form and you can start another groundcover bed.

Piedmont and Coastal Plain gardeners can wait until next month when the cooler temperatures make planting more enjoyable.

CARE

ANNUALS

Take cuttings of your annual plants to bring indoors to carry through the winter. Coleus, geranium, impatiens, wax begonia, and others do best when stem cuttings are rooted and kept in pots indoors during cold weather. Be sure to place pots where they receive plenty of light and cool temperatures.

Trim back leggy annuals and continue removing faded flowers to encourage more blooms.

BULBS

If you cannot plant bulbs right away, store them in a cool (60 to 65 degrees Fahrenheit) location to prevent them from drying out before planting. Temperatures higher than 70 degrees Fahrenheit

HERE'S HOW

TO PLANT A CONTAINER-GROWN TREE

1. Dig a hole no deeper than the depth of the root ball but at least twice as wide, preferably three or four times wider.

2. Place the plant in the hole and adjust the hole depth so that the plant is about 1 inch higher than it was planted in the nursery to allow for settling of soil. Use a shovel handle laid across the hole to help determine the proper depth.

3. Shovel in the soil around the root ball, stopping to tamp down the soil when the hole is half full. Continue filling the rest of the hole with loose soil and tamp down again to ensure good contact between the soil and the roots.

4. Soak the planting area with water. Once the soil has settled, build up a 2- to 3-inch basin around the plant to catch rainfall and irrigation water. However, do not build a basin if your soil is very heavy and doesn't drain well.

5. Apply 2 to 3 inches of organic mulch such as shredded bark or wood chips, keeping the mulch a few inches away from the trunk.

can damage the flowers inside spring-flowering bulbs. They can be stored in ventilated bags but not in paper or plastic bags unless specified. Because rhizomes, tubers, and tuberous roots dry out faster than bulbs and corms, store them in peat, perlite, or vermiculite.

Bulbs can be stored for several weeks in a cool place (35 to 55 degrees Fahrenheit) such as a refrigerator. Vegetable crisper drawers can be used, but avoid storing bulbs in the same drawer as ripening fruit or vegetables, which give off ethylene, a gas that can cause problems with flowering. Because some bulbs are poisonous, this storage method is not recommended for households with young children.

Mountain gardeners should dig and store caladium bulbs before frost.

EDIBLES

Harvest herbs to dry for winter use. Freeze chives. Take cuttings for a windowsill garden.

Start drying herbs such as basil, oregano, sage, summer savory, and tarragon. Alternatively, use your microwave oven to dry herbs. Heat them between paper towels for one minute or until

■ *Harvest luffa gourds when they begin to turn brown, feel light and dry, and rattle when shaken. Let any that remain after the first killing freeze dry on the vine.*

HERE'S HOW

TO STORE CALADIUM BULBS

1. Lift the tubers from the ground before frost. Shake the soil from the tubers and leave them in a sunny location to dry for seven to ten days. If rain or frost is forecast, move the tubers indoors temporarily. After this drying period, pluck off the withered leaves from the tuber and brush off any remaining soil.

2. Store the tubers over the winter in a box or basket filled with dried vermiculite or perlite. Place the container where the temperature will not drop below 60 degrees Fahrenheit.

3. Next spring, plant the tubers in the garden when the soil temperature rises to 70 degrees Fahrenheit.

leaves are crisp. They'll keep their color and flavor stored in the dark in jars.

Dig sweet potatoes before frost, being careful to avoid bruises and scrapes. Cure them for two or three weeks in the warmest room in the house to toughen the skin. Then store them where it is cool and dark. Every two weeks, cull out any showing signs of decay.

Harvest luffa gourds when they begin to turn brown, feel light and dry, and rattle when shaken. Let any that remain after the first killing freeze dry on the vine. To make useful, biodegradable scrubbers for you and your pots and pans, prepare the luffa:

- Soak in warm water until the sponge can be slipped out of the skin.

- Whiten sponges by dipping them into a 10 percent solution of household bleach.

- After thorough drying, store them in mesh bags.

- Discard worn-out sponges in your compost pile.

Harvest winter squash and pumpkins when fully mature but before they are damaged by frost. Cut the fruits from the vine, leaving a short piece of stem attached. They will keep for several months in a cool, dry basement.

Harvest garlic when the tops die. Cure the bulbs for six weeks in a warm, dry, shady, airy place, then move them to a cool, dry, airy spot.

After mid-month, pinch new blossoms off tomatoes, peppers, and eggplants to help smaller fruits mature before cold weather.

Tomatoes won't ripen when average daily temperatures fall below 65 degrees Fahrenheit. Then is the time to nip off all blossoms so plant nutrients flow to tomatoes already set. Not all green tomatoes ripen off the vine to an acceptable taste. Rescue from frost for later ripening only those showing a white or yellow star or a pink tinge at the blossom end. Delay ripening by storing at 50 to 60 degrees Fahrenheit. Light is not needed, so put them where you can keep an eye on them.

LAWNS

Don't retire the lawn mower—as long as the grass grows, it should be mowed.

PERENNIALS & ORNAMENTAL GRASSES

Pull out stakes and remove cages as plants finish for the year. Clean the stakes and cages and store them where you can locate them next spring.

Deadhead silvermound artemisia (*Artemisia schmidtiana* 'Nana') to remove the flowers. It tends to decline after flowering, so channeling the plant's energy to the leaves will prevent it from self-destructing.

ROSES

Roses in the Piedmont and Coast areas can be deadheaded and pruned to encourage new growth now that the cooler temperatures of fall are on the way. In the Mountains, stop deadheading roses so the seedpods, or rose hips, will mature. Instead, hand-pluck faded petals from the hip. The colorful hips add an attractive feature to the winter garden. Producing them also encourages the rose to focus its energy on "hardening off" in anticipation of winter dormancy.

SHRUBS, TREES, AND VINES & GROUNDCOVERS

As the leaves fall, rake them up, shred them, and use them as mulch.

Prune out only branches that are dead, diseased, or broken. Hold off on major pruning such as rejuvenation until late winter. Pruning now will only stimulate tender, new growth, which can be killed by our first freeze. A certified arborist should repair any storm damage to large trees.

Wait until next year to prune your crapemyrtles. Research shows that late-summer, fall, and early-winter pruning may predispose woody ornamental plants, especially crapemyrtles, to cold injury. Delay pruning until late winter or early spring before bud-break.

WATER GARDENS

Before freezing weather arrives, bring tender marginals and others indoors, where you will store them. Continue to trim spent flowers and foliage that has matured on your marginals. Clean up any leaves that may have sloughed off into the pond, and compost them.

WATER

ANNUALS, PERENNIALS & ORNAMENTAL GRASSES, AND ROSES

Fall is the driest season in the Carolinas. Keep newly set-out transplants well watered to help them establish quickly.

BULBS, SHRUBS, TREES, AND VINES & GROUNDCOVERS

September and October tend to be dry months in the Carolinas. Continue watering regularly, especially new plantings until they become established. Check moisture in the rootball prior to watering.

EDIBLES

Keep watering. Many crops, such as corn, pepper, squash, and tomato, won't mature nicely if stressed due to lack of water.

LAWNS

Water the lawn if necessary.

WATER GARDENS

Maintain the water level in the pond.

FERTILIZE

ANNUALS

Apply a slow-release fertilizer when planting cool-season annuals.

BULBS

It's not necessary to fertilize newly planted spring-flowering bulbs if they're going to be treated like annuals for one season of bloom. The bulbs can grow and bloom without any additional nutrients.

If you want your bulbs to naturalize or perennialize, fertilize newly planted spring-flowering bulbs with a slow-release fertilizer. Instead of making one annual application of a controlled-release fertilizer, apply a fast-release fertilizer at planting and a second application the following spring when the new shoots emerge. Water after fertilizing to make nutrients available to the roots.

Winter-blooming bulbs such as cyclamen and crocus do not have to be fertilized in most well-prepared garden soils. A light topdressing, however, with a balanced fertilizer such as 10-10-10 will encourage abundant blooms and keep corms healthy.

EDIBLES

Apply fertilizer to vegetables as needed.

LAWNS

Do not fertilize warm-season grasses at this time. Heavy amounts of nitrogen can predispose them to winterkill. Often potassium is recommended for winter hardiness and drought tolerance.

Fertilize Kentucky bluegrass or tall fescue according to a soil test. In the absence of soil-test recommendations, use a 3:1:2 analysis (such as 12-4-8 or 16-4-8) fertilizer where one-fourth to one-half of the nitrogen is slowly available (look for "water-insoluble nitrogen" or "slowly available nitrogen" on the label). Apply ½ or 1 pound of nitrogen per 1,000 square feet of lawn. If you accidentally spread fertilizer on the sidewalk, driveway, or road, sweep it up and return it to the lawn.

PERENNIALS & ORNAMENTAL GRASSES

Fertilizing is not necessary this late in the season. Allow the perennials to go dormant.

ROSES

Stop fertilizing roses six weeks before the average first freeze date in your area to allow the new growth to harden off, preparing the roses for their winter rest.

If you didn't do so last month, Piedmont and Coastal gardeners can fertilize everblooming roses with a fast-release fertilizer, if necessary. Water

■ *Mountain gardeners with cool-season Kentucky bluegrass lawns should fertilize them in the fall based on soil-test recommendations.*

afterward to make the nutrients available to the roses.

SHRUBS AND TREES

If your shrubs and trees have produced sufficient growth this year, fertilizing may not be necessary. If you choose to fertilize, rely on soil test results to apply the nutrients required by your shrubs and trees.

For blue flowers on your French hydrangeas, maintain a soil pH between 5 and 5.5. Apply aluminum sulfate or sulfur to reduce the pH to this ideal range. To avoid having to adjust the pH, grow a blue-flowered hydrangea such as 'All Summer Beauty', 'Blue Wave', or 'Nikko Blue'.

VINES & GROUNDCOVERS

If your vines and groundcovers have produced sufficient growth this year, fertilizing may not be necessary. If you choose to fertilize, rely on soil test results to apply the nutrients required by your plants. If they are showing their fall colors, wait until next year.

WATER GARDENS

As the water temperature cools, the plants will cease growth and begin to go dormant. They do not have to be fertilized.

PROBLEM-SOLVE

ANNUALS

Discouraged by powdery mildew on your zinnias? This late in the season, fungicides may not be warranted. Zinnias will soon be removed to make way for cool-season annuals. Make a note in your gardening journal to select mildew-resistant zinnias next year.

Check for evidence of snails and slugs. Set out baits or traps for them as the weather turns cooler and wetter. Look for silvery slime trails and irregularly shaped holes in the leaves, which are the most characteristic signs of slugs. A close inspection of plants at night, early in the morning, or on cloudy, wet days is the best way to catch slugs feeding.

Do not turn your back on the weeds in your flowerbeds. Summer annual weeds like crabgrass and goosegrass have matured and are going to seed. Winter annual weeds like annual bluegrass, chickweed, and Carolina geranium are germinating. Hoe them out or handpull them now.

BULBS

Aphids and spider mites may still be active. Evaluate the extent of injury and decide if pest control measures are warranted. Use a water wand on a weekly basis, preferably early in the morning, to wash mites from plants.

Clean up dead, fallen leaves. They can harbor disease and insect pests over the winter if allowed to remain on the ground.

Handpull any young winter annuals, or cover them with a shallow layer of compost. Weeding is never fun, but the cooler temperatures can make it more bearable.

Voles, rabbits, and deer relish many kinds of flower bulbs, such as crocuses and tulips. To protect bulbs from voles, cover the bulbs with heavy wire mesh screening that allows the shoots to grow through.

■ *A pit-fall trap baited with beer must be filled and emptied regularly.*

Dig down about 10 to 12 inches and spread the ½-inch mesh across the bottom, up the sides, and over the top. A simpler technique that offers less protection is to spread a handful of sharp crushed gravel around the bulbs at planting.

EDIBLES
Cucumber beetles, squash bugs, Colorado potato beetles, and European corn borers pass the winter in garden debris. Compost or plow under dead plants. This will limit your pest population next year to insects that migrate into the garden.

LAWNS
Sample several damaged areas to get an average number of white grubs per square foot to decide if control is necessary. Lawns can tolerate lower or higher numbers of grubs, depending on the health of the lawn and the kind of grub. Submit the grubs to your Cooperative Extension Service office for identification to help you decide if an insecticide is warranted.

Scout for adult mole crickets in the Coastal Plain and treat if necessary. Examine the yellowish to brownish spots in your St. Augustinegrass lawn for chinch bugs. Use the coffee can technique (see May, Problem-Solve) to sample for them at the edge of the damaged area.

Dollar spot or brown patch may be present. Refer to April and June, Probem-Solve sections, to learn how to manage these fungal diseases.

If annual bluegrass (*Poa annua*) and other winter annuals have been a problem, apply a pre-emergent herbicide to control the germinating seeds before they appear. Annual bluegrass germinates in late summer and early fall when temperatures drop consistently into the mid-70s. A pre-emergent herbicide forms a barrier at or just below the soil surface and kills the emerging seedlings. Look for annual bluegrass in shady or moist areas.

PERENNIALS & ORNAMENTAL GRASSES
Handpick slugs and drop them into soapy water. Setting out an inverted clay pot, board, or grape-fruit rind near favorite plants will give the slugs a

place to congregate. Pit-fall traps baited with beer or a simple mix of sugar water and yeast attract and drown the slugs. More effective are strips of copper foil (Snail-Barr) or even copper screen attached to the edges of pots, raised beds, and tree trunks. Poison baits containing iron phosphate (Sluggo®) are also effective.

Finally, because slugs prefer moist conditions, eliminating trash and other debris in the garden, limiting irrigation, and delaying mulching until seedlings have grown larger will reduce problems with slugs.

Remove infected leaves and clean up fallen leaves and discard them. Fungicides may not be warranted this late in the season. Make a note in your gardening journal about varieties that were highly susceptible to powdery mildew, and consider replacing them with more resistant cultivars next year. Powdery mildew-resistant garden phlox cultivars include: 'Bright Eyes', 'David', 'Eva Cullum', 'Franz Schubert', 'Natascha', 'Robert Poore', and 'Starfire'. The following beebalm cultivars are less prone to infection by powdery mildew: 'Claire Grace', 'Colrain Red', 'Elsie's Lavender', 'Jacob Cline', 'Vintage Wine', 'Raspberry Wine', and 'Marshall's Delight'.

Don't turn your back on the weeds in your flowerbeds. Summer annual weeds like crabgrass and goosegrass have matured and are going to seed. Winter annual weeds like annual bluegrass, chickweed, and Carolina geranium are germinating. Hoe them out or handpull them now.

ROSES

Rose aphids and spider mites may still be active. Evaluate the extent of injury and decide if pest control measures are warranted. Use a water wand to wash mites off plants weekly, preferably early in the morning.

Clean up fallen rose leaves. They can harbor diseases and insect pests over the winter if allowed to remain on the ground. Keep the rose plants clean and the area around their feet tidy and free of debris. During the growing season, pick up and remove fallen leaves

Keep the area around the roses free of weeds to eliminate any overwintering hideouts for two-spotted spider mites.

SHRUBS

Aphids and spider mites may still be active. Evaluate the extent of injury and decide if pest control measures are warranted. Use a water wand to wash mites off plants on a weekly basis, preferably early in the morning.

Clean up fallen leaves, which can harbor disease and insect pests over the winter if allowed to remain on the ground.

Don't turn your back on the weeds in your shrub beds. Summer annual weeds like crabgrass and goosegrass have matured and are going to seed. Winter annual weeds like annual bluegrass, chickweed, and Carolina geranium are germinating. Hoe them out or handpull them now.

Rabbits and deer can be a problem. Various commercially available mammal repellents can be applied to your shrubs. See October, Problem-Solve for a homemade repellent recipe.

TREES

Fall webworm is a North American native insect that attacks more than 100 species of deciduous trees and shrubs. Unlike the eastern tent caterpillar, which constructs similar nests, the fall webworm does not become conspicuous until late summer and early fall. Two generations hatch each year, the second being more conspicuous.

Fall webworms are a cosmetic nuisance. The defoliation typically involves only a few branches and occurs late in the season (by which time the tree is ready to shed its leaves naturally).

In most years, a large number of natural predators and parasitoids keep fall webworms in check. The bacterial insecticide *Bacillus thuringiensis* (*B.t.*) can be applied in June when the caterpillars are small and sprayed onto leaves next to the nest, on which the caterpillars will soon feed. Nests that are easy to reach can be pruned off or torn apart with a stick and the caterpillars dislodged with a strong stream of water. The simplest course of action, however, is to do nothing in the confidence that the fall web-worms aren't doing your plants any real harm.

Root rot caused by Phytophthora, which means "plant destroyer," attacks a wide variety of plants, including dogwood, deodar cedar, Fraser fir, white pine, and many others. Look for wilted, dying plants. Scrape the bark near the crown and look for a reddish brown discoloration where the fungus has moved into the stem. These fungi are often found in wet or poorly drained sites. They'll attack plants in moderate to dry sites if they're planted too deeply. Overwatering plants in moderate to dry sites also favors these fungi. When symptoms are evident, fungicides are often ineffective in controlling this disease. See August, Problem-Solve.

Prepare now to protect your trees from deer and rodents. Protect trees from deer with fencing or repellents. Rabbits can be deterred by installing wire or plastic guards around the trunks of young shade trees and fruit trees. To discourage voles, pull the mulch away from the trunk about a foot.

Rabbits and voles will feed on the thin bark of young trees. To protect trees, shrubs, and ornamentals, use hardware cloth cylinders to keep voles away. First use a shovel to cut the ground around the plant just enough to insert a wire cylinder. Then add the hardware cloth. The bottom edge of the cylinder should be buried at least 6 inches below the ground. If kept in place permanently, the mesh will girdle the tree's roots. To avoid injury, remove it after one or two years or bury it further away from the trunk without harming the feeder roots.

VINES & GROUNDCOVERS

Aphids and spider mites may still be active. Evaluate the extent of injury and decide if pest control measures are warranted.

Clean up fallen leaves. They can harbor diseases and insect pests over the winter if allowed to remain on the ground.

Watch out for germinating winter annuals such as annual bluegrass, chickweed, and henbit. Remove them now while they're young and easy to remove. Don't wait until spring when they'll be well established and poised to go to seed.

WATER GARDENS

Trim away any damaged, dead, diseased, or pest-ridden leaves. Compost them or bring them into the garden to be buried to enrich the soil.

■ *To protect young trees from rabbits and rodents, place a cylinder of ¼-inch mesh hardware cloth around the trunk. The cylinder should extend 18 to 24 inches above the soil and 6 inches belowground.*

October

It has become an autumn ritual for me when I saddle up my white steed with plastic trash bags and a short-handled rake and become the "Leaf Ranger." I drive through subdivisions and neighborhoods in search of fallen leaves, determined to recycle them back into gardens and landscapes. Unlike the Lone Ranger, I have no faithful companion like Tonto by my side. I don't have any room for him or anyone else in my hatchback. It's just me and as many bags of leaves that I can fit into my car without hampering my ability to drive.

The leaves I acquire end up as mulch or compost. For that coarse-textured look, mulch with leaves right out of the bag. For a finer-textured look, shred the leaves with a lawn mower or a leaf shredder. Finely cut leaves look more attractive and tend to stay where you put them.

To compost leaves, build piles at least 4 feet in diameter and 3 feet in height. To keep the piles to a manageable size, make them no larger than 5 feet high and 10 feet wide. You can compost leaves by themselves, or add fresh vegetable peelings, grass clippings, or other kitchen or yard trimmings. To speed-up the composting process, shred the leaves before putting them into the pile. Be sure to avoid adding meat or grease, which may cause odors and attract pests.

To create compost quickly, keep the ingredients moist enough so you can squeeze water droplets from a handful of leaves. Aerate or supply air to the pile by turning the materials.

In 4 to 9 months your compost should be ready. Amend your soil with this crumbly, earthy-smelling "black gold." Compost supplies very small amounts of plant nutrients and trace elements needed for plant growth. It also attracts and feeds earthworms and other beneficial soil microorganisms.

Compost makes an attractive mulch. A 2- to 3 inch layer around shrubs and trees, vegetable gardens, or flowerbeds will help suppress weeds, conserve soil moisture, and keep the soil cool during the summer months. According to research findings, mulch promotes faster growth of trees and shrubs than does grass or groundcovers.

So, if some early weekend morning you happen to hear a "Hi yo' Silver," rest assured that the leaves in your neighborhood will be recycled by the Leaf Ranger.

PLAN

ANNUALS

With the onset of cooler temperatures, begin planning new beds or converting the beds to new plantings of perennials or shrubs. Refer to your journal to guide your decisions to expand your beds, reduce them, or add different kinds of plants. Start making lists of the plants you will need. You will be ready when catalogs arrive in the next couple of months.

To help you design new beds, use a garden hose to outline the shape. Enrich the soil with organic matter. Take a soil sample and send it in for testing.

BULBS

Though not as famous as "major" bulbs like daffodils, hyacinths, and tulips, "minor" spring-flowering bulbs such as crocus, cyclamen, Dutch iris, snowdrops, and winter aconite are quite easy to grow and can be used in a variety of landscape situations:

- Plant them beneath the rising stems of tulips and daffodils to highlight the color and forms of their taller brethren.

- Interplant early-spring-flowering crocuses with groundcovers such as vinca.

- Plant anemones, grape hyacinths, or crocus *en masse* in borders.

- Plant them as a focal point for a perennial border or mixed planting with shrubs. Eye-catchers include giant onion (*Allium giganteum*), with its towering purple globe-shaped flower heads, and crown imperial (*Fritillaria imperialis*), with pendulous flowers topped by a pineapple-shaped crown.

EDIBLES

Envision an indoor winter herb garden. Most herbs do very well on a south-facing windowsill. Sweet basil, lemon verbena, summer savory, and tarragon are the exceptions. They either go dormant or shed their leaves excessively.

Oregano, thyme, parsley, and sage can all be grown in small pots and trimmed as needed for the kitchen. Pots of rosemary and sweet bay (*Laurus nobilis*) are equally valuable, though they need more space.

■ *Plant crocus bulbs en masse for a showy display next spring.*

■ *Marjoram, rosemary, and lemon balm grow nicely in pots inside the house on a south-facing windowsill.*

In the onion family, windowsill candidates include chives, onion sets, and garlic. The onions and garlic can be started in pots.

If you have only an east- or west-facing windowsill, try mints such as peppermint, spearmint, or lemon balm. Provided they are sheared regularly, these make excellent houseplants.

If you find you have insect pests, it's best to discard infested plants rather than use pesticides indoors.

Indoor herbs grow best in a mixture of two parts potting soil to one part coarse sand or perlite. Setting the pots in trays lined with gravel will keep them from getting wet feet should you overwater. Cool temperatures (60 degrees Fahrenheit), especially at night, will keep herbs at their best.

LAWNS

As you rake up the fallen leaves from your lawn, recycle them as mulch or compost. For a fine-textured mulch, shred the leaves with a lawn mower or a leaf shredder. Finely cut leaves look more attractive and tend to stay where you put them.

To compost leaves, researchers recommend building piles at least 4 feet in diameter and 3 feet high. To keep the piles a manageable size, make them no larger than 5 feet high and 10 feet wide.

Compost leaves by themselves or add fresh vegetable peelings, grass clippings, or other kitchen or yard trimmings.

PERENNIALS & ORNAMENTAL GRASSES

With the onset of cooler temperatures, expand old beds, create new ones, or rearrange plants. When starting new beds, have the soil tested through your Cooperative Extension Service office. Test old flowerbeds every three years.

ROSES

Identify beds whose soil needs to be tested. Soil testing is best done every two or three years.

■ *Roses in Mountain gardens benefit from an insulating blanket of soil or mulch for winter protection.*

Sasanqua camellias herald the beginning of camellia season with a profusion of fall flowers.

Contact your Cooperative Extension Service office for soil-testing materials. You can take samples this month or wait until the cooler fall weather arrives. This is also a good month to think about creating new beds, keeping in mind the three basic requirements of roses: 1) six hours of direct sunlight per day; 2) a well-drained, fertile location; and 3) room to grow.

Mountain gardeners who live where the temperatures reach 10 degrees Fahrenheit should plan to put their roses to sleep under protective blankets of soil or mulch. This will insulate them from freezing temperatures and the seesaw weather patterns of winter, which can tease a dormant bud into waking up too early. Find and stockpile dry mulching materials such as wood chips, shredded leaves, and evergreen branches.

SHRUBS

Late-season flowering plants could be considered the "Rodney Dangerfields" of the plant kingdom. They don't get any respect. How can they? During the spring months when winter-starved gardeners are looking for a floral feast, they skip over these late bloomers for the sumptuous flowers of azaleas and a multitude of other spring bloomers. "You're doomed without blooms" is the credo of plant merchandisers.

Even when they reach their peak in late summer and fall, late-season flowering plants still go unappreciated. At this time of year, deciduous shrubs are sporting their fall colors. But give these late-summer treats a second look: holly tea olive (*Osmanthus heterophyllus*), Fortune's osmanthus (*Osmanthus × fortunei*), fragrant tea olive (*Osmanthus fragans*), senna (*Cassia corymbosa*), sasanqua camellia, and tea-oil camellia are standard fare. Japanese fatsia (*Fatsia japonica*) is another fall-flowering choice. Learn more about these and other late-season flowering plants that will thrive in your corner of the Carolinas.

TREES

Deciduous trees light up the autumn skies with an assortment of fiery reds, oranges, and yellows. These colors result from the interaction of several pigments, including yellow xanthophylls, orange carotenoids, and red anthocyanins. The anthocyanins are manufactured by the conversion of sugars in the fall; the other pigments have been there all along but are not visible until the masking green chlorophyll has disappeared.

Okay, so maybe it's not that important to know where these brilliant colors came from. But it's good to know the names and cultivars of trees whose fall color would make an important addition to your landscape.

VINES & GROUNDCOVERS

If you have a slope whose steepness makes mowing a dangerous gardening activity, plan a few low-maintenance solutions:

1. Plant groundcovers on the existing slope. Some good slope-stabilizers include Asian star jasmine, daylily, English ivy, juniper, liriope, periwinkle (*Vinca minor*), willowleaf cotoneaster, and winter jasmine (*Jasminum nudiflorum*). Be sure to choose hardy groundcovers adapted to your region and match their preferences for sunlight or shade with the site.

2. On very steep slopes, build a retaining wall to reduce the height of the slope. Above and below the wall create usable gardening space. If the wall is less than 1½ feet in height, it could be a do-it-yourself project.

3. Long and steep slopes can be terraced with a series of walls to create several layers of gardening space.

WATER GARDENS

Make plans this month to evaluate the plants in your water garden and decide whether you're going to save questionable plants: those that have become too invasive for your garden, some that looked shabby all season long, and tender plants that will have to be overwintered indoors. Some gardeners treat tender floating-leaved and marginal plants like annuals and replace them. But if you want to save your tropical water lilies, plan to find some room indoors.

PLANT

ANNUALS

In the Piedmont and Coastal Plains, sow seeds of calliopsis, foxglove, Johnny-jump-ups, larkspur, money plant, stock, and Shirley, Iceland, and California poppies directly into well-prepared garden soil before the first expected freeze. These plants need cool temperatures to germinate. Fall sowing tends to produce stronger plants than seeds sown in early spring. Leave the soil surface bare or use a very light mulch.

Plant ornamental cabbage and kale, pansies, and violas to help them get established quickly before cold weather sets in. Allow at least six weeks before the first expected freeze. Mulch pansies in the Mountains after the ground freezes. Now is also a good time to set out calendula, dianthus, sweet William, snapdragons, stock, and sweet alyssum before the night temperatures drop consistently below 40 degrees Fahrenheit.

BULBS

Spring-flowering bulbs require an extended cold period to bloom reliably. When bulbs do not receive sufficient weeks of cold treatment (usually in the warm Coastal areas of Zone 8b), they produce flowers close to the ground on shortened stalks, often hidden by the leaves. Coastal gardeners can purchase precooled tulips and other spring-flowering bulbs. Alternatively, chill them yourself by storing them in an old refrigerator for a minimum of ten weeks (and up to sixteen weeks) prior to planting in December or January. After chilling, plant the cooled bulbs immediately.

Interplant spring-flowering bulbs with your groundcovers for splashes of color next year.

EDIBLES

Chives, cilantro, dill, and parsley can be direct-sown in the fall in the milder areas of the Piedmont and Coastal Plain so they will grow during the fall and winter months.

Piedmont and Coastal Plain gardeners can divide chives, thyme, mint, and tarragon when new growth emerges.

Plant garlic now for harvest in late summer next year. It likes a sunny, well-drained spot. Set bulb tips 2 inches beneath the surface.

Most herbs have lost their best flavor by now; discontinue drying for winter use. Chives and parsley, however, taste better than ever in cool weather; use them lavishly. (French cooks mince fresh chives and parsley together and let diners spoon desired amounts onto fresh vegetables or baked potatoes. The flavors complement each other and parsley cuts the oniony aftertaste of chives.)

Extend the gardening season well into the winter. Lettuce, radish, and spinach can all be grown in cold frames. Piedmont and Mountain gardeners might consider buying transplants for quicker results. In cooler weather, insulate the outsides of the frame with banked soil or sawdust. Cover the top with sacks stuffed with straw or other insulation during cold nights.

Plant onion sets and garlic cloves now to mid-November in the Coastal Plain. Plant spinach in October to do well this fall and winter.

■ *Woodland ferns like this native cinnamon fern* (Osmunda cinnamomea) *prefer a moist, shaded, humus-rich location.*

LAWNS

In the Piedmont there's still time to reseed bare areas of a cool-season lawn or start a new one, but hurry. Try to get it completed by mid-month.

If you want to overseed your warm-season lawn with ryegrass in the Coastal Plain, start working on it early this month.

PERENNIALS & ORNAMENTAL GRASSES

Herbaceous peonies can remain undisturbed for many years. When they become overcrowded, however, and blooms are few and far between, they will have to be divided. Divide them when the leaves and shoots are killed by frost. Mountain gardeners should be aware that peonies need six to eight weeks to develop roots before the ground freezes.

Ferns can be planted or transplanted in fall. Hardy ferns are best divided in early fall or very early spring before new growth emerges. Ferns such as hay-scented fern (*Dennstaedtia punctilobula*) and ostrich fern (*Matteuccia struthiopteris*) have branching rhizomes on or near the soil surface. These can simply be cut; make sure, however, that you have a growing tip and one or two intact fronds. Replant the divisions at the same level.

Other species such as cinnamon fern (*Osmunda cinnamomea*) develop a tangle of rhizomes and roots—you will have to dig up the whole clump and do your best to separate individual plants. Occasionally ferns develop multiple crowns that can be cut apart. The important thing is not to cover the crowns of the new transplants with more than ½ inch of soil, and to keep them well watered until they are established. A shallow layer of mulch throughout the growing season will help retain moisture in the soil.

There's still time to dig, divide, and replant crowded perennials. In the higher Mountain elevations, wait until spring, as winter may kill the young divisions before they have time to become established. Look for perennials that have grown out-of-bounds or have declined due to overcrowding and have developed a ring of growth with an empty center.

HERE'S HOW

TO DIVIDE PERENNIALS

1 *Dig up the plant that you want to divide. Dig all the way around the plant clump, about 4 inches away from the edge of the plant. If you water the plants you're planning to dig up and divide the night before you're dividing them, they'll be easier to dig up.*

2 *Divide the plant with either a spade or two gardening forks. Garden forks work well for plants like daylilies because they have relatively small roots. Hostas have large roots, and ornamental grasses are often so dense that it is impossible to pry pieces of the plant apart with the forks, so you might have to use a spade to chop the plant apart.*

When using a spade, put the spade in the center of the plant clump and chop the clump in half. Plants are tougher than you think, so don't worry about hurting them. Sharpen the spade before chopping—you'll be glad you did!

3 *To divide with two forks, put the forks back to back in the center of the plant clump, push both down, and pry apart.*

Replant the divided halves immediately, or put them in pots or plastic bags, and give them to friends. Plants that have been divided shouldn't be left out of the ground for more than a day. The tiny root hairs on their roots (which soak up most of the water a plant uses) have been disturbed, and the plants need to get back in the ground to grow new ones.

ROSES, SHRUBS, TREES, AND VINES & GROUNDCOVERS

Fall is a perfect season for planting in the Carolinas. Gardeners in the Coastal Plain and in the milder parts of the Piedmont can even plant throughout late fall and into winter. The cooler temperatures allow the plants to settle in comfortably and concentrate on producing roots.

Now is a good time to move roses and shrubs that have outgrown their location. Shrubs normally transplant more readily than trees. Small plants transplant more successfully than do large ones of the same species. Piedmont and Coastal gardeners can postpone moves until next month or December, depending on how mild the temperatures are. Mountain gardeners should be mindful of this transplanting rule-of-thumb: allow at least four weeks of soil temperatures above 40 degrees Fahrenheit after planting to give the shrubs some time to settle in before cold winter temperatures.

VINES & GROUNDCOVERS

When planting a groundcover on a steep slope, reduce the need for handweeding by using a geotextile or landscape fabric, which will curb weed growth. Follow these steps for installing landscape fabric.

HERE'S HOW

TO PLANT ON A SLOPE USING LANDSCAPE FABRIC

1. Kill the existing vegetation with a clear plastic sheet or a nonselective herbicide.

2. When the vegetation has been killed, lay down the fabric, making sure you overlap the pieces of fabric and tack them down tightly with U-shaped nails.

3. Place the potted groundcovers on top of the fabric in staggered rows. Stagger the plants across the slope to reduce the occurrence of soil erosion from water runoff (and to keep them from looking like rows of soldiers when you're finished).

4. Cut an "x" through the fabric and dig a planting hole. Avoid spilling any soil on top of the fabric because it may contain weed seeds.

5. Fold the "x" back down after planting. Try to avoid leaving any large gaps, which can be invaded by weeds.

6. Apply a 2- to 3-inch layer of pine straw over the fabric.

CARE

ANNUALS

Piedmont and Coastal Plain gardeners can pull up frost-tender plants like marigolds, impatiens, and zinnias toward the end of the month before the first expected freeze. Although it may be disconcerting to lift up completely healthy plants, you need the space to plant cool-season annuals, like pansies in their place. The cool-season annuals will need time to settle in before temperatures cool down.

Deadhead spent flowers from pansies planted last month.

BULBS

In the fall, cut back lily stalks to soil level after they have turned yellow. Mountain gardeners should lift cannas, dahlias, gladioli, and tuberous begonias after their foliage is killed by frost. Because they won't survive the winter outdoors, they need to be cleansed of soil and stored indoors in a cool but frost-free location. Dig and store caladium bulbs before frost in the Piedmont and Coastal Plain. See September, Care.

EDIBLES

Listen for frost warnings and be prepared to cover tomatoes, eggplants, peppers, and other tender vegetables. The weather often warms up again after the first frost, so this protection can prolong the harvest for weeks.

When there is a threat of frost, harvest your beans, cucumbers, eggplant, okra, pepper, and summer squash, to avoid frost-damage. Bring in tomatoes for ripening when daytime temperatures are consistently below 65 degrees Fahrenheit. Pick only those fruits that have begun to change color.

Harvest sweet potatoes before frost as well as gourds, pumpkins, and winter squash. To store pumpkins, pick only solid, mature pumpkins of a deep orange color. Try not to injure the rind; decay-causing fungi attack through wounds. Dip them in a chlorine solution of 4 teaspoons bleach per gallon of water. Allow the fruit to dry, but do not rinse until ready to use. Cure them at room temperature for a week to harden the rind,

then store in a cool place. They will keep about two months.

When you can no longer protect your plants, pull them and add them to the compost heap. Till or spade the soil in cleared areas to expose insects that are planning to overwinter. Then plant a hardy cover crop or mulch with shredded leaves, fresh manure, or spoiled hay to minimize winter erosion and provide nutrients for next year. Mountain gardeners can plant a cover crop of clover or winter grain as described in September.

■ *No other cool-season annual can compete with pansies in diversity of flower colors, length of flowering, and celebrated cold tolerance.*

■ *To protect pumpkins from rot, place a barrier underneath the ripening fruits to keep them off the soil. An old shingle is better than paper or plastic, which will trap water. Harvest only solid, mature fruit with a deep orange color. Be careful not to injure the rind, as decay fungi will attack through wounds. After harvest, dip the fruit in a dilute chlorine solution of 4 teaspoons bleach per gallon of water. Allow fruit to dry, but do not rinse until you use them.*

Semihardy vegetables that can survive repeated light frosts in the 30 to 32 degrees Fahrenheit range include beets, Chinese cabbage, cauliflower, celery, collards, green onions, potatoes, Bibb and leaf lettuces, mustard, parsnips, radishes, salsify, spinach, and Swiss chard. The flavor of some of these, such as collards and parsnips, is much improved by exposure to a spell of below-freezing temperature.

Hardy vegetables that can survive temperatures as low as 20 degrees Fahrenheit before finally being killed include cabbage, broccoli, Brussels sprouts, carrots, kale, leeks, rutabagas, and turnips. Upon thawing out, these hardy vegetables will continue to grow between freezes. Even when the tops of such vegetables as carrots and turnips are killed by cold, the roots will remain in good condition if plants are mulched with a generous layer of insulating material such as hay or leaves. This will prevent the ground itself from freezing and allow you to harvest the fresh roots as you wish during the winter. You may, however, find that voles discover and enjoy your cache of overwintering produce first.

For bigger and better Brussels sprouts, pinch out the top of the plant when sprouts at the bottom are fully grown. The smaller, upper sprouts will grow larger than they would otherwise.

Thin turnip and radish plantings to give each root enough room to develop.

LAWNS

Mow cool-season lawns often enough so that no more than one-third of the grass height is cut. Recycle grass clippings by leaving them on the lawn.

Remove tree leaves from the lawn to reduce lawn problems. Compost them or shred them to use as mulch around your flower or shrub border.

PERENNIALS & ORNAMENTAL GRASSES

Before the first freeze, Mountain gardeners can take cuttings of Confederate rose (*Hibiscus mutabilis*), a fall-blooming perennial that's marginally hardy in Zone 7b, where the top growth gets winterkilled and resprouts from the crown the following spring. The peony-like flowers can be either single or double, depending on the cultivar, and go through subtle color changes from light pink to red, or white, to pink, to crimson.

If you're concerned that the plant will not survive the upcoming winter, or if you choose to share this plant with friends, it roots very easily in water from cuttings taken in the fall. Pot up rooted cuttings and transplant them outside after the last freeze in spring to an area in full sun or partial shade.

■ *Harvest home-grown sweet potatoes, the official state vegetable of North Carolina, 90 to 120 days after planting. Carefully dig them before or immediately after a frost because cool soil temperatures can reduce their quality and storability.*

TO OVERWINTER A TROPICAL WATER LILY

1. When they stop blooming in the fall and are going dormant with the cooler fall temperatures, take them out of the pool. Gently remove the plant from the pot and wash away the soil.

2. Look for a smooth, black walnut-sized tuber (many form when the parent is potbound) beneath the crown. Separate the tuber and put in water. If the tuber sinks, it's alive and can be stored over the winter. If the tuber floats, discard it.

3. Store the tubers over the winter in a plastic bag filled with cool damp sand. Put the tuber inside the bag and top it off with more sand. Seal and label the bag with the name of the variety. Store the bag in a cool 55 to 60 degrees Fahrenheit location.

Cut back peonies hard after the first frost and compost the trimmings to reduce the chances of disease outbreaks.

Prune perennials when their tops are nipped by cold. Some perennials produce seeds that are attractive to birds. Leave these plants standing as long as there are still seeds in them.

ROSES

If your climbing roses are in an exposed location, tie them up firmly with broad strips of rags so that the wind will not whip them against the trellis and bruise the bark. Roses grown in containers need to be put in the ground, container and all, in a protected area of the landscape. Mulch with a layer of compost.

Stop deadheading spent flowers. Remove petals with your hand to allow the rose hips to form, which helps trigger winter dormancy.

SHRUBS & TREES

Don't shear your shrubs now, it's too late. You'll have brown-edged leaves all winter and you may spark tender new growth that will be killed by the first freeze. If there are a few wayward branches, cut them back by hand. Wait until spring to do any major shaping. Continue to prune out dead, damaged, and diseased branches.

Do not become alarmed if your yews, pines, arborvitae, and junipers begin to shed their interior needles. It is natural for them to do so at this time of year.

VINES & GROUNDCOVERS

Dig up sweet potato tubers of 'Blackie', 'Margarita', 'Pink Frost', and others of the Sweet Caroline Sweetheart series, and store them in a cool, dry location for replanting next year. The tubers have eyes that will sprout once they're back in the ground.

In the Mountains, mulch newly planted vines and groundcovers after the ground freezes. (After the ground freezes the pests should have found other winter quarters, reducing the chances of their bedding down in the mulch next to your new plantings.) Annual vines that have been killed with the first freeze should be cut back from their supports and composted or buried in the vegetable garden.

WATER GARDENING

Oxygenating plants should be cut back hard in the fall. Remove dead leaves from marginals. Move any cold-hardy aquatic plants to the lowest part of the pond or water garden. After the first killing frost, trim away the dead leaves of your hardy water lilies. In the Mountains where ice will form on the ponds, move the pots to the deepest part of your pond (at least 2 feet or more in depth). Rest assured that hardy water lilies will overwinter in the Carolinas (they're hardy to Zone 3) as long as their roots are protected from freezing. To store a tropical water lily, follow the steps above.

If you want to overwinter your tropical marginal plants, move them indoors and treat them like houseplants. Set them on a water-filled saucer in a bright, south-facing window. They need ten to twelve hours of light to remain healthy throughout the winter months, so consider supplementing natural sunlight with fluorescent light. Prevent the pond from freezing—any organic matter trapped at the bottom of the pond may decay, producing toxic levels of methane gases that can be toxic to fish. Install a pump or a heater designed for water garden pools. Remove any fallen debris or dead plants in the water.

After the first hard frost, trim away any dead leaves from marginals and compost them.

WATER

ANNUALS

Keep an eye on the watering needs of your annuals, especially emerging seedlings and newly set-out transplants. Check the soil for moisture; don't wait until the plants begin to wilt. Rake up fallen pine needles and use them for mulch.

BULBS

If fall is dry, provide sufficient water to newly planted spring-flowering bulbs. Check bulbs being forced in beds or cold frames and water them to keep the potting medium moist (but not sopping wet).

EDIBLES

Cool-season vegetables perk up in the milder areas and grow vigorously. Water during dry spells and feed as necessary.

LAWNS

Newly seeded or sodded lawns should be watered frequently. As the seedlings emerge and the sod "knits" into the soil, gradually water less frequently but more deeply.

PERENNIALS & ORNAMENTAL GRASSES

Add mulch to your perennial border. A 2-inch layer of weed-free straw or chopped leaves will

HERE'S HOW

TO TEST SOIL AND ROOTBALL MOISTURE

1. Dig a small hole in the loosened backfill soil just outside the rootball.

2. Squeeze a handful of the soil from the top and another from the bottom of the hole. If water drips between your fingers or the soil feels sticky, the soil is too wet. If it crumbles and falls from your hand as you open your fingers, you need to add water. If the soil stays together in your hand as you open your fingers, the moisture in the backfill is just right. But you'll still need to test the rootball.

3. Insert your fingers into the rootball. If it's dry, go ahead and water.

help conserve soil moisture, protect root systems, and reduce plant loss from soil heaving during the winter.

Keep new plantings watered if the weather is dry. Established gardens may need water as well so they won't go into winter with insufficient moisture.

ROSES AND SHRUBS

Water newly planted roses and shrubs if there's insufficient rain. Fall can be dry time in the

Carolinas, so don't rely on Mother Nature to water newly planted shrubs. Water frequently, checking the soil and rootball before watering. Water deeply and infrequently.

TREES

Water evergreens thoroughly before the ground freezes in the Mountains. Evergreens continue to lose water by transpiring during the winter, but when the ground is frozen they cannot replenish the water.

In fall and early winter, don't forget to water newly planted trees to help them become established. A few weeks after planting, start reducing watering to every few days or longer, especially with cloudy, rainy, or cool weather. Eventually, water on an "as-needed" basis by testing the soil and rootball for moisture.

VINES & GROUNDCOVERS

See September.

WATER GARDENS

Maintain the water level in your pond. The plants and fish that overwinter outdoors in the pond can use the depth.

FERTILIZE

ANNUALS

Use a slow-release fertilizer at planting time to lightly fertilize hardy annuals such as calendulas, pansies, and sweet alyssums. This will encourage establishment and flowering.

BULBS

See September.

LAWNS

Wait until next month to fertilize cool-season lawns.

PERENNIALS & ORNAMENTAL GRASSES

Do not fertilize this late in the season. Allow the perennials to go dormant so they can tolerate the winter weather.

ROSES

Stop fertilizing your roses six weeks before your expected first freeze.

SHRUBS, VINES & GROUNDCOVERS

To add nutrients, supplement mulch with well-rotted horse or cow manure. Do not fertilize when these plants are displaying their fall colors—wait until next year.

TREES

See September.

PROBLEM-SOLVE

ANNUALS

Inspect the annuals you brought inside for the winter. Whiteflies and spider mites could have hitchhiked their way inside. Keep the plants quarantined, and control pests before you introduce them to your other indoor plants. Insecticidal soap applied to the upper and lower leaf surfaces will control these pests. If the plant is not listed on the label, you may have to test a small area on your plant for injury. It may take seven to ten days to see if any damage occurs. If your plant shows sensitivity, rinse the soap off once the whiteflies and spider mites are killed.

Leaf spots may be a problem on zinnias and other warm-season annuals. Because they're going to be removed, or killed by impending cold temperatures, a fungicide may not be necessary. Any heavily infected plants can be pulled out immediately.

See September for details about weed controls.

BULBS

Watch out for storage diseases, including Fusarium bulb rot and botrytis. Avoid damaging bulbs and tubers when lifting them out of the ground to be stored.

Weeds, especially weedy grasses, may be in beds. Handpull or hoe out the clumps.

EDIBLES

Clean up the garden. Remove any diseased or insect-infested plant debris. That's where pests spend the winter. Cabbage loopers and cabbage-worms are the bane of the fall garden. If your cabbage leaves resemble lace, spray with BTK (sold as Dipel® or Thuricide®). This microbial insecticide will not harm humans but will put a stop to hungry caterpillars. Control aphids with insecticidal soap.

LAWNS

If fire ants have cropped up in your lawn or land-scape, control them with the "two-step method" described in August, Problem-Solve.

Examine the yellowish to brownish spots in your St. Augustinegrass lawn for chinch bugs. Use the coffee can technique (see May, Problem-Solve) to sample for them at the edge of the damaged area.

"Fairy rings" may appear as a ring of mushrooms or simply as a dark green ring of lush grass. The ring may vary from a few inches to several feet in diameter. Fairy rings are caused by soil-inhabiting fungi that feed on old roots, stumps, and thatch. Fairy-ring fungi are not plant parasites, but they can cause the lawn to dry out because their fungal bodies make the soil repel water. Fairy rings are difficult to control. Be patient and allow them to disappear over time. Watering the ring to saturate the soil for several hours and over several days may help. As a last resort, replace the infested soil occupied by the fairy ring with clean soil.

Large patch is a devastating disease, espe-cially on St. Augustinegrass in the fall. See November, Problem-Solve.

Handpull or spot-treat chickweed, henbit, and other winter annuals with a broadleaf herbicide. Use a herbicide labeled for your lawn grass and for the weeds you're trying to control.

Florida betony is a cool-season perennial weed that emerges from seeds and tubers during the cool, moist months of fall. Throughout the winter months it grows and spreads rapidly. Spot-treat with herbicide while it's actively growing this month. See April, Problem-Solve for more information.

PERENNIALS & ORNAMENTAL GRASSES

Clean up the dead leaves from around your peren-nial flowers. If left on the ground, leaves and stems can harbor diseases and provide convenient places for pests to spend the winter.

Hoe or handpull any weeds in the beds to pre-vent them from going to seed, and to prevent the younger weeds from settling in for the winter. Mulch with a shallow layer to suppress emerging weeds.

ROSES

Sorry, but spider mites can still be active in the warmer parts of the Carolinas. Because your roses will shed their leaves soon, control may not be necessary. Controlling the overwintering eggs with a dormant horticultural oil this fall when the rose goes dormant may be all that's needed.

Rake and clean up the garden to get rid of black-spot spores that can overwinter on the leaves. If powdery mildew is a problem, control may not be necessary, because we're approaching the end of the season and leaves will be shed.

SHRUBS

Spider mites can still be active in the warmer parts of the Carolinas. Control the overwintering eggs with a dormant horticultural oil this fall when the shrubs go dormant (see January, Problem-Solve).

Prune out infected limbs and rake up dead leaves to remove any overwintering fungal diseases.

Keep the area around your shrubs free of weeds to eliminate any overwintering hideouts for two-spotted spider mites.

If you'd like to make your own repellent, mix 2 tablespoons of homemade hot pepper sauce per gallon of water or blend 2 or 3 rotten eggs in a gallon of water and spray it on your plants. Dried ground red peppers, ground black pepper, or chili powder are other repellents that can be dusted on or near flowers. To be effective, they will have to be reapplied after rain or heavy dew, and quite often to new plant growth.

Be aware that some of the repellents designed for mammals may kill non-targeted, beneficial insects. Before choosing a course of action, weigh the benefits of the treatment versus the level of acceptable damage.

TREES

Control the overwintering bagworm eggs with a dormant horticultural oil this fall when the plants go dormant. It may be all that's needed to kill the eggs and any active mites that may be present.

Remove and destroy bagworm bags on narrow-leaved evergreens. Eggs overwinter in the bags produced by the females and will hatch-out next spring.

Old, fallen leaves contain the disease spores for next year's plant infections. If you have diseased plants, prune out infected branches in the late fall and winter when the disease-causing organism is inactive. Remove any infected debris from around the plant's base and dispose of it.

To protect young trees against whitetail deer damage, there are a number of deterrents. Remember, deer will become accustomed to any object, so alternating items will help. Hang bars of strong-scented soap or mesh bags filled with human hair

on the outer branches with no more than 3 feet between them. Chemical deer repellents also can be applied. To be effective, repellents will have to be reapplied if there is rain or heavy dew; they will have to be applied often to new plant growth.

The only technique that ensures safety from deer is fencing. Both woven wire fences and multi-strand electric fencing will do the job, but their construction can be elaborate and expensive. An alternative fencing material—7½-foot black plastic mesh—is nearly invisible and can be used to completely surround your plantings. To learn more about these and other techniques for keeping deer at bay, contact your local Cooperative Extension Service.

VINES & GROUNDCOVERS

Clean up plantings to get rid of diseased leaves.

Weeds continue to germinate and emerge. Hand-pull them while they're young and suppress their growth with mulch.

WATER GARDENS

Trim away any damaged, dead, diseased, or pest-ridden leaves. Compost them or bring them into the garden to be buried to enrich the soil.

■ *The only surefire way of keeping white-tailed deer out of your garden is with a tall fence.*

November

Anticipation. It reminds me of that ketchup commercial from the late '70s with Carly Simon singing "Anticipation . . . is making me late . . . is keepin' me waiting." It also reminds me of gardening. Waiting— anticipating the appearance of flowers, fruits, or fall color—that's what we do.

I'm already looking forward to next year. Sure, I appreciate the flowering dogwoods donning their red and purple finery and the light pink Confederate rose flowers changing to red, but I want to see my fall-planted bulbs in bloom next spring. I hope to see the deciduous magnolias escape any springtime freezes as their large, fuzzy green flower buds give rise to magnificent, jaw-dropping flowers. I'll have to wait until next fall to see the green globs of 'Goldrush' goldenrod, 'Taipei Silk' toad lily, and 'First Light' swamp sunflower explode into bloom.

Not everyone is willing to wait for a plant to do something. That's why annuals exist. Their sole mission is to flower every waking moment until the first frost, perfect for folks who want immediate gratification. What you see is what you get, day after day after day.

Fortunately, not all plants behave like annuals. Asiatic lilies, for example, make gardening fun and exciting. Over several weeks they produce long, slender green stems that eventually bear clusters of balloon-like flower buds. Soon they open to reveal majestic flowers that last for a brief but glorious time.

The same goes for 'Color Guard' yucca, which flaunts a 3-foot-tall flower stalk in midsummer. The days go by as I watch and wait for those white flower buds to open.

For those gardeners who are willing to delay their gratification, they do it for economic reasons. One gardening friend is slowly converting her tall fescue lawn to bermudagrass. Her cost-effective and clever approach involves cutting out 2-foot wide circles of turf and planting 6-inch plugs of bermudagrass in the center of each bare spot. From a distance the lawn looks pockmarked. In an area plugged last year, I can see a clash of textures between the fine-leaved bermuda and the wide-bladed, coarse-textured fescue. (The fescue is rapidly losing ground.) It may take a few years for the lawn to become completely bermudagrass, but what is time to a seasoned gardener? Her plugging approach saves money and curbs soil erosion. It also reminds me that if anticipation is good for ketchup, then it must be a whole lot better for gardening.

PLAN

ANNUALS AND EDIBLES

Garden tools can add up to a large investment. Make plans this month to clean them off and repair or replace any broken ones. As soon as seed flats and pots are emptied of fall transplants, wash and sterilize them with a 10-percent bleach solution (1 part bleach to 9 parts water) before storing them so they'll be ready in the spring.

This is also a good month to think about building a cold frame, which is like a halfway house for seedlings as they make their way from the windowsill or light table to the outdoors. The cold frame is basically a bottomless box made of wood, stone, or brick, with a transparent or translucent cover—like a miniature unheated greenhouse outdoors.

Cold frames are typically rectangular in shape, 3 by 6 feet or so. The back of the cold frame should face north and should be 18 to 30 inches high. The front should be slightly lower, between 12 and 24 inches to allow enough headroom for the plants inside. Tilt the cover to the south by sloping the sides about 1 inch per foot. More adventurous gardeners can even add an automatic opener to the cover. These devices lift the cover automatically as the temperature rises during the day, and gradually close it with the falling evening temperatures.

BULBS

While bulbs are commonly planted in formal beds, borders, and even containers, many lend themselves to naturalized plantings where they bloom and spread in ever-widening drifts. Plan to create some naturalized areas in your landscape in the following ways:

1. Randomly scatter crocuses, daffodils, grape hyacinths, snowdrops, and snowflakes, and plant them where they fall. They look better when planted in clumps or drifts, so you may have to move them around. These bulbs will root and establish themselves by spring.

2. Plant spring-flowering bulbs along the edges of woodland areas or beneath the canopies of deciduous trees. They should receive plenty of sunlight there and finish blooming by the time the trees leaf out.

3. Insert bulbs such as crocuses in your warm-season lawn. The crocuses will brighten up the lawn before it awakens from its winter dormancy in the spring. By the time the crocuses finish replenishing themselves, it will be time to mow the grass and remove the spent crocus leaves.

Keep in mind that naturalized bulbs need to be fertilized on an annual basis to encourage perennialization. Failure to fertilize them often results in a gradual reduction in their numbers.

LAWNS

"A rolling stone gathers no moss," but expect moss to collect in the moist, shaded areas of your lawn. In addition to shady places, mosses are especially fond of acidic (low pH) soils with low fertility, poorly drained or wet soils, or combinations of these. These primitive, nonflowering plants spread by dust-fine spores carried on the wind that alight on moist soil, rocks, bricks, or tree trunks. The spores germinate and form a network of green

It's time to clean and store your gardening tools.

■ *Moss will typically grow in cool, shady areas.*

threads that develop into tiny matted plants. Most grow only ¼ inch to 2 inches high.

Although mosses are harmless, folks either court them or hate them. I love the velvety, cushiony look and feel of moss. Mosses are cultivated as ornamentals in Japanese gardens. A famous thirteenth-century garden in Kyoto called Saiho-ji ("Moss Temple") has over forty species and varieties of rolling green mosses spread over 4½ acres. If you're planning to rid your lawn of moss by raking it out and then reseeding, be aware that in most cases, the moss will return. Only when you make the growing conditions less appealing to the moss and more favorable for the grass will you be able to halt the moss's advance.

Before you choose to fight a "turf war" with moss, figure out your chances of winning. If your moss-covered lawn gets less than four hours of sunlight a day, it will be too shady for turfgrasses. You're going to lose the battle unless you can improve sunlight penetration by selectively pruning tree limbs. If there's always going to be insufficient sunlight, your best bet is to forget about grass. If you really dislike moss, plant shade-tolerant groundcovers or mulch with leaves, needles, or wood chips. Ideally, extend the mulch layer to the drip line or outermost branches of the tree.

If your lawn is receiving adequate sunlight but still seems to be losing ground to moss, follow these steps to improve the health, density, and appearance of your lawn:

- Test your soil at least every three years and fertilize according to a soil test and at the proper time.

- Improve poorly drained areas by regrading to direct water away from the site.

- Cultivate compacted, heavy clay soils with a core aerifier—a machine that removes plugs of soil. Rent, purchase, or contract this service through lawn care companies. For small areas, use a spading fork to punch holes in the soil to improve drainage.

- Mow grasses growing in the shade at the top of their recommended mowing height range to promote deep rooting and to leave as much leaf area as possible to manufacture food.

PERENNIALS & ORNAMENTAL GRASSES

Keep your garden looking good while nourishing birds with perennials that offer attractive leaves, stems, and seedheads. Ornamental grasses are at the top of the list with their beautiful seedheads and leaves that turn yellow, orange, red, or purple with the onset of cooler winter temperatures.

HERE'S HOW

TO PLANT BULB CONTAINERS WITH ANNUALS

1. Use a plastic container (so it won't crack during the winter), and fill it about one-third full with potting soil. Use potting soil, which is a lightweight mix made especially for container gardens.

2. Next, place the bulbs in the pot, pointy end up. Really pack the bulbs into the container. You can place the bulbs so they're almost touching one another. A secret of the pros: more bulbs equals more excitement. You can also plant a mixture of bulbs that bloom at different times to extend the flower show on your front porch.

3. Then, add potting soil to the container so that it is two-thirds to three-fourths full of potting soil. This will ensure that the bulbs are deep enough. Leave room in the container to add more potting soil and annual flowers on top.

4. Plant cool-weather annuals on top of the bulbs. Pansies and flowering kale are the most cold-tolerant, but snapdragons and calendula are good choices for warmer climates as well. You can also plant perennials like coral bells on top of the bulbs. Plant the annuals and perennials close together in the pot. This container uses twelve pansy plants.

5. Fill in around the flowering annuals with more potting soil, and leave ½ to 1 inch between the top of the soil and the rim of the container so that the soil doesn't wash out when you water the plants.

6. Last, water the container. Make sure to water the flowers at least once a week throughout the winter, unless the soil in the pot is frozen solid. Leave the flower pot outside all winter. While the bulbs are "chilling," you can enjoy the flowering annuals. In the spring, the bulbs will grow up through the annual flowers.

ROSES

Plan for improvements next year. What were the most troublesome insects and diseases this season? Were there problems with the pest control measures you selected? Perhaps you need to dig out some roses and replace them early next year.

Think about the roses that seemed to "take a lickin' and keep on tickin'." Was it the rose itself, or could its performance also be attributed to the growing environment—plenty of air circulation, diligent removal of infected leaves, adequate water and fertility? Spend some time pondering these factors, along with others, and document them in your journal.

SHRUBS

Identify shrub beds and borders whose soil will have to be tested. Soil testing is best done every

particularly 'Natchez' and 'Fantasy' Japanese crape-myrtle (*Lagerstroemia faurei* 'Fantasy').

VINES & GROUNDCOVERS

Throughout history gardeners have showcased their vines on structures that ranged from the simple to the elegant. Buy ready-made fan-shaped or rectangular trellises at garden centers. If you're a do-it-yourselfer, plan to build your own this month after you decide on the kinds of vines you're going to support. Twining vines with long flexible stems—hyacinth bean, morning glory, moonvine, and trumpet honeysuckle—need to wrap themselves around something like a string, wire, or trellis. They climb best on narrow, vertically oriented supports.

■ *While crapemyrtle flowers and fall-colored leaves draw attention in the summer and fall, in winter the cinnamon-colored, mottled bark takes center stage.*

two or three years. Contact your Cooperative Extension Service agent for soil-testing materials.

TREES

When planning to include trees in your landscape, take advantage of a their winter interest. Bark, branches, and architectural forms give deciduous trees character. Look at the peeling or exfoliating bark of a wide variety of trees such as crapemyrtle,

Climbing vines that use tendrils need a support that's small enough for their threadlike "fingers" to grasp. Fine latticework or a structure that includes wire, string, or plastic mesh is suitable for passionflower (*Passiflora*) and sweet pea (*Lathyrus odoratus*). Chicken wire can be wrapped around a freestanding pole or pillar to give the vines something to hold onto. A tripod is a simple way of mixing these climbers into borders of annual and perennials.

If you're going to be growing a heavyweight like Japanese (*Wisteria floribunda*) or Chinese wisteria (*W. sinensis*), be prepared to build a sturdy structure and foundation. Arbors need to have 6 × 6 posts set in concrete with 4 × 4 crossmembers. American wisteria isn't as heavy and doesn't require an arbor of this magnitude.

WATER GARDENS

It is hoped that you have had an enjoyable water gardening experience that inspired you to learn more about this exciting field. Remember that many water gardeners are happy to share their experiences (and their plants and fish) with you. To learn about a water gardening society in your area, speak to an aquatic nursery staff or water garden supplier. Surf the Internet for water gardening information to learn about different approaches and techniques.

PLANT

ANNUALS
Set out forget-me-nots, snapdragons, pansies, sweet William, pinks, violas, and other hardy plants for flowers and leaves in winter and early spring.

If you didn't sow them last month, Piedmont and Coastal Plains gardeners can go ahead and sow the seeds of calliopsis, foxglove, Johnny-jump-ups, larkspur, money plant, stock, and Shirley, Iceland, and California poppies.

BULBS
Now is a good time to plant spring-blooming beauties such as anemones, crocus, daffodils, scillas, and snowdrops. Use a timed-release bulb fertilizer at planting time. When in doubt, follow this general rule: Plant bulbs at a depth equal to three times the height of the bulb.

Summer bulbs, which could be killed by winter freezes, should be lifted, dried, and stored (if you did not already do so last month). Divide and replant crowded dahlias after a freeze kills their top growth. Where they won't survive the winter outdoors (in zones colder than 7b) they will have to be lifted and overwintered indoors in a cool (35 to 50 degrees Fahrenheit), dry place. Here's how: Cut the tops back to 6 inches, lift out the

■ *Sweet William is a hardy plant that will provide early flowers next year.*

■ *Plant dormant, bare-root peonies that so the "eyes," or buds, are covered by no more than 1½ to 2 inches of soil. In milder areas, the eyes should be no deeper than ½ to 1 inch below the ground.*

clumps with a spading fork, brush off the soil, and turn them upside-down to dry. Inspect each clump and pare away any damaged parts. Remove infested or dead tubers at the neck. Dust the tubers with sulfur to prevent rot in storage, making sure all the surfaces are coated. Store them in a ventilated crate or basket filled with peat moss. Place each tuber upside-down, stacking them no more than two deep. Inspect them monthly and discard any rotting tubers.

EDIBLES

Plant lettuce and hardy vegetables such as beets, cabbage, and spinach in cold frames for winter or early spring crops. Grow leafy vegetables such as lettuce, Chinese cabbage, and spinach in a cold frame or beneath a row cover for harvesting all winter long.

Continue enjoying fresh-picked cool-weather crops as they mature.

Harvest kale by picking just a few leaves from each plant; this will encourage continued production of new leaves.

LAWNS

Install cool-season sod as long as the soil isn't frozen. Postpone seeding, plugging, or sodding a warm-season lawn until next spring.

PERENNIALS & ORNAMENTAL GRASSES

Continue to set out perennials in the Piedmont and Coastal Plain if good selections are available from garden centers. Mountain gardeners can set out or transplant no later than four to six weeks before the ground is expected to freeze. Late-planted perennials will benefit from a 3- to 5-inch layer of mulch after the ground freezes to protect them from being lifted by the freezing and thawing of the soil.

Start perennial seeds that need to be stratified or exposed to moist chilling conditions (check the seed packet for the length of cold exposure); otherwise, they won't germinate.

Plant peonies now in the Piedmont and Mountains. For best results, choose a variety that blooms in early to mid-season. Peonies are long-lived, reliable, and extremely cold-hardy plants (Zones 3 to 7) that produce magnificent flowers in spring and early summer and attractive compound leaves throughout the season. Plant dormant bare-root herbaceous peonies so the "eyes" or buds on the division are covered by no more than 1½ to 2 inches of soil. In milder areas, the eyes should be no deeper than ½ to 1 inch below the soil surface. Peonies planted too deeply will never bloom. Plant container-grown peonies so the top of the rootball is less than an inch below the soil surface.

ROSES

This is a good month to plant. In the Mountains, mulch with compost, shredded bark, or shredded leaves soon after planting to keep the ground thawed so roots can become established. Water them thoroughly and mulch to keep them from freezing.

SHRUBS

Got a shrub that's "too big for its britches"? Move it.

TREES

Fall is the best time of year for moving trees. To ensure success, transplant trees when they're dormant. Where circumstances necessitate very late planting of trees, remember to mulch the area heavily to keep the ground thawed so roots can become established.

Planning on having a live balled-and-burlapped Christmas tree? Then dig a planting hole now before the ground freezes in the Mountains. Fill the hole with straw or hay to keep it from freezing. Store the soil in a garage or shed so you will have workable soil when you need it for planting the tree.

HERE'S HOW

TO MOVE A SHRUB THAT HAS OUTGROWN ITS LOCATION

1. Tie up the branches of wide, low-spreading shrubs with soft twine.

2. Use a ribbon to mark the side of the shrub that faces north so it can be properly oriented when replanting.

3. Create a good-sized rootball. Shrubs less than 3 feet in height can be moved bare root. Bare root means that most or all of the soil is removed from the roots after digging the plant. Bare-root plants should be moved when they're dormant.

   Shrubs greater than 1 inch in trunk diameter and all broadleaf and narrowleaf evergreens should be moved with the soil attached. The size of the rootball should be large enough in diameter and depth to include as much of the fibrous and feeding roots as possible. It also depends on how much you or a friend can physically manage.

4. With your shovel, dig a trench around the shrub to create a rootball that's 12 to 14 inches wide. This will be adequate for deciduous shrubs up to 2 feet tall and sprawling evergreens with a spread of 2 feet.

5. Use a spade to dig under the shrub. Undercut all around the plant with the spade before rocking it.

6. Once the rootball is free, tip the shrub to one side and slide a tarp beneath it as far as possible. Then lay down the shrub in the opposite direction and pull the tarp all the way under the plant. Now slide the shrub out of the hole.

7. Use a shovel handle to measure the depth and width of the rootball to determine how wide to make the hole.

8. Plant the shrub so the rootball is a few inches higher than the surrounding soil.

9. Backfill around the plant and tamp down the soil lightly with the end of your shovel handle to settle the soil around the roots.

10. Water the plant thoroughly making sure the rootball and surrounding soil are completely wet.

11. Water it in to settle the soil, and follow up with a 2- to 4-inch layer of mulch.

CARE

ANNUALS

Clean up the garden. Remove spent plants, chop them up, and compost them. Add organic matter to beds. Either shred leaves and use them as mulch or compost them to improve soil. Cover the garden with mulch to prevent soil loss.

Move containers of live plants to a protected spot if possible. Protect the roots by covering the soil and the container with a thick layer of straw or leaves. Check the moisture level of the pots every few weeks and water if needed. Annuals overwintered indoors should be kept in a cool location in bright light.

BULBS

Mulch plantings with compost, pine straw, or salt hay to protect tender and semihardy bulbs from the winter cold.

Clean up and remove old, dried iris leaves, stems, and other debris in the fall to help eliminate over-wintering eggs or iris borers.

EDIBLES

A light mulch of shredded leaves or straw on carrots, turnips, and other root vegetables will help protect against freezing. Pick tomatoes when frost is predicted and store in a single layer in a cool location. Harvest broccoli while the heads are still compact. Tie the leaves around cauliflower heads to blanche the curds.

Remove asparagus foliage after frost kills it.

PERENNIALS & ORNAMENTAL GRASSES

There's still time to dig, divide, and replant crowded perennials. Look for perennials that have grown out-of-bounds or have declined due to overcrowding and have developed a ring of growth with an empty center. Divide peonies when the leaves die back (see October, Plant).

Reduce peony botrytis blight and powdery mildew on beebalm and phlox by trimming away and disposing of old, dead stems.

■ *Allow rose hips to form on your roses to encourage dormancy and for you to appreciate as well.*

Avoid pruning Monch's aster, ferns, salvias, mums, and other marginally hardy plants so the crowns will be insulated during cold weather. Prune them when new growth emerges in the spring. Plants such as leadwort (*Ceratostigma plumbaginoides*) that also emerge late in the spring should not be pruned; the old stems and leaves will let you know where they are so you won't damage them by digging.

Perennials with winter interest should not be pruned until winter takes its toll.

ROSES

If you haven't done so already, have a soil test done of your rose beds. At least every two or three years, have your soil tested through your Cooperative Extension Service to determine soil pH and fertility levels.

Allow the hips to signal dormancy. It's not necessary to prune back roses to make them attractive in winter. If you do this before a freeze, you may awaken dormant buds, which will produce new growth that will only be killed by freezing temperatures. Even gardeners along the warmer coast should wait until January (at the earliest) to begin pruning roses. If a rose's height will put it in peril of being damaged by strong winter winds, prune back only after a freeze.

SHRUBS, TREES, AND VINES & GROUNDCOVERS

Limit any pruning to the removal of diseased, damaged, or broken branches. Wait until after the coldest part of winter has passed next year before pruning summer-flowering shrubs and trees.

SHRUBS AND TREES

Rake up and compost fallen leaves and fruit around shrubs because this litter offers overwintering places for insects and diseases.

Broadleaved and tender evergreens exposed to drying winds and sun may need to be shaded on the south and southwest sides to reduce moisture loss and leaf injury. Enclose your evergreens in these exposed locations with a burlap screen.

Protect tender palms with tall, solitary trunks during the winter by tying up their leaves and wrapping the trunk with insulating blankets. Small specimens can be enclosed in a wire circle and buried with pine straw. Check guy wires around newly planted trees to be sure hose sections still cover the supporting wires or ropes so they will not damage the trunks in windy weather. Mulch plantings to protect against winter cold.

VINES & GROUNDCOVERS

Don't hesitate to tie uncooperative vines in place with twine or twist ties. This will help your clematis, climbing hydrangeas, and Confederate jasmine find their way across arbors.

WATER GARDENS

If your pond is too shallow or you have tender plants that won't survive the winter, you need to overwinter them indoors. Lift hardy water lilies out of the pond, cut away the leaves, and move them to a cool location (40 to 50 degrees Fahrenheit is ideal). Keep the soil moist. (This also works for most hardy marginal plants.)

Tropical floating plants are inexpensive to replace, so they can be discarded after the first frost. Allowing them to remain in the pond can cause them to rot and foul the water.

Aboveground water containers such as tub gardens can freeze during extended cold periods, so move them into a greenhouse or indoors in the colder parts of the state.

To prevent ice from forming on the surface of your pond—trapping carbon dioxide and other noxious gases that can kill fish—keep the water pump running. This will create water movement, preventing at least a small area from freezing so the top of the pond won't be completely sealed.

If the water does ice up, avoid the urge to smash a hole in the ice; this could damage plants and injure the fish. Set a kettle or pan of hot water on the surface of the ice to melt an opening.

To prevent ice from cracking the walls of the pool, float a tennis ball, soccer ball, or other air-filled or rubber object before hard freezing weather. The ball will absorb the expanding pressure from the ice and will relieve pressure from the pool walls.

WATER

ANNUALS

If the month is dry, water newly planted transplants.

BULBS

Check potted bulbs that will be forced during the winter months. Bulbs stored outdoors in cold frames or in the ground may need to be watered. Water newly planted bulbs to encourage rooting before cooler temperatures arrive.

LAWNS

Do not allow newly sodded cool-season lawns to dry out. When the sod has "knitted" or rooted into the soil, reduce the frequency of irrigation and water deeply as the roots begin to penetrate the soil.

Dormant warm-season lawns may need to be watered to prevent them from drying out, especially when warm windy weather prevails. Water warm-season lawns overseeded with ryegrass as needed.

PERENNIALS & ORNAMENTAL GRASSES AND ROSES

Keep newly planted transplants well watered to help them get established.

As cold weather sets in, reduce water, but do not allow roses, especially those that have recently been planted, to dry out completely. Plants need water during dry spells, even during the winter months.

SHRUBS, TREES, AND VINES & GROUNDCOVERS

Fall is usually dry in the Carolinas, so don't rely on Mother Nature to water new plantings. A few weeks after planting, start cutting back on watering to every few days or longer, especially with cloudy, rainy, or cool weather. Eventually water on a weekly or as-needed basis, testing the soil and rootball for moisture. Established plants, especially evergreens, should be watered during the winter months so they won't go into the winter on the dry side.

If fall rains have been scarce in the Mountains where the ground freezes, keep broadleaf evergreens such as hollies and rhododendrons well watered. Give them a deep watering once every two weeks. Evergreens continue to lose moisture from their leaves all winter, but once the ground is frozen they'll be unable to take up enough water to replace it. Sending them into winter well watered reduces the potential for damaged foliage.

FERTILIZE

ANNUALS

If you didn't incorporate a slow-release fertilizer last month at planting, lightly fertilize with a liquid fertilizer such as 20-20-20 now.

BULBS

Fertilize new and established beds with a slow-release nitrogen fertilizer. Don't wait until spring, because the bulbs are producing roots and foraging for nutrients now.

LAWNS

Fertilize Kentucky bluegrass, tall fescue, and dormant, overseeded bermudagrass and zoysia-grass lawns according to the results of a soil test. Fertilizing in the fall promotes root development without excessive top growth. With a strong root system, your lawn will be better able to withstand drought conditions next summer. Do not apply a fertilizer containing phosphorus and potassium if adequate levels are already present in the soil. See September, Fertilize.

PERENNIALS & ORNAMENTAL GRASSES, ROSES, SHRUBS, TREES, AND VINES & GROUNDCOVERS

Do not fertilize at this time of the year. If vines and groundcovers have already filled in their allotted space and have grown vigorously this past year, fertilizing may not be necessary. In fact, it can result in a lot of excess, jungle-like growth that would have to be removed by machete.

■ *When fertilizing your cool-season lawn, apply the appropriate amount of fertilizer according to soil-test results.*

hyacinth (*Muscari*), Grecian windflower (*Anemone blanda*), spring star flower (*Ipheion*), snow iris (*Iris reticulata*), ixiolirion, ornamental onions (*Allium*), star-of-Bethlehem (*Ornithogalum nutans*), puschkinia, scilla, snowdrop (*Galanthus*), snowflake (*Leucojum*), Spanish bluebell (*Hyacinthoides hispanica*), and winter aconite (*Eranthis hyemalis*) all resist attack. Be mindful, however, that extremely hungry animals will eat almost anything.

LAWNS

Rust and dollar spot are fungal diseases that attack bluegrass and fescue lawns. Rust causes grass leaves to turn yellow before turning brown and dying. Take a close look at the leaves for red, orange, or brown spores. Heavy infestations cause thinning. Many grass varieties have good-to-moderate levels of resistance to rust, so this disease shouldn't be much of a problem. Avoid keeping the grass wet for long periods by watering in the early morning.

Dollar spot produces small circular areas of straw-colored grass, which range from 1 to 6 inches across. If you examine individual grass blades you'll find straw-colored lesions with reddish brown borders. Dollar spot is more common during the spring and fall months. Maintain adequate levels of fertility, especially nitrogen, because this disease favors "hungry" lawns. Fungicides are generally unnecessary.

Large patch is a devastating disease, especially on St. Augustinegrass in the fall. Look for circular, brown dead patches in the lawn. Take a close look at the infected grass plants at the edge of the dead area and you'll find rotting leaf sheaths near the crown at the soil surface. Rake up dead areas and remove the infected grass. Reduce the occurrence of this disease by not overfertilizing in the fall or spring when the disease is likely to appear.

Treat wild garlic with a broadleaf herbicide when the air temperature is above 50 degrees Fahrenheit. Handpull wild garlic when the soil is moist to remove the entire plant—bulb and all. If you leave the bulb behind, it will resprout. Pull young, emerged weeds now while the task is easier and the weather is comfortable. By eliminating the weeds before they set seeds, you'll also reduce next year's problem.

■ *Divide and replant crowded dahlias after a freeze kills their top growth. Inspect the underside of each clump and pare away any damaged parts. Remove infested or dead tubers at the neck.*

PROBLEM-SOLVE

ANNUALS

See September, Problem-Solve for weed information.

BULBS

Some bulbs resist attacks by squirrels, chipmunks, voles, and their kin. In addition to the popular choices of daffodils and colchicums (also known as autumn crocuses), you have several other choices. Common hyacinth (*Hyacinthus orientalis*), glory-of-the-snow (*Chionodoxa*), tommies (*Crocus tommasinianus*), crown imperial (*Fritillaria imperialis*), dogtoothed violet (*Erythronium*), grape

If your lawn has a history of weed invasions, determine why the weeds invaded and correct the problem. Weeds are often found in lawns with a thin or weak stand of grass. The most common causes of a poor lawn are using a grass that's not adapted to your region or improper mowing, watering, and fertilizing. Other factors that affect the condition of the lawn include insects, diseases, compacted soil, and thatch.

PERENNIALS & ORNEMENTAL GRASSES

See October, Problem-Solve for disease information.

Handpull any young winter annuals, or cover them with a shallow layer of compost. Weeding is never fun, but the cooler temperatures can make it more bearable.

ROSES

Clean up rose beds. Rake fallen leaves and compost them or bury them in the vegetable garden.

SHRUBS

Watch out for the "cool-weather" mites: spruce spider mites that feed on arborvitae, juniper, spruce, and other conifers. They attack in the spring and fall, although at higher elevations they may be active all summer long.

Those small cone-shaped bags aren't the fruits of your arborvitae or juniper. They house the eggs of bagworms, which have been feeding on your conifers. Remove and destroy bagworm bags on narrow-leaved evergreens. Eggs overwinter in the bags produced by the females and will hatch out next spring.

If there is any evidence of scale on shrubs, spray with dormant oil in late fall and again in early spring. See January, Problem-Solve.

To protect young shrubs against deer damage, try a number of deterrents. Remember, deer will become accustomed to any object, so alternating items will help. Hang bars of strong-scented soap, mesh bags filled with human hair, paper bags of dried blood (bloodmeal), or strips cut from white plastic bags on shrubs that are likely to be attacked. Chemical deer repellents also can be applied. Be sure to reapply any chemicals after two to three weeks of normal weathering.

TREES

Remove all mummified fruit from fruit trees, and rake up and destroy those on the ground. Rake and dispose of dropped apple and cherry leaves. Good sanitation practices reduce reinfestation of insects and diseases the following season.

Inspect trees and shrubs for bagworm capsules and the silvery egg masses of tent caterpillars. Remove and destroy them to reduce next year's pest population. If there is any evidence of scale on trees and shrubs, spray with dormant oil in late fall and again in early spring.

See December, Problem-Solve for information on animal problems.

VINES & GROUNDCOVERS

If there is any evidence of scale on vines and groundcovers, spray with dormant oil in late fall and again in early spring when the plants are dormant.

Rake up fallen leaves from your groundcovers and compost them or bury them in the vegetable garden.

Geotextile or landscape fabrics are synthetic mulch underliners that are used to suppress weeds on a long-term basis. There are woven and nonwoven fabrics of polypropylene or polyester that have been developed to replace black plastic. Black plastic, a solid polyethylene material, has been used underneath mulches to provide excellent control of annual weeds and suppress perennial weeds. Black plastic isn't porous, however, and doesn't allow for air and water movement. Geotextiles overcome this disadvantage by admitting air and water. They should not be used in plantings where the fabric would inhibit rooting and spreading of the groundcover.

WATER GARDENS

Trim away any damaged, dead, diseased, or pest-ridden leaves. Compost them or bring them into the garden to be buried to enrich the soil.

December

Now that the oaks have shed their leaves, look for the green azalea-sized clusters of mistletoes (Phoradendron serotinum) nestled comfortably in the bare branches. This half-parasitic plant has been a part of our culture for centuries.

The modern tradition of using mistletoe around the Christmas holiday season dates back to the Celts of northern Europe. Druids, the holy men of Celtic society, used mistletoe in winter solstice ceremonies. Fearing the cold, short days of winter, the Druids used this green symbol of growth to ensure the return of the sun's warmth in the spring.

Some cultures associated mistletoe with fertility because of its ability to bear fruit in winter. The Ainu of Japan chopped up mistletoe leaves and sprinkled them on their fields to ensure a good crop. In Austria, a sprig of mistletoe was placed in a couple's bed to encourage conception.

Of more modern origin is the act of kissing under the mistletoe on Christmas Eve. It probably drew upon age-old rituals and traditions involving druidism and fertility rites. It began as a fad in England and Wales in the eighteenth century and has become a Christmas tradition in many households today.

In our trees, the mistletoe leaves allow it to produce its own food but steals water and nutrients from its host. In some cases, mistletoe is simply a cosmetic problem; in others, it can affect the growth and vigor of its host and expose the tree to attacks by diseases and insects.

The only effective way of ridding your tree of a mistletoe infestation is by cutting the infected limb 1 to 2 feet below the plant because mistletoe "roots" may extend up to a foot on either side of the point of attachment. Breaking off the tops only encourages regrowth. If you're a do-it-yourselfer, avoid butchering the tree with haphazard cuts. Find a certified arborist.

If you decorate your home with store-bought or homegrown mistletoe, hang it up high out of the reach of children and pets. The berries are toxic and the sap may irritate the skin of some people. Watch out . . . it also can turn Scrooges into smoochers.

PLAN

ANNUALS

There's not much to be done with annuals this month, and you must not expect much from them—they expect little from you. If you've kept up with the autumn chores outdoors and your green thumb still itches, swing your focus to your houseplants.

BULBS

Evaluate the performance of your bulbs this past year. What bulbs stopped you in your tracks when you first noticed them in bloom? Were any troubled by insects or diseases? Did any "minor" bulbs stand out among the rest? Make plans to experiment with new bulbs and those recommended by others.

HERE'S HOW

TO WINTERIZE A LAWN MOWER

1. Run the engine dry. Untreated gasoline stored for long periods can cause a gummy buildup in the carburetor that can make it impossible to start after a few months. Run the engine until it stalls. Alternatively, add a small amount of gasoline stabilizer to the fuel tank and run the engine for a few minutes to distribute it with the fuel.

2. Drain and replace the oil. Disconnect the wire from the spark plug for safety. Change the oil at least once a year (refer to your owner's manual) and check the oil level each time you use the machine. Recycle the used oil.

3. Clean the air filter. Foam-element air filters should be removed and cleaned with hot, soapy water. Before replacing it, pour a couple of tablespoons of clean engine oil onto it and distribute it by squeezing the foam.

4. Oil the spark plug. Remove the spark plug and pour a tablespoon of clean engine oil into the hole. Replace the spark plug and pull the starter cord a couple of times to crank the engine and distribute the oil. This will protect the engine from corrosion during the winter.

5. Clean and store the engine by brushing the cooling fins to make sure they're not plugged. Scrape off any dirt or grass clippings on the underside with a screwdriver, putty knife, or wire brush. If the blade is dull, remove and sharpen it or replace it.

EDIBLES

Take inventory of your seed collection. Decide what to save, trade, or toss out. See the January chapter introduction.

LAWNS

Plan to winterize the lawn mower before putting it away for the winter. Nothing could be more exasperating next spring than a lawn mower that won't start. The secret to getting it to start on the first (or second) pull next spring is to winterize it.

PERENNIALS & ORNAMENTAL GRASSES

Start a "wish list" of perennials. Some information that should be included:

- Name (common name and botanical name) and cultivar

- Expected bloom time (for example, early spring, midsummer, early fall)

- Cold/heat hardiness

- Flower color

- Ornamental characteristics (flowers, leaves, seedheads)

- Height and spread

- Pest problems

- Additional comments (self-sows, requires staking, needs regular deadheading, and so forth.)

ROSES

Review what happened during this past year. If this was your first year growing roses and you've been pleased by your performance and theirs, make plans to get better.

SHRUBS

The best way to prevent winter damage to shrubs is to select hardy species. Remember that it is better to select cold-hardy species in the first place rather than attempt to protect tender plants later.

HERE'S HOW

TO CHOOSE A LIVE CHRISTMAS TREE FOR INDOORS OR OUTDOORS

1. Choose a balled-and-burlapped tree with a firm rootball. Grab the trunk and push it back and forth once or twice. If the root system is healthy and unbroken, the tree will bend along its length. It's damaged if it rocks at its base before it bends.

2. Store the tree in a protected location before bringing it inside. Put it in a place where it won't freeze such as an unheated garage, porch, or cool basement.

3. Once you bring the tree indoors, keep it inside for as short a time as possible: no more than ten days, but five to seven days would be better. Keep the tree away from heating vents, fireplaces, and other heat sources.

4. Place the rootball in a large tub and water from the top. Check the rootball daily and water often enough to keep the soil moist.

5. After the holiday, plant your tree immediately. The rootball will be very heavy, so enlist the help of any holiday guests to help you carry it outside.

6. Plant the tree in a sunny well-drained location with plenty of room to spread out.

7. Water thoroughly and mulch with 2 to 4 inches of compost, shredded bark, or pine straw. Keep the tree well watered during the winter months to help it become established.

TREES

The first Friday in December is Arbor Day in South Carolina. Only South Carolinians in the warmer areas of Zone 8a can expect cabbage palmetto to survive the winter, but other adapted trees can be planted this month as long as the weather is mild and the soil does not freeze and thaw during the winter months. Try something new. Just as you may feel comfortable with a particular entrée at a restaurant but sometimes want something different, get adventurous—*carpe diem*—and try something new.

If you want to purchase a live Christmas tree, choose one that will thrive in your area, and make sure you know where you're going to plant it. Here are some choices for Carolinas gardeners. In Zone 6 try Colorado spruce, Norway spruce, white fir (*Abies concolor*), Douglas fir, red cedar (*Juniperus virginiana*), Scotch pine. Gardeners in Zones 7 and 8 can try Arizona cypress (*Cupressus arizonica* var. *arizonica*), deodar cedar (*Cedrus deodara*), red cedar, Virginia pine, and Leyland cypress. If you live in Zone 9 try Arizona cypress, deodar cedar, Leyland cypress, and southern red cedar (*Juniperus virginiana* var. *silicicola*). Follow the steps on page 215 to choose the right live tree this holiday season.

VINES & GROUNDCOVERS

Evaluate and plan to make improvements next year. See if you've cured any of your troubled spots with vines and groundcovers. Perhaps you'll have to replace the annual vines with perennial woody types to give you year-round privacy. Were pests a problem this season? Learn more about

controlling the most troublesome insects and diseases by refining your pest control techniques or simply replacing the pest-prone plants with more resistant ones.

WATER GARDENING

There's not much to be done with the water garden this month except to plan for next season. As with most garden maintenance, monitoring the garden on a regular basis will prevent many serious problems from occurring.

Plan to spruce up your water garden next year with some exciting plants. The nursery industry is responding to the popularity of water gardening with new colors and forms of water lilies and marginal and edge-of-the-pond plants that have variegated stems and leaves. And "smaller is in," with a greater selection of smaller water lilies and compact marginal plants.

PLANT

ANNUALS

Hardy cool-season annual transplants may still be set out in the Coastal Plain, particularly near the coast.

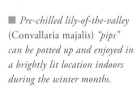
■ *Pre-chilled lily-of-the-valley (Convallaria majalis) "pips" can be potted up and enjoyed in a brightly lit location indoors during the winter months.*

BULBS

Buy commercially prepared lily-of-the-valley pips from your florist or garden center. Plant as many as possible in pots to secure an abundance of fragrant blooms. One bonus of these bulbs is that they tolerate more heat than other commonly forced bulbs. Spring bulbs, which are late bloomers, can still be planted, though bulbs that bloom in February (crocuses, snowdrops, and so forth) may not flower if planted now. Try to get them in the ground before midmonth.

EDIBLES

Sow onion seeds in the Piedmont. Piedmont and Coastal Plain gardeners can sow lettuce and other greens in cold frames for winter use.

LAWNS

Sod of cool-season grass can be installed as long as the soil is not frozen. Wait until next spring to seed, plug, or sod your warm-season lawn. You and your lawn should take the month off.

PERENNIALS & ORNAMENTAL GRASSES

Seeds that need an exposure to cold temperatures can be sown this month and set outdoors.

ROSES

Weather permitting, Coastal Plain and Piedmont gardeners can plant bare-root roses or move roses to other parts of the landscape.

SHRUBS, TREES, AND VINES & GROUNDCOVERS

Continue planting container-grown and balled-and-burlapped shrubs in the Piedmont and Coastal Plain where the soil doesn't freeze and thaw during the winter months. Take hardwood stem cuttings of evergreens such as boxwood, camellia, holly, and juniper this month, and root them in a cool greenhouse or cold frame.

For good establishment, transplant at least four weeks before the soil temperature goes below 40 degrees Fahrenheit. Newly planted trees should be watered immediately after planting. Continue to water them during the winter months if the soil isn't frozen. However, don't keep them waterlogged.

Root hardwood stem cuttings of coniferous evergreens such as juniper, cypress, falsecypress, and cryptomeria. Some broadleaved evergreens that can be propagated now are holly, arborvitae, and hemlock.

CARE

ANNUALS

Pansies and other winter annuals can be pushed out of the ground in the winter in the colder Mountains and Piedmont. This frost-heaving (when the freezing and thawing of the soil lifts plants out of the ground and damages roots) can be minimized by mulching. Cut up your Christmas tree and lay some of the branches over flowerbeds to insulate the soil.

BULBS

Take soil samples from your beds if not done in the past two or three years. Because lime can take up to six months to react and increase the soil pH, the sooner you have your soil tested, the sooner you can apply lime to your beds if necessary.

EDIBLES

Continue to harvest chives, cilantro, and parsley. In the Piedmont and Mountains, protect winter greens with a fabric row cover or with plastic tunnels—plastic stretched over metal hoops for protection from hard freezes. Brussels sprouts, broccoli, mustard, cabbage, turnips, and most lettuces will be damaged by a hard freeze (more than six hours below 26 degrees Fahrenheit).

LAWNS

You may still have to mow your cool-season lawn this month. Continue practicing the "one-third rule": Do not remove any more than one-third of the height at each mowing.

Mow overseeded bermudagrass lawns at 1 inch before the grass gets taller than 1½ inches. Dormant bermudagrass that has not been overseeded does not need mowing.

PERENNIALS & ORNAMENTAL GRASSES

Late-planted perennials in the Mountains and the colder parts of the Piedmont where the soil freezes

You can continue to harvest chives throughout the winter.

should be mulched to insulate the soil and reduce the occurrence of frost-heaving.

Continue to cut back dead, damaged, or dying perennial top growth that offers no winter ornamental interest or food for birds. Cut down to within 2 to 3 inches of ground level or just above the new foliage at the base.

Perennials such as coneflower, heliopsis, and black-eyed Susan, whose seedheads offer food for birds, are best left unpruned until late winter.

ROSES

Roses that are newly planted in the fall will benefit from winter protection, especially in the higher elevations in the Mountains and valleys. Late-summer and early-fall-planted roses also need to be protected. Tender roses such as teas, Chinas, and Noisettes should be protected with mulch to protect their roots and aboveground canes.

Winter winds can aggravate tall-growing hybrid teas, breaking their canes and injuring their roots as they're tossed about by the wind. Wait until they're dormant to cut them back to 3 feet, thereby lessening their chances of getting tousled by the wind.

SHRUBS, TREES, AND VINES & GROUNDCOVERS

When cutting branches from hollies or other evergreen shrubs for indoor decoration, maintain the natural form and beauty of the plant.

Limit pruning of other shrubs to the removal of damaged or dead branches. Wait until after the coldest part of winter has passed before doing any major structural pruning that would remove large limbs. That may encourage new growth or make the tree susceptible to winter injury.

SHRUBS

Construct windbreaks around broad-leaved evergreens predisposed to winter damage. Drive four wooden stakes around the shrub, wrap it with burlap, and staple the burlap to the stakes.

TREES

Check the water in your Christmas tree stand daily and replenish it so it won't go dry.

VINES & GROUNDCOVERS

Keep vines off wooden walls—the vines trap moisture and slow the drying of wood, which can encourage decay. When shading brick or masonry walls with clinging vines that have aerial rootlets or adhesive disks such as English and Boston ivies, climbing fig, and climbing hydrangea, think twice before allowing them to cling to the walls. After you tear down the vine you're left with rootlets and disks that can only be removed with a stiff scrub brush.

Give English ivy a trim and pull it off house walls or trees. Ivy which grows up into a tree may eventually cover too much of the crown and cause the tree to die. Heavy infestations have been known to break tree limbs. Once ivy climbs it also flowers and sets seeds, leading to seedlings, which can be a nuisance.

WATER GARDENS

In the milder Coastal Plain gardeners need to thin out the submerged plants if that wasn't done last month. Remove the dead leaves from your marginal plants.

Trim dead leaves from hardy water lilies and cold-hardy aquatic plants and discard them. If there's a threat of ice forming on your pool, move the plants to the lowest part of the pond or pool.

Aboveground water containers, such as tub gardens, can freeze during extended cold periods, so it's best to locate them in a southern exposure for most of the winter. Cover them during the cold nights to trap stored heat and to offer some protection from freezing. Prevent the pond from freezing because any organic matter frozen at the bottom of the pond may eventually decay, producing levels of methane gases that can be toxic to fish. Install a pump or a heater designed for water garden pools.

Remove dead leaves and other debris that may gather around the pond or on the surface of the water.

WATER

ANNUALS

Water cool-season annuals after fertilizing. Newly planted transplants should be watered more often to speed up establishment. If there is a warm spell, check to be sure nothing in the garden is getting too dry; water as necessary.

BULBS

See November.

LAWNS

For cool-season grasses, if dry weather persists and the lawn shows signs of drought stress, apply an inch of water per week in the absence of precipitation. Newly seeded or sodded lawns should be watered frequently. As the seedlings emerge and the sod "knits" into the soil, gradually water less frequently but more deeply and less often.

For warm-season lawns, periodic watering may be necessary to prevent the grasses from drying out, especially when the weather is warm and windy.

PERENNIALS & ORNAMENTAL GRASSES

Keep newly planted transplants well watered to help them get established.

ROSES, SHRUBS, TREES, AND VINE & GROUNDCOVERS

Mountain gardeners should make sure their new plantings are well watered before the ground freezes.

Never allow the reservoir of your Christmas tree holder to go dry; an air lock can form in the trunk that can keep the tree from absorbing any more water. Researchers have shown that plain water is best.

WATER GARDENS

Maintain the water level in your pond for the plants and fish who spend the winter outdoors.

FERTILIZE

ANNUALS

Lightly fertilize winter annuals such as pansies and ornamental cabbage and kale between bouts of cold weather. If you didn't fertilize last month and the weather is mild, apply a complete fertilizer such as 10-10-10 in the absence of a soil test.

BULBS

See September.

■ *The colorful rosettes of ornamental cabbage intensify in color after the first frost.*

LAWNS

Do not fertilize the lawn at this time. Overseeded bermudagrass lawns can be fertilized this month. Use a fertilizer recommended by soil-test results. Do not apply a fertilizer containing phosphorus and potassium if adequate levels are already present in the soil.

PERENNIALS & ORNAMENTAL GRASSES, ROSES, SHRUBS, TREES, AND VINES & GROUNDCOVERS

Do not fertilize this month. Wait until spring when new growth begins.

PROBLEM-SOLVE

BULBS

Discard any bulbs that show signs of rot, which attacks improperly stored tubers in warm, humid conditions.

Handpull any young winter annuals or cover them with a shallow layer of compost. Weeding is never fun, but cooler temperatures can make it more bearable.

Mice may get into outdoor bulb beds or cold frames. Use hardware cloth to keep them out.

Voles, also called meadow or field mice, can feed on a wide variety of plants, including your bulbs. Two kinds of voles, pine voles and meadow voles, reside in the Carolinas.

LAWNS

Handpull or spot-treat chickweed, henbit, and other winter annuals with a broadleaf herbicide.

PERENNIALS & ORNAMENTAL GRASSES

Diseases can be carried over the winter on plant parts and infect the plants in spring. Remove all fallen leaves and dead stems from the perennials before mulching.

ROSES

Apply a dormant oil spray early in the month, before new growth emerges, to control overwintering insect and spider mite eggs.

Blackspot overwinters on fallen leaves and canes. Rake out the leaves and compost them or bury them in the flower border or vegetable garden away from any roses.

Handpull any young winter annual weeds, or cover them with mulch. Weeding is never fun, but the cooler temperatures can make it more bearable.

TREES

If scale insects and mites have been a problem this past season, apply a dormant horticultural oil when the plants go dormant. Be sure to spray the trunk, branches, and stems and both sides of the leaves thoroughly. Read the label for precautions regarding the high and low temperature limits at the time of application.

Check your plants for the spindle-shaped bags of bagworms, which contain 500 to 1,000 eggs that will hatch next spring.

Take precautions against deer and rodents. Protect trees from deer with fencing or repellents. Rabbits can be deterred by installing wire or plastic guards around the trunks of young shade trees and fruit trees. To discourage voles, pull the mulch away from the trunk about a foot.

VINES & GROUNDCOVERS

Apply a dormant oil spray early in the month before new growth emerges to control overwintering insect and spider mite eggs. Read the label for cautions regarding the limits of high and low temperatures at the time of application.

■ *Henbit (top) and Chickweed (bottom) can produce pretty flowers, but they interfere with lush lawn growth. Remove these weeds by hand or with a broadleaf herbicide.*

First Fall Freeze Map

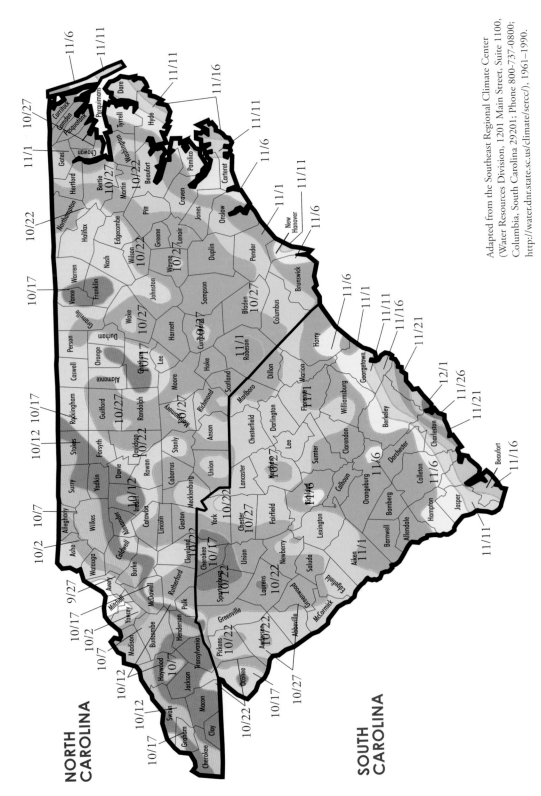

Adapted from the Southeast Regional Climate Center (Water Resources Division, 1201 Main Street, Suite 1100, Columbia, South Carolina 29201; Phone 800-737-0800; http://water.dnr.state.sc.us/climate/sercc/), 1961–1990.

Last Spring Freeze Map

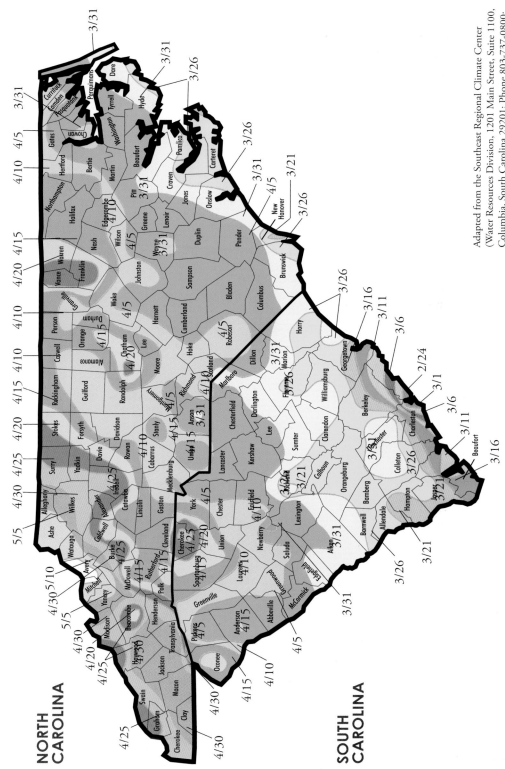

Adapted from the Southeast Regional Climate Center (Water Resources Division, 1201 Main Street, Suite 1100, Columbia, South Carolina 29201; Phone 803-737-0800; http://water.dnr.state.sc.us/climate/sercc/), 1961–1990.

Chilling Hours

Some plants not only like but need colder air. Most fruit trees need a certain number of hours with air temperatures below 45 degrees Fahrenheit, called chilling hours. Plants with chilling hour requirements must meet the minimum number of chilling hours in order to break dormancy and bloom. (Remember: no blooms, no fruits!) During warmer winters, fruit trees can get physiologically "confused," blooming early, late, or not at all.

In the Carolinas, it's important to select fruit tree varieties with relatively low chilling hour requirements. Gardeners in the mountains of western North Carolina will experience more chilling, but the whole region gets less chilling than areas of the Midwest, Pacific Northwest, or Northeast.

Before buying fruits, look at the number of chilling hours your area gets.

MINIMUM CHILLING HOURS AVAILABLE BY REGION

Mountains: more than 1,200
Foothills and Piedmont: 800–1,000
Coastal regions (northern): 600–800
Coastal regions (southern): 400–600

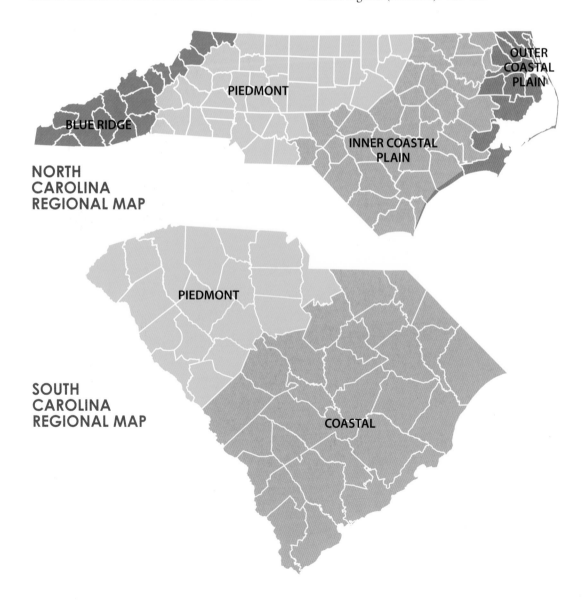

NORTH CAROLINA REGIONAL MAP

BLUE RIDGE

PIEDMONT

INNER COASTAL PLAIN

OUTER COASTAL PLAIN

SOUTH CAROLINA REGIONAL MAP

PIEDMONT

COASTAL

Glossary

Alkaline soil: soil with a pH greater than 7.0. It lacks acidity, often because it has limestone in it.

Annual: from a botanist's perspective, an annual lasts no longer than one year. To the gardener, an annual is a seasonal plant, growing until winter's cold or summer's heat causes it to decline or die.

Balled-and-burlapped: tree or shrub grown in the field whose rootball was wrapped with protective burlap and twine when the plant was dug up to be sold or transplanted.

Bare root: plants that have been packaged without any soil around their roots. (Often young shrubs and trees purchased through the mail arrive with their exposed roots covered with moist peat or sphagnum moss, sawdust, or similar material, and wrapped in plastic.)

Barrier plant: a plant that has intimidating thorns or spines and is sited purposely to block foot traffic or other access to the home or yard.

Beneficial insects: insects or their larvae that prey on pest organisms and their eggs. They may be flying insects, such as ladybugs, parasitic wasps, praying mantises, and soldier bugs, or soil dwellers, such as predatory nematodes, spiders, ants, and beetles.

Berm: a temporary narrow raised ring of soil around a newly planted tree, used to hold water so it will be directed to the root zone.

Bract: a modified leaf structure on a plant stem near its flower that resembles a petal. Often it is more colorful and visible than the actual flower, as in dogwood or poinsettia.

Bud union: the place where the top of a plant was grafted to the rootstock; usually refers to roses or fruit trees.

Canopy: the overhead branching area of a tree, usually referring to its extent including foliage. Also called the crown.

Cold hardiness: the ability of a perennial plant to survive the winter cold in a particular area.

Complete fertilizer: powdered, liquid, or granular fertilizer that contains the three key nutrients—nitrogen (N), phosphorus (P), and potassium (K).

Compost: organic matter that has undergone progressive decomposition by microbial and microbial activity until it is reduced to a spongy, fluffy texture.

Corm: the swollen energy-storing structure, analogous to a bulb, under the soil at the base of the stem of plants, such as crocus and gladiolus.

Crown: the base of a plant at, or just beneath, the surface of the soil where the roots meet the stems.

Cultivar: a CULTIvated VARiety. It is a naturally occurring form of a plant that has been identified as special or superior and is purposely selected for propagation and production.

Deadhead: a pruning technique that removes faded flower heads from plants to improve their appearance, abort seed production, and stimulate further flowering.

Deciduous plants: unlike evergreens, these trees and shrubs lose their leaves in the fall.

Desiccation: drying out of foliage tissues, usually due to drought or wind.

Division: the practice of splitting apart perennial plants to create several smaller-rooted segments. The practice is useful for controlling the plant's size and for acquiring more plants; it is also essential to the health and continued flowering of certain ones.

Dormancy: the period, usually the winter, when perennial plants temporarily cease active growth and rest. Dormant is the verb form, as used in this sentence: Some plants, like spring-blooming bulbs, go dormant in the summer.

Established: the point at which a newly planted tree or shrub has generated enough roots in its new location to keep it alive without supplemental watering.

Evergreen: perennial plants that do not lose their foliage annually with the onset of winter. Needle or broadleaf foliage persists and continues to function on a plant through one or more winters, aging and dropping in cycles of three or four years or more.

Foliar: of or about foliage—usually refers to the practice of spraying foliage, as in fertilizing or treating with insecticide; leaf tissues absorb the liquid directly.

Floret: a tiny flower, usually one of many forming a cluster that comprises a single blossom.

Germinate: to sprout. Germination is a fertile seed's first stage of development.

Girdling root: root that encircles all or part of a trunk/woody stem or other roots and interrupts the movement of water, minerals, and sugars.

Graft (union): the point on the stem of a woody plant with sturdier roots where a stem from a highly ornamental plant is inserted so that it will join with it. Roses are commonly grafted.

Hardscape: the permanent, structural, nonplant part of a landscape, such as walls, sheds, pools, patios, arbors, and walkways.

Herbaceous: plants having fleshy or soft stems that die back with frost; the opposite of woody.

Hybrid: a plant that is the result of intentional or natural cross-pollination between two or more plants of the same species or genus.

Included bark (bark inclusion): bark embedded between two adjacent stems or between a branch and a trunk, which indicates a weak union or attachment.

Mulch: a layer of material over bare soil to protect it from erosion and compaction by rain, and to discourage weeds. It may be organic (compost, wood chips, bark, pine needles, shredded leaves, compost) or inorganic (gravel).

Naturalize: (a) to plant seeds, bulbs, or plants in a random, informal pattern as they would appear in their natural habitat; (b) to adapt to and spread throughout adopted habitats (a tendency of some nonnative plants).

Nectar: the sweet fluid produced by glands on flowers that attract pollinators such as hummingbirds and honeybees for whom it is a source of energy.

Organic material, organic matter: any material or debris that is derived from plants. It is carbon-based material capable of undergoing decomposition and decay.

Peat moss: organic matter from sphagnum mosses, often used to improve soil texture, especially sandy soils. It is also used in seed-starting mixes and in container plantings.

Perennial: a flowering plant that lives over two or more seasons. Many die-back with frost, but their roots survive the winter and generate new shoots in the spring.

pH: a measurement of the relative acidity (low pH) or alkalinity (high pH) of soil or water based on a scale of 1 to 14, 7 being neutral. Individual plants require soil to be within a certain range so that nutrients can be available to them.

Pinch: to remove tender stems and/or leaves by pressing them between thumb and forefinger. This pruning technique encourages branching, compactness, and flowering in plants, or it removes aphids clustered at growing tips.

Pollen: the yellow, powdery grains in the center of a flower. A plant's male sex cells, they are transferred to the female plant parts by means of wind or animal pollinators to fertilize them and create seeds.

Raceme: an arrangement of single stalked flowers along an elongated, unbranched axis.

Rhizome: a swollen energy-storing stem structure, similar to a bulb, that lies horizontally in the soil, with roots emerging from its lower surface and growth shoots from a growing point at or near its tip, as in bearded iris.

Root-bound (or potbound): condition of a plant that has been confined in a container too long, its roots having been forced to wrap around themselves and even swell out of the container. Successful transplanting or repotting requires untangling and trimming away of some of the matted roots.

Root collar: region between the base of the trunk and the roots which swells as trees grow. Also called root crown, root flare, and trunk flare.

Self-seeding: the tendency of some plants to sow their seeds freely around the yard. It creates many seedlings the following season that may or may not be welcome.

Semievergreen: tends to be evergreen in a mild climate but deciduous in a colder one.

Shearing: the pruning technique whereby plant stems and branches are cut uniformly with long-bladed pruning shears (hedge shears) or powered hedge trimmers. It is used when creating and maintaining hedges and topiary.

Slow-acting/slow-release fertilizer: fertilizer that is water insoluble (contains more than 50 percent water insoluble nitrogen) and therefore releases its nutrients gradually as a function of soil temperature, moisture coating, and related microbial activity. Typically granular, it may be organic or synthetic.

Sucker: a new growing shoot. Underground plant roots produce suckers to form new stems and spread by means of these suckering roots to form large plantings, or colonies. Some plants produce root suckers or branch suckers as a result of pruning or wounding.

Tuber: a type of underground storage structure in a plant stem, analogous to a bulb. It generates roots below and stems above ground. A dahlia is a tuberous root. A potato is a tuber.

Variegated: having various colors or color patterns. The term usually refers to plant foliage that is streaked, edged, blotched, or mottled with a contrasting color, often green with yellow, cream, or white.

White grubs: the larvae of scarab beetles, including Japanese beetles, masked chafers, and May and June beetles. They have plump, cream-colored, C-shaped bodies and distinctive yellow to brown heads. Most have life cycles lasting from several months to three years.

Wings: (a) the corky tissue that forms edges along the twigs of some woody plants such as sweetgum; (b) the flat, dried extension of tissue on some seeds, such as maple, that catch the wind and help them disseminate.

Public Gardens

Public Gardens
Along the Carolina Coast
Airlie Gardens
Wilmington, NC
(910) 763-4646

Boone Hall Plantation
Mt. Pleasant, SC
(843) 884-4371

Brookgreen Gardens
Pawleys Island, SC
(800) 849-1931

Cypress Gardens
Moncks Corner, SC
(843) 553-0515

Elizabethan Gardens
Manteo, NC
(919) 473-3234

Greenfield Gardens
Wilmington, NC
(910) 341-7855

Magnolia Plantation and Gardens
Charleston, SC
(843) 571-1266

Middleton Place
Charleston, SC
(800) 782-3608

Nancy Bryan Luce Garden
Moncks Corner, SC
(843) 761-8509

New Hanover County Extension Service Arboretum
Wilmington, NC
(910) 452-6393

Orton Plantation Gardens
Wilmington, NC
(910) 371-6851

Roycroft Daylily Nursery
Georgetown, SC
(800) 950-5459

Tryon Palace and Gardens
New Bern, NC
(800) 767-1560

Off the Carolina Piedmont and Coastal Plain
Cape Fear Botanical Garden
Fayetteville, NC
(910) 486-0221

Chinqua-Penn Plantation
Reidsville, NC
(336) 349-4576

Clemson University
Sandhill Research and Education Center
Columbia, SC
(803) 788-5700

Daniel Stowe Botanical Garden
Belmont, NC
(704) 825-4492

Davidson College Arboretum
Davidson, NC
(704) 892-2596

De Hart Botanical Gardens
Louisburg, NC
(919) 496-4771

Edisto Memorial Gardens
Orangeburg, SC
(803) 533-6020

Fearrington Village
Pittsboro, NC
(919) 542-1145

Flora Macdonald Gardens
Red Springs, NC
(910) 843-5000

Francis Beidler Forest
Harleyville, SC
(843) 462-2150

Gardens of Greensboro
Greensboro, NC
(336) 373-2199

Hamlin Sensory Garden
Salisbury, NC
(704) 637-1881

Of the Carolina Piedmont and Coastal Plain
Hatcher Gardens
Spartanburg, SC
(864) 574-7724

Hemlock Bluffs Nature Preserve
Cary, NC
(919) 387-5980

Hezeldan Alexander Homesite
Charlotte, NC
(704) 568-1774

Memorial Garden
Concord, NC
(704) 786-8009

Mordecai Historic Park
Raleigh, NC
(919) 834-4844

Municipal Rose Garden
Raleigh, NC
(919) 821-4579

NC Botanical Garden
Chapel Hill, NC
(919) 962-0522

NC Wesleyan College
Rocky Mount, NC
(252) 985-5100

NC Zoological Park
Asheboro, NC
(800) 488-0444

Old Salem
Winston-Salem, NC
(800) 441-5305

Park Seed Co. Trial and Display Gardens
Greenwood, SC
(803) 223-7333

Reynolda Gardens of Wake
Forest University
Winston-Salem, NC
(336) 758-5593

Ribbon Walk
Charlotte, NC
(704) 365-9080

Riverbanks Zoological Park
and Botanical Garden
Columbia, SC
(803) 779-8717

Robert Mills Historic House
and Garden
Columbia, SC
(803) 252-1770

Rose Hill Plantation State Park
Union, SC
(803) 427-5966

Sarah P. Duke Memorial
Gardens
Durham, NC
(919) 684-3698

Sandhills Horticultural
Gardens
Pinehurst, NC
(910) 695-3882

SC Botanical Garden
Clemson, SC
(864) 656-3405

Swan Lake Iris Gardens
Sumter, SC
(803) 773-3371

Tanglewood Park
Clemmons, NC
(910) 766-0591

UNC-Charlotte Botanical
Gardens
Charlotte, NC
(704) 547-2555

White Pines Natural Area
Raleigh, NC
(919) 833-3662

Wing Haven Gardens and Bird
Sanctuary
Charlotte, NC
(704) 334-0664

WRAL Gardens
Raleigh, NC
(919) 821-8555

Historic Bethabara Park
Community/Medical Gardens
Winston-Salem, NC
(336) 924-8191

Historic Mill Hill Plantation
Concord, NC
(704) 786-3990

Hopeland Gardens and Rye
Patch
Aiken, SC
(803) 642-7630

Hurley Park
Salisbury, NC
(704) 638-5260

Iron Gate Gardens
Kings Mountain, NC
(704) 435-6178

JC Raulston Arboretum
Raleigh, NC
(919) 515-3132

Kalmia Gardens of Coker
College
Hartsville, SC
(843) 383-8145

Of the Carolina Mountains
Biltmore House and Gardens
Asheville, NC
(800) 543-2961

Blue Ridge Community
College
Flat Rock, NC
(828) 692-3572

Botanical Gardens of Asheville
Asheville, NC
(828) 252-5190

Campus Arboretum of
Haywood Community College
Clyde, NC
(828) 627-4640

Cherokee Botanical Garden
Cherokee, NC
(704) 497-2111

Chimney Rock Park
Chimney Rock, NC
(800) 277-9611

Daniel Boone Native Gardens
Boone, NC
(828) 264-2120

Grandfather Mountain
Linville, NC
(828) 733-2013

N.C. Arboretum
Asheville, NC
(828) 665-2492

Pearson's Falls
Tryon, NC
(828) 749-3031

Wilkes Community College
Gardens
Wilkesboro, NC
(336) 838-6100

Selected Bibliography

Aquatic Plants and their Cultivation, Helen Nash with Steve Stroupe, Sterling Publishing Co., Inc., NY, 1998.

Armitage's Manual of Annuals, Biennials, and Half-hardy Perennials,
Allan M. Armitage. Timber Press, Portland, OR, 2001.

Bulletproof Flowers for the South, Jim Wilson, Taylor Publishing Co., Dallas, TX, 1999.

Carolinas Gardener's Handbook, Toby Bost and Bob Polomski, Cool Springs Press, Minneapolis, MN, 2012.

Diagnosing Turfgrass Problems: A Practical Guide,
Ralph W. White and L. B. McCarty, Clemson University Public Service Publishing, Clemson, SC, 2012.

Easy Roses for North American Gardens, Tom Christopher, The Reader's Digest Association, Inc., Pleasantville, NY, 1999.

The Encyclopedia of Ornamental Grasses, John Greenlee, Michael Friedman Publishing Group, Inc., NY, 1992.

The Encyclopedia of Roses, Judith C. McKeon, Rodale Press, Inc., Emmaus, PA, 1995.

The Evening Garden; Flowers and Fragrance from Dusk Till Daw, Peter Loewer, Timber Press, Portland, OR, 2002.

Garden Bulbs for the South, 2nd. ed., Scott Ogden, Timber Press, Portland, OR, 2007.

Garden Guide to the Lower South, Trustees' Garden Club (P. O. Box 24215, Savannah, GA 31403-4215), 1991.

Growing and Propagating Showy Native Woody Plants, Richard E. Bir, The University of North Carolina Press, Chapel Hill, NC, 1992.

Herbaceous Perennial Plants, 3rd ed., Allan M. Armitage, Stipes Publishing L. L. C., Champaign, IL, 2008.

Hutchinson's Tree Book: A Reference Guide to Popular Landscape Trees, Bob H. Head, Hutchinson Publishing Corporation, Taylors, SC, 2006.

An Illustrated Guide to Pruning, Edward F. Gilman, Delmar, Cengage Learning, Clifton Park, NY, 2012.

Landscaping with Natives, Guy Sternberg and Jim Wilson, Chapters Publishing Ltd., Vermont, 1995.

Manual of Woody Landscape Plants, 6th ed., Michael A. Dirr, Stipes Publishing L. L. C., Champaign, IL, 2009.

Ortho's All About Roses*, Tommy Cairns, Meredith* Books, Des Moines, Iowa, 1999.

The Practical Science of Planting Trees, Gary W. Watson and E. B. Himelick, International Society of Arboriculture, Champaign, IL, 2013.

Rose Gardening in the Carolinas: Culture and Care, C. Douglas Baker, Thomas W. Estridge, and Roderick J. Humphreys, The Greater Columbia Rose Society, Columbia, SC, 1997.

The Southern Garden Advisor, Barbara Pleasant, Cool Springs Press, Nashville, TN, 2003.

The Southern Kitchen Garden, William D. Adams and Thomas R. LeRoy, Taylor Trade Publishing, NY, 2007.

The Southern Living Garden Book*, Steve Bender, ed., Oxmoor House, Inc., Birmingham, AL, 2004.

Southern Living Garden Problem Solver*, Steve Bender, ed., Oxmoor House, Inc., Birmingham, AL, 1999.

Southern Seasons: Month-by-Month Gardening in the Piedmont Plateau, Frances Worthington, Shurcliff Press, Greenville, SC, 1993.

Trees for Urban and Suburban Landscapes, Edward F. Gilman, Delmar Publishers, Albany, NY, 1997.

Water Gardening, Joseph Tomocik, Pantheon Books, Knopf Publishing Group, NY, 1996.

Water Gardening: Water Lilies and Lotuses, Perry D. Slocum and Peter Robinson with Frances Perry, Timber Press, Inc., Portland, OR, 1996.

Water Gardens, Thomas C. Cooper, Ed., Primedia, Inc., Peoria, IL, 1998.

Weeds of Southern Turfgrasses, Tim R. Murphy et al., EB 150, PSA Publishing, Clemson University, Clemson, SC, 2010.

The Well-Tended Perennial Garden: Planting and Pruning Techniques, Tracy DiSabato-Aust, Timber Press, OR, 1998.

MAGAZINES

Carolina Gardener, P. O. Box 4504, Greensboro, NC 27404 (www.carolinagardener.com)

ASSORTED PUBLICATIONS FROM:

Clemson University Cooperative Extension Service Home & Garden Information Center (www.clemson.edu/extension/hgic)

North Carolina Cooperative Extension Service (www.ces.ncsu.edu)

State of North Carolina Department of Environment and Natural Resources Division of Water Resources (www.ncwater.org/Education_and_Technical_Assistance/ Aquatic_Weed_Control)

South Carolina Department of Natural Resources Aquatic Nuisance Species Program (www.dnr.sc.gov/invasiveweeds/ illegal1.html)

Index

Photo Credits

Meet Bob Polomski

Bob Polomski is widely known and respected for both his down-to-earth gardening expertise and knowledge of the latest technical information. He shares his gardening know-how with gardeners across the Carolinas through numerous print and electronic articles, books, radio broadcasts, and television appearances.

The author's numerous publications range from scientific papers and extension publications to magazine, newspaper, and Internet articles. For twelve years he was the "Questions & Answers" columnist for *Horticulture* magazine. Polomski has also published articles in *Carolina Gardener*, *Fine Gardening*, *American Rose*, and *American Nurseryman*. He appears on television programs devoted to gardening and hosts a monthly public radio program that's broadcast statewide with listeners in portions of North Carolina and Georgia. He has also conducted garden study tours in England and France.

Polomski was a contributing writer for the *Better Homes and Gardens New Garden Book* and the *Southern Living® Garden Problem Solver*. He was technical editor of several books, including the *Miracle-Gro Guides*, the *Yard and Garden Owners Manual*, and *The Complete Perennials Book*.

Attesting to his expertise and communication skills, the author has accumulated many honors, among them national awards from the National Association of County Agricultural Agents (NACAA) for his columns and books (2008, 2006, 2003, 2000, 1998, and 1992) and radio program (2008, 2006, and 1996), Garden Writers Association Silver Award of Achievement for radio on-air talent (2006), a Quill & Trowel Award for his "Listen to Your Lawn: Recycle Your Grass Clippings" public service announcement videotape (1977), and the National Extension Materials Award from the American Society of Horticultural Science (2008, 2003, and 1995).

As co-author of *Home Lawn Management in South Carolina* (Clemson Ext. Circ. 687, Clemson University Public Service Publishing), he received the Notable State Document Award conferred by the South Carolina State Library to "recognize state government publications of outstanding merit and usefulness to the citizens of South Carolina." In 2012 Polomski received the Rowland P. Alston Sr., '42 Award for Excellence in Public Relations. The award was established in 2009 to "recognize outstanding Clemson University faculty or staff who, through programs and activities related to agriculture and/or natural resources, have provided Clemson University with positive visibility throughout South Carolina, the United States, and the world."

The author directed his lifelong study of horticulture toward earning a Ph.D. in Plant & Environmental Sciences at Clemson University in 2009. Presently he lectures and conducts research at Clemson University where he continues his pursuit of evaluating and promoting noteworthy, sustainable landscape plants.

Polomski is the author of three regional Month-by-Month Gardening books for the Carolinas, Mississippi, and Alabama published by Cool Springs Press. His most recent book, co-authored with Toby Bost, is the *Carolinas Gardener's Handbook: All You Need to Know to Plan, Plant & Maintain a Carolinas Garden* (Cool Springs Press, 2012).

Polomski lives in Easley, South Carolina, with his wife, Susan, who are proud parents of three children and soon-to-be empty-nesters.